The Bridge

A nine-step crossing into authentic and wholehearted living

DONNA LANCASTER

PENGUIN LIFE
AN IMPRINT OF
PENGUIN BOOKS

PENGUIN LIFE

UK | USA | Canada | Ireland | Australia
India | New Zealand | South Africa

Penguin Life is part of the Penguin Random House group of companies
whose addresses can be found at global.penguinrandomhouse.com.

First published 2022

001

Copyright © Donna Lancaster, 2022

The moral right of the author has been asserted

Set in 12/14.75pt Dante MT Std
Typeset by Jouve (UK), Milton Keynes
Printed and bound in Great Britain by Clays Ltd, Elcograf S.p.A.

The authorized representative in the EEA is Penguin Random House Ireland,
Morrison Chambers, 32 Nassau Street, Dublin D02 YH68

A CIP catalogue record for this book is available from the British Library

HARDBACK ISBN: 978-0-241-51309-5
TRADE PAPERBACK ISBN: 978-0-241-58634-1

www.greenpenguin.co.uk

'If you always look up and never down, you will be seeking your whole life from the heavens, for something that was always meant to be found in the dirt.'

For Corinne – my favourite sister

The Welcome: A prayer for the Worthy (that means you)

I welcome each and every one of you and every part of you.
The part of you that feels anxious and afraid
the part of you that is full of rage
the part that feels excited and curious
the part of you feeling shut down and disconnected.
You are welcome here.

I welcome the part of you that feels heartbroken and overwhelmed
the part of you that feels too broken to ever heal
the parts of you that feel fake, and those that you know are real.
You're all welcome.

The parts carrying your trauma; the body carrying your soul.
The abused and violated parts, too,
the addicted you and your shadowy layers
the secret-carrying, guilt-filled shameful parts.
Guess what? Welcome!

The part of you that has been hurt and that has hurt others
made mistakes, screwed up BIG time.
And the resulting self-loathing and low self-worth.
Oh, you are all so welcome here.

For the parts of you that are confused and lonely
the ones that feel they can't go on another day . . . and yet they do.
And for the courageous you that gets back up again and again.
And those parts of you that yearn to live in love and truth.
The parts that remember everything. Welcome.

And welcome to the Queen in you, who has forgotten her crown.
Welcome to the innocence of you and the joyful part, too.
You are all so beyond welcome. Yes! All parts of you are welcome.

You Belong. You Matter.
You are Worthy. You are Loved.
And I'm so very glad that you came.

Contents

Introduction: Everybody Hurts Sometimes

Face down on the floor in a ladies' loo might seem like an unlikely place for personal transformation, but that's where mine began.

The day I experienced my breakthrough began as a day like any other. I took my children to school and then drove to work, my mind already on my caseload. I was a social worker working in child protection and felt compelled to do everything I could to help vulnerable children. My mind would buzz day and night with their stories.

As I was parking my car that morning, I noticed my heart was beating very fast. My breathing was shallow and my palms were sweaty. *What's wrong with me?* I thought impatiently. *I haven't got time for this.* As I entered the building, I began to realize I was in serious trouble. I was sweating heavily, my heart was pounding and I felt really sick.

I stumbled into a staff toilet and locked the door. Pain flooded my chest. *Was I having a heart attack?* I sank to my knees and began to sob. I was terrified that I was going to die. (On a dirty toilet floor of all places. Oh, the glamour.) Pain coursed through my whole body and tears poured out for what seemed like hours. Eventually I lay face down and surrendered to my fate.

I don't know how long I was lying there for, but eventually the pain and tears subsided enough for me to stand up on my wobbly legs. I splashed water on my face and tried to work out what had just happened to me and what I should do now. Was I out of danger? I felt wired. There was no way I could work. I dragged myself out to my car, my whole being focused on my need to get home. I couldn't think beyond that goal. I took some deep breaths and started the car. I set off. Very slowly.

I never went back to the office after that day. I was signed off sick for three months and eventually decided I could not return to social work. I didn't realize it then but my transformation had begun. I had hit rock bottom. The only way from here was up.

In diagnostic terms it was a panic attack that I was suffering from that day, over twenty years ago now. But, in a way, my hunch about a heart attack was more accurate. My poor heart had been shattered so many times and so completely over the years. I was exhausted, burnt out and the cumulative weight of my unhappiness had become unbearable. Although my mind had refused to acknowledge this devastating truth, my body found a way to make me feel it.

Although this experience was agonizing at the time, it was also my way out of the half-life of the walking wounded that I'd been existing in for the best part of thirty years. I didn't know it then but I had found an opening, a portal to a very different way of living, right there in the darkness of my pain. It took courage (heavily laced with desperation) to decide to crawl through it and begin my journey towards the life I live today. Which, let me be clear, is not all sunshine and rainbows, but is most definitely a life of authenticity, lightness and truth where I do not pretend to feel or be something I am not. This is my version of a wholehearted life. My deepest hope is that this book will enable you to discover your own.

Everyday heartbreak

Every person's life has its sorrows and struggles. We all know this on some level and yet we are often blindsided when painful things happen to us. The shock we might feel at the unexpected ending of a significant relationship, for example, can leave us feeling helpless. Sometimes we are surprised a particular event has hit us so hard. If a casual friend cuts us off without explanation, for example, that can feel more hurtful than we would have predicted. Many of us don't realize the impact of the 'smaller' losses or hurts in our life. Hurt and loss come in so many forms, from being teased at college to being passed over for promotion to failing an exam to falling out with our grown-up children. Whatever our stage of life and personal circumstances, all of us experience everyday heartbreaks and would benefit from being better equipped to deal with them.

There are a lot of misunderstandings about loss, as we will see throughout this book. Many people understand it to mean bereavement. I will be showing you that the death of a loved one is not the only loss that needs to be grieved. Far from it. That's why I also use the slightly different term 'heartbreak' to refer to all our significant pains and losses. For some people, heartbreak makes them think of the loss of romantic love. For me, it encapsulates the visceral reaction to *any* painful event that hurts our heart and leaves us feeling bereft, wounded or abandoned.

The events may be different for each person, but the feelings they provoke tend to be similar for many of us: anguish, fear, anger, disappointment, sorrow, confusion, guilt, to name but a few. These are just some of the emotions that make up the complex human experience called 'grief'.

My work has shown me that these feelings, though uncomfortable and potentially damaging if left unexpressed, are pretty much universal. We will all experience loss and feel grief at some point in our lives, perhaps many times. Fortunately, most of us will also feel happiness, contentment, joy and wonder.

They're all part of being deliciously human. Our heartbreaks and our grief, however, can also teach us to live a more authentic and wholehearted life, if only we let them.

What I finally learned on that day when I couldn't stop crying in the loo at work was that my pain needed an outlet. It needed somewhere to go. I had tried so hard to keep busy, ignore it, tough it out, file it away and wait for it somehow to magically disappear. I had denied the impact of my heartbreaks for years, telling myself and others that I chose to think positively, look forward not back and 'keep on keeping on'. I felt that there was no alternative. Anything less would be weakness, a personal failure.

It got more and more frightening to acknowledge that this strategy wasn't really working. I refused to recognize my chronic low mood or self-sabotaging behaviour (damaging relationships, use of illegal drugs) as distress signals. And all the time, my ungrieved pain was slowly bubbling up towards boiling point.

I was mistaken about so much from that period of my life, before my breakthrough. I was mistaken about the best way to react to my feelings of deep sadness, anger and fear. I was completely wrong to imagine that allowing them expression would mean I was weak or a failure. I was mistaken in thinking that if I ignored the past it would leave me be. Or that the events that had wounded me were unusual or that there was something wrong with me for not being able to move on. I had lost sight of one of the fundamental truths about life, which is that tough things happen to everyone and when we are hurt or we lose something or someone we love and value, it is completely natural to feel shit about it.

Ask yourself, who do you know who hasn't been hurt or let down, lost someone they adored or been betrayed? I'll hazard a guess: no one. The pain that we feel when these things happen to us is not a mistake or a failure or a tragic exception to the rule. It's part of what it means to be human.

So given all that, the really crucial question is this: how can we learn a kinder, gentler, more effective way to process our emotional pain? Our lack of preparation in how to deal with life's inevitable losses is a serious disadvantage, given that they are coming for all of us.

Perhaps your early heartbreaks began as a child, when your parents divorced or when they let you down or didn't listen to you. Maybe it was when you were bullied at school or when you were ignored all night at the youth club disco. Maybe later you failed your exams, or were dumped by your first love, or went on to leave your marriage, or lost a company that you'd slogged for years to build up. Perhaps you missed the opportunity to become a parent. Maybe you betrayed yourself, or were betrayed. You lost a parent, a partner, a friend or a pet. Perhaps you lost your innocence, your hope or even your mind.

However it happened, each time you lost something or somebody valuable, your heart broke. And since, like most of us, you may not have been shown how to express your emotions healthily, or how to heal, you may still be feeling stuck and hurting in some aspects of your life. Some of you might feel you're not good enough; some might feel angry or afraid. Some of you might feel disappointed, disconnected, numb or just plain sad; others will suffer from anxiety or depression. Or perhaps your heartbreak speaks through your body in the form of chronic back pain, IBS, headaches or skin problems.

Rather than pay attention to these distress signals, many of us develop coping mechanisms to allow ourselves to ignore them and carry on living our lives. We distract ourselves by pursuing relationships, sex, money or status. We exhaust ourselves by keeping so busy and working so hard that we are too tired to feel anything at all. We self-medicate, abusing food, alcohol or other drugs. We scroll Instagram or watch Netflix for hours until we've completely zoned out. We do almost anything to ease or numb the pain of the past. Above all, we do not go looking for the reasons that we feel so bad. In fact, we will often go to any lengths to conceal our hurt from our friends, partner, doctor and family. And, crucially, from ourselves.

How has this happened? Partly, it's a cultural thing. Many of us have been brought up in a society that lacks the tools to understand and process our distress in more healthy ways: through grieving. In some cultures, such as in Mexico with its Day of the Dead, they still have rituals and rites that support the bereaved. Others, such as many of the countries of West Africa, encourage elders to pass on their wisdom to younger people, equipping them with insights and resilience to see them through a crisis.

I have spent decades now supporting people to recognize and release their ungrieved losses. Having found a way to uncover my own buried pain and to heal from it, I wanted to pass on anything that might be useful to others. Along the way I co-founded and facilitated a retreat called The Bridge, where people came to take part in a residential programme of radical and transformative healing for their loss and hurt.

The people who came on The Bridge were of different eth-nicities and nationalities and of all ages, sexual identities and orientations. Some of them had been in therapy for years, some of them were just starting out. Some had mental health issues but many did not. They were simply tired of feeling unhappy or 'not enough'. They sensed there was more to life than merely slogging away, more than just existing. These people came to share their stories in a safe place and learn how to put their broken hearts back together. The one thing they had in common was a sense that they were ready to do the work to heal from their emotional pain in order to find a different and more vibrant way to live.

Some of the people who came on The Bridge had been treated for mental health issues for years. Their backlog of blocked emotions led to a range of symptoms, some of which looked and felt very similar to depression or anxiety. Eventually, though, they had begun to suspect that their diagnosis wasn't telling the whole story. In the end, their hunch that it was unreleased pain that was holding them back from a full life brought them to a place where they could approach that pain differently.

Of course, some people *do* develop clinical depression or anxiety disorders, for a whole range of reasons. Medication can be a profoundly powerful tool and I am certainly not saying that medical interventions are necessarily wrong for any individual. But our culture is certainly quick to medicate people for emotional distress. Rather than teach ourselves to simply *be with* and to process life's inevitable emotional suffering, we typically tell ourselves that if we're feeling sad, there's something wrong with us. We might allow ourselves a (short) grace period to deal with a socially recognized loss such as a bereavement, but in general, if we are struggling with persistent distress, we receive the message that our feelings are unacceptable and we 'should be grateful for what we do have'. We should leave the past in the past and move on.

I encourage you to look beyond this unhealthy message. I am here to help you explore an alternative. During more than thirty years of working therapeutically with people, I have observed over and again that if they are allowed a safe, loving and nurturing space to share their story in front of others, to be seen, heard and understood, and to express their pain without judgement; to cry and grieve with their whole body, then what happens is this . . . quite simply, they start to get better. You can too.

You can heal your hurt

Whatever your past looks like, whatever poor decisions you might have made, however inauthentic or lost you might feel today, a different future is possible for you. There is so much more to any life than heartbreak and pain. In even the toughest life there are moments of grace and fun and laughter. Please take courage and inspiration from those moments, however fleeting they may have been for you. You, like me, are not just a heartbroken person with a sad story to tell. You are not merely a collection of wounds and you are certainly not – and this is so important to say and to really hear – you are *not* and have never been broken. Far from it. You might be wounded, hurting and perhaps making some poor life choices as a result. But you are, and will always be, whole. In this book we will be exploring together how you can learn to welcome, support, encourage and eventually love all parts of yourself back to that wholeness. (Hard to believe, I know.) It's not that I am going to *teach* you how to do this. It's that I can guide you to *remember* how to do it, learning from that wise part of yourself that is deep inside of you.

Some of you might find it hard to connect to this part of yourself. You may not be feeling particularly wise or resilient right now. You may not even feel worthy of healing. Perhaps you prefer the safety of the hurts you know to the risk of ones you don't. Some of you may feel damaged, exhausted, lacking the energy for any more fight or slog. That's all understandable and welcome. Remember, you are not building a different version of yourself, but merely returning to the person you were before your heart was broken one too many times. You can start where you are, work at your own pace and with whatever you've got to give. You can begin now or when you feel ready. All you need is courage and a commitment to yourself to do this inner work.

So how does this work take place? I will be asking you to take some time to investigate your past in order to find the original sources of your pain. Then, once you've brought more awareness to your hurts, you will be guided to safely grieve them. Allowing yourself to express and feel what you were perhaps unable to when you were originally hurt, or what you haven't allowed yourself to feel for many years since. You will mourn all you have lost, including the lost parts of yourself: those elements of your personality or experience that were judged unacceptable by you or by somebody else. And alongside your grieving, you will learn how to soothe and comfort yourself, how to build your resilience and eventually learn to love, honour and cherish yourself with every thought, word and action you take. You will be guided to remember your full worth. The truth of who you are. Now this is true healing in action.

Rest assured that you will not have to do this work unsupported. Throughout the book there will be stories from others who have been where you are, and I will be sharing my own stories of healing and helping others to heal themselves. There is so much love and lightness that is waiting for you on the other side of your own portal, if you can just find the courage and energy to climb through and begin.

Redefining the 'G' word

I love talking about grief. If that sounds ghoulish or a bit tragic, I get it. I used to be able to clear a room at a party just by mentioning the 'G' word. I've reined that in lately (I need friends in my life!) but grief remains both my specialist subject and a personal passion because I know what it can offer people. I know what lies on the other side of it. I want to tell every person on the planet that, through grief, we can heal the wounds of our past and return to a state of wonder and playfulness, wholeheartedness and even joy. It's like a secret that nobody tells us, or the missing piece of the puzzle hidden down the back of the sofa: grieving our pain is the gateway to remembering who we really are and living a more grateful, connected and joyful life.

I understand the fears and resistance around grief, believe me. Pain, loss, wounding, heartbreak and betrayal are not exactly laugh-a-minute topics are they? Why would we spend any longer on them than necessary? We might need to acknowledge them to move past them, but if we want lightness in our lives, why delve into the darkness? Shouldn't we aim for a swift closure and then set our best foot forward? Focus on positivity and on being the best version of ourselves?

This approach might seem convincing on the surface and it certainly sounds like an attractive option in many ways, but experience has shown me that denying or avoiding our painful feelings just doesn't work. Down there in the darkness, left unattended, they simply fester. The truth is this: we can't heal a loss if we don't acknowledge its full impact on our life. In fact, when we minimize, dismiss or run from our grief, we *maximize* its impact. We literally extend and expand the original hurt. The avoidance of our pain can keep us trapped within it for decades (and for some of us, sadly, a whole lifetime).

It doesn't have to be this way.

Speaking my truth

I discovered all this the hard way (of course) by experiencing it for myself. By the time I was thirty, my life was a complete mess. I was desperately unhappy even though I had two daughters, a loving partner and a successful career as a social worker, working in children's services. I was burnt out, not only from the stress of my job but from the relentless struggle to deny that my old hurts and emotional wounds still caused me pain.

On one level, I absolutely *was* the strong, determined, successful, competent adult (the warrior woman as I named her) that I tried to model to the children I worked with. But on a deeper level, I was also a wounded little girl myself, pretending to be 'fine'. I had never grieved the hurts and losses I suffered as a child, which meant that in the end they grew tired of tugging on my sleeve for attention and just let rip. My hurt tore through my body and brought me to my knees.

I acquired my first emotional wounds early. Like many people, I had a childhood home that felt more like a war zone than a place of safety. My parents were both addicts. My father was an alcoholic and my mother was addicted to him and his drama. Neither of them was emotionally mature enough to be a healthy parent and they simply didn't know how to really love and care for me and my siblings; they could barely take care of themselves.

I grew up feeling that I was unsafe and unwelcome. I did not belong anywhere, least of all in my family. By the time I was born my mother was already exhausted from caring for my older brother and sister and coping with the stresses and dramas of being married to an alcoholic. She had three kids (including my dad), really, so when I arrived her tank was well and truly empty and she had very little left to give. One of my earliest memories, from when I was about four, centres on a feeling of not being good enough to make either of my parents notice or love me. So I reasoned – with all my four-year-old powers of logic – that I was unloved because I was unlovable. It was all my fault.

There was a lot of chaos and violence in our home and I remember being almost permanently afraid. In addition, other hurts piled on top, which led to more painful feelings and later huge levels of self-criticism. When I was six, I was rejected at school by my peers for looking different. I was the only mixed-race child in my class and was made to believe that my brown skin was the wrong colour. When I was nine and struggling with maths, I had a particularly cruel teacher who made me believe I was stupid.

On and on the heartbreaks went. Over the years, I started to reject all those 'weak' or 'bad' and vulnerable parts of myself, just as others had rejected them. I sent them packing, banishing them out into the cold, dark night. They were like my 'emotional orphans', the parts of me that I disowned. I ignored them for years but they patiently waited: cold, hungry and sad. Desperate to be invited back in.

Unsurprisingly, I suffered with low mood throughout my teenage years and as I moved into my twenties it only got worse, as did my self-loathing. I took on a number of roles to try to protect myself from my painful emotions. To start with, I tried so hard to be the good girl. I became an expert people-pleaser, both with my parents and the bullies at school who taunted me for being the 'brown girl'. By the time I was a teenager, my anger had surfaced. I'd moved on to being a rebel and a bad girl, raging against any authority or attempts to control me. By early adulthood I was very comfortable being the numb warrior woman who never went round an obstacle if she could plough straight through it. Honestly, it was exhausting always being strong, always being capable, always being 'positive' – except when I lost it and was angry as hell.

On one level, I have to admit, these defences and masks served me well. I got a lot done being a warrior. I decided to train in child protection because (and you don't have to be Freud to see how this one works) I wanted to 'save' vulnerable children. I worked hard. I had my own children and worked harder still. The hardest thing of all was pretending that I was 'fine'. Fine with working for a system that claimed to have children's needs at its heart but forced me to split up siblings when they were taken into care. Fine with my past. Fine with myself.

I was 'fine' for years, until that day when I found myself sobbing uncontrollably on the floor in the toilet at work. Finally, I was able to hear what my body, heart and soul were trying to tell me. 'Enough.' Enough of the lies, Donna, enough of the stress, enough pretence. Stop it.

For weeks afterwards I could barely function. I had panic attacks if the phone rang or the doorbell went. I slept as much as I could, lived only to get back to my bed. I intuitively knew that I needed help. This was not something that was going to get better all on its own. My first port of call was to visit my GP, who prescribed me antidepressants. Then I began weekly sessions with a brilliant psychotherapist. Jackie was warm, down to earth and funny, which made her the perfect fit for me. I needed a therapist who could be with me in the darkness, while also seeing see the funny side when appropriate.

I had never done any therapy before but I was familiar with that world thanks to my job in social work. I also began regular sessions of acupuncture because, even though money was tight, I knew I had to invest in myself. I had to help my mind and body to heal. I felt I had no choice if I wanted to truly live. Which I did, very much. But first of all, an old way of living had to die. Looking back, I can see that I was in fact dying my way back to life. No wonder it was exhausting.

I spent the next few years on and off antidepressants, which had been a lifeline in the early days but increasingly came to feel like a deadening weight. They stopped me feeling sad, for sure, but they also stopped me feeling pretty much anything at all. I felt numb, as if I were flat-lining through life. I was still existing rather than thriving, so I explored and then eventually trained in various healing techniques, therapies and spiritual practices, seeking out the mentors who could help me and teach me to help myself. It got easier and then harder and then easier again. Sometimes it felt like two steps forward, one step back, but I reassured myself that I was at least still heading in the right direction. Even at the beginning I knew something big was happening, that I had passed through the portal of my heartbreak. I was determined not to fall back. However challenging the journey, I felt the positive energy that comes from moving in the right direction. I sensed that I was slowly but surely becoming fully alive once again.

This book, and how to use it

Whatever your level of experience with therapy, personal development or self-help, you are completely welcome here.

Some of you might have done a lot of personal development work. For others, this might be the first book on this subject you've ever picked up. I have tried to aim at a point roughly in between these two positions, in order to make the book accessible and inclusive to as many people as possible. You won't find lots of statistics or graphs. I've avoided jargon where I can and, when a specialist term is the best fit for what I'm trying to say, I've explained what it means in everyday language.

You can't get this work wrong because heartbreak and grieving are simply too personal for there to be a single 'correct' way to do it. This book is an offering for you to use in the way that feels most appropriate for you. It's not based on any one particular theory; it's more a collection of what I've observed on the ground and what I've learned through training and over thirty years of professional and personal experience. My expertise is based in practical trial and error and I know for sure that everyone must experiment to find what works best for them. This is not a one-size-fits-all approach.

On that note, please do set your own pace and spend as long as you need on any particular section. The book is structured as a step-by-step programme so I suggest that you work through it in chronological order rather than dipping in and out, but there is no obligation to complete each stage within a week, or even a month. All I would ask is that if you do take a break, you commit to coming back when you're ready for the next step. There might be a temptation, when the work touches into your wounds and you begin to feel some of the painful related feelings, to say, 'Sod that,' and put the book away. But I urge you to stick with it. Abandoning the work before it's complete is a bit like getting up off the operating table mid-surgery and saying, 'That's OK, no need to stich me up. I think I'll leave it there.' Not a great idea if you want your wound to heal.

There are guided exercises called Over to You throughout the book, and short summaries of key ideas and questions for you to reflect on at the end of each chapter. Nothing is compulsory, but the more actively you read and engage with the material the more you are likely to get out of it.

You might find it helpful to take notes at various points, so I invite you to buy yourself a lovely notebook and perhaps a special pen to write in it. When we bring focused attention to any task and honour its importance with particular actions and tools, we are turning it into a ritual. Rituals of all kinds are a key element of the way I approach healing from heartbreak, and will be coming up as elements of the work throughout the book.

This book will not be right for everyone. If you are suffering from chronic emotional distress and mental health issues or severe trauma, I urge you to get professional support. Please contact your doctor or call one of the helplines listed at the back of the book.

If you are a member of a marginalized or discriminated group, you may be carrying a huge amount of pain and loss connected to the abuse or inequality you experience in your day-to-day life. You may also be dealing with the effects of intergenerational trauma and systemic injustice, as are, for example, many Black people and people of colour. You are all more than welcome here and I hope that you will still find the book useful, but I acknowledge that there may be elements of your wounding that lie beyond the scope of its work. Whoever you are, I honour you and I do hope you find what you need.

For every single one of us, the most important resource for healing isn't contained in the pages of this book. It's inside of us. It lies in our willingness to stop running and turn to face what's been holding us hostage for years: our emotional pain.

It's in our decision to stop digging the hole we're in and learn a new, healthier and happier way to live.

From hole to whole

Every heartbreak we suffer creates a wound inside of us, like a hole in our being, and because we are generally not taught how to hold ourselves in this hurt, nor shown how to tend to our precious wounds, we fill them up with 'stuff' so that they might hurt a little less (if only for a moment). We cram these holes in our heart and soul with drink, drugs, relationships, sex, money, food, work, gadgets, shoes – you name it, we will stuff anything in there. We close down our battered heart to protect ourselves and try to forget the past. But we end up crawling through life with this *huge* gaping hole at the core of our very identity.

Sounds painful, doesn't it? I know because I've lived it. Maybe you have too? The alternative can feel pretty scary – terrifying even – and I won't lie to you, it is not a walk in the park. But in the end, it's the difference between existing and living. Between stagnation and growth. Between healing and pain management. And here's the thing: the pain of healing is temporary whereas the impact of ignored pain can last a whole lifetime. It can even affect the generations that follow you.

When tended to properly, your emotional wounds can and will heal. And the secret that so few people get to discover, because they are too busy anaesthetizing their pain away, is that in daring to look closely at your wounds, through a lens of courageous tenderness, you will discover that they are the resolution for your pain. Yes, those holes inside of you that you have been avoiding for years, decades even. For when you gently trace your fingers around their shape, you will discover that they are in fact a doorway – an opening back to your own soul.

When I finally had the courage to stop running and to fill the holes inside me with my un-shed tears and self-compassion instead of substances, men and internalized misogyny, I found something extraordinary: those holes became WHOLE.

Time to cross the bridge

From the majesty of the Sydney Harbour Bridge to a simple set of stepping stones across a stream, bridges offer us support and invite us to travel across in search of new experiences and adventures. A bridge is such a beautiful metaphor for the journey of human life. It connects where we have come from with where we are headed.

I invite you now to safely cross your own bridge, one step at a time. Travel at your own pace – looking back at where you came from as well as forward to a future that is no longer defined by your (negative) past.

On this side of your bridge you might be living a lie, covering up pain, hiding behind masks that offer you protection but keep you from being your true self. On the other side authentic and wholehearted living awaits. This journey will take you across, step by step, until you arrive on the other side of the pain you've been struggling with. And, once on the other side, you will be able to look back and see that you could not have arrived at your new place without it.

So my question to you is this: are you ready to cross? If the answer in your gut is yes, take a deep breath, slowly step on to the bridge and let's begin . . .

Step One: Heartbreaks and Tears – how and why we get hurt

Over the years I have invited many people to describe to me how their hearts got broken. I have listened to many and varied stories of loss and wounding. Some people struggle to begin with but, once they get going, their story gushes out of them. Others seem almost to have a script that they know by heart. Some people tell me they don't know how they got hurt or grew sad, all they know is that they feel it.

I remember a woman called Rachel, who came on The Bridge years ago. She told us on the first day that she didn't really know why she was there. She couldn't recall any significant loss or hurt. She had a stable family and had never suffered a major bereavement or been divorced. It was a mystery to her why she had wrestled with low mood since she was a teenager, but she couldn't face living like that any longer, so here she was.

That first day, she looked totally blank when everyone began to share stories about what had brought them there. I could see her getting more and more nervous. When it came to her turn she told us she felt like a fraud. She couldn't explain, except to say that there was what felt like a 'terminal sadness' deep inside her.

Rachel wasn't a fraud. She was somebody who had never been helped to understand the broader definition of grief or how to mourn her losses. She was somebody who had a particular idea about which life events were serious enough to count as 'proper' heartbreaks. As she told it, nobody had died, she hadn't been abused, nothing awful had happened. Perhaps she was making a fuss about nothing?

Except she never actually made a fuss. She just got sadder and sadder without understanding why she felt that way and without knowing what to do to feel better. She had never been to her doctor with her problems – she was too stoical for that. She didn't think she deserved to do therapy or take medication or burden her friends. So she kept it all inside and stayed sad, until one day she realized she couldn't live that way any more and booked herself on to The Bridge.

As we all began to talk about how everyday heartbreaks can wound us deeply and come with emotions attached, and how each experience feeds into another over time, Rachel began to cry. A lot. It was as if her tears were saying what her words could not. It turns out she had been teased at school. And that her parents (although lovely people) were both career-focused, meaning that Rachel spent long periods on her own as an only child. She often felt very lonely.

As an adult she found herself making and clinging to bad friendships and relationships, in a desperate attempt to feel loved and avoid ever feeling alone again.

Through her work on The Bridge, Rachel was able to 'join the dots' and understand that she had, in fact, felt very abandoned and rejected by her parents as a young child and that this unprocessed heartbreak had rippled through all the relationships in her life, especially the one she had with herself. Only in turning towards this original hurt and feeling its impact was she finally able to heal.

Wherever you are in relation to the story of your own heartbreak, trust that it is the perfect place for you to begin. I invite you to explore with gentle curiosity and an open heart.

Mapping loss: following the trail . . .

We will start our work together by looking more closely at what we mean by loss and hurt. We will look at how context shapes our reaction to losses and how, if we don't mourn them, the impact of painful events stacks up throughout our lifetime. How can we begin to relate differently – with more emotional language and less intellectual distance – to that ungrieved loss and pain? We will be talking generally, using lessons and stories I've built up from my years of practice, but I will also invite you to investigate how the ideas apply to your specific situation.

Later in the chapter, I'm going to show you how to map out a timeline of loss and heartbreak for your own life. For example, what happened when you were five, or six? Did a parent leave the family through divorce or separation? Did you move house across the country and lose all your friends? What about when you were twelve and struggled to find your place with your peers at a new school? And so on, all the way through to the present day.

Once you've completed your timeline, you will begin to track your emotional reactions to these painful events and ask yourself honestly how they made you feel at the time. How did it feel when a parent went away? Did you feel rejected, abandoned, unlovable? What about when you moved house? Did you feel alone, frightened, angry? This is a little like detective work, following threads and asking questions about what happened and how you felt as a result.

You will 'follow the trail' back in time to make connections between your heartbreaks and the wounded parts of yourself that were not supported, to make sense of what happened or healthily express the related emotions. These wounded parts may have become frozen inside you, as if they've got stuck at the age you were when they were hurt. In psychology this is known as 'arrested emotional development'.

So, for example, by the time I was four years old I already knew that my parents could not really love and care for me, but I did not know how to process the feelings of rejection and abandonment I had as result. I didn't even know how to name them, let alone release them. That four-year-old me remained trapped inside me, unable to grow up emotionally because she had been unable to release her grief at the time. My adult self then developed strategies for handling this unprocessed pain. My warrior persona, for example, was very effective at denying that vulnerable, hurting part of me, but if a partner innocently forgot to call me one day or (heaven forbid) turned up late to meet me, then bam! There I was, feeling and behaving like that abandoned and rejected four-year-old girl. (Anyone else recognize this or is it just me?!)

Your detective work is absolutely crucial in laying the groundwork for the rest of your healing journey. We cannot understand or release our pain unless we can access and name it, using specific and emotional language.

By the end of the chapter, I hope that you will have begun to identify what happened to hurt you and acknowledge the feelings associated with those painful events. This will prepare you for the next steps in your journey.

Innocence, heartbreak and wholeness

During my thirty-plus years of working in therapeutic and personal development settings, I've heard literally hundreds of people's stories of heartbreak. Every single one was unique but contained within it recurring themes and strands of meaning. I've come to believe that as part of being human we travel along a timeline of events that includes losses, betrayals and disappointments. This is not to say of course that all life is miserable (that's clearly not the case, thank God) but that there will be a certain amount of unavoidable struggle, confusion and pain for us all.

Every single one of us was born an innocent being of love with an infinite capacity for joy. It's that simple. Babies have only one agenda and that is to survive. Their innocence is radiant. I mean, have you ever met a cynical baby? I didn't think so. I am in awe of how my four-year-old grandson, Theo, naturally spreads love and joy to everyone he meets. His heart is so open. He hasn't yet learned to close it for protection. I am deeply moved to watch him as he looks in the full-length mirror just before bath time and says to his naked reflection, 'I really love you, Theo.' He absolutely means it! It breaks my heart because we were all like Theo once. We all felt worthy of love and belonging, simply by being our fabulous naked selves.

Each of us then experiences hurts. Our little hearts get broken and we begin to journey away from the boundless capacity for love, delight in play and easy emotion of early childhood, towards the entrenched attitudes, repression of playfulness and general wariness of an adult's defences. Life slowly becomes a much more serious business.

You could say that's just growing up, and it's true that much of it is necessary and even beneficial. The knowledge and experience we acquire allow us to form our personality and tastes, to discover how to be both an individual and a member of the group, how to live and work together. The fact that not all our life experiences are positive certainly doesn't make them a tragedy. The events that hurt us can still be incorporated into our story of who we are, if we can learn to integrate them in a healthy way.

But some of those experiences are not just hurtful; they are harmful. This might be because they are such huge losses or injuries that we find we cannot healthily incorporate them into our story. They create wounds – like holes in our heart – and until we are shown how to attend to them we cannot flourish.

Other events are harmful because we, like Rachel, haven't been shown how to recognize them as heartbreaks, let alone how to heal them. These might be so-called minor losses (the death of your beloved family pet) or something more ambiguous or complex like becoming a parent, which though positive can also entail loss of identity and freedom. Even if we can't recognize these experiences as losses, we carry their impacts inside us regardless.

A third category of loss or hurt, and one of the most toxic, is the ones we barely register because they are all but invisible to us. An example of this is the loss of aspects of our own self. What happened to the part of us that was once like Theo: open-hearted, confident, loving of self and others, for example? Where has it gone? When and why did we start to become 'half-hearted' rather than 'whole-hearted' in our lives?

The sad answer is that we banished those elements when we learned that they were unacceptable. There is a particular pain attached to this kind of loss, precisely because it is a protective mechanism we adopt in response to external heartbreaks. We defend our hearts from hurt and, in doing so, lose parts of ourselves, which in turn causes more heartbreak . . . This happens repeatedly, throughout our lives. Certain aspects of ourselves are judged inappropriate, unacceptable or unlovable, so we hide or disown them. I call these parts of ourselves our 'emotional orphans' because they are the self-abandoned parts of ourselves left without a home.

This, for me, is a truly soul-destroying loss that virtually all of us need to mourn: the lost aspects of ourself that have been frozen out. Somewhere inside us there is still a little girl whose daddy left when she was four. Or a little boy who heard all the way through primary school that he wasn't good enough. Or a shy teenager who was bullied. All of these heartbroken parts of us are still frozen in time, waiting for us to return for them, scoop them up, invite them back into the warmth of our heart and soul.

What I wish for you is that by the end of this book you will be able to recognize and integrate all of the wounded and frozen aspects of yourself, welcoming them back to their rightful place within you. And you will discover, as I did all those years ago, that this is what it really means to feel 'at home'.

What have you lost? How have you been hurt?

Healing from our heartbreaks starts when we dare to pause long enough to ask ourselves the question, 'What happened to make me feel so bad?' and then stick around to listen for the honest answers. Only when we're willing to do this are we ready to begin to heal. We often have to get to the point where we're finally so sick and tired of all the emotional crap we're lugging around, and inflicting on ourselves and others, that we decide something has got to change.

Sometimes there is a sort of rock-bottom moment, as there was for me when I was forced by my body to recognize that I was really unwell. For some people that rock bottom can literally be a question of life or death.

It isn't always this dramatic, though. It could also be a comment from a friend that makes you question your choices, whether that's your need to always be in a relationship or your reliance on social media to raise your self-esteem. Or it could be when you cross a personal boundary such as drinking too much too regularly, or it might be watching somebody close to you do their own personal development work and realizing that there is an alternative to living wrapped in hurt, apathy and sadness.

The pathways to this moment are different for all of us, but one day we find that we're ready to stop clinging on to whatever we use to distract or numb ourselves. We're ready to try to find a different way to live. To ask and answer the courageous question, 'What happened to make me feel so disconnected, sad, angry or afraid?'

So if that's where you are right now, whatever your particular circumstances, you have come to the right place. In deciding that you want things to change and that you are willing to do the necessary work, you have taken the first important step on to the bridge. Your work now is to begin to investigate the losses and hurts that brought you to this place in your life.

Lessons in loss

To get us warmed up, I've listed some of the key things I've learned about loss, both what it is, and what it isn't. These ideas have all come straight out of my personal experience of shifting my own understanding of loss, and helping other people to do the same. They are not objective 'truths' so much as insights that some people have found useful.

See whether any of them resonate with you. Perhaps some seem obvious. Do you find any of them surprising, or challenging? You might find it helpful to unpick your reactions. You could pause your reading and give yourself the space and time to explore your thoughts and feelings. I encourage you to jot down notes or add to this list if that feels helpful, but there is no obligation to do so. This is just the beginning of our explorations and we will be returning to many of these ideas throughout the book.

Loss is . . .

- What happens when someone or something that we value highly either leaves us or is taken away.
- A normal part of life.
- Inevitable.
- Something that occurs many times in a lifetime.
- Relative, and exists on a spectrum.
- Personal – what wounds you might not wound me, and vice versa.
- Sometimes complex in its consequences, sometimes very clear, sometimes ambiguous and often confusing.
- Necessary in order for us to learn and grow.

Loss isn't . . .

- Confined to being bereaved or getting divorced.
- Hierarchical or a competition. Your loss is not more important than mine. Mine is not worse than yours. There is plenty to go around!
- A once-in-a-lifetime tragedy.
- Something that happens to other people.
- A petty grievance or an excuse for aggressive behaviour.
- A life sentence. It is possible to heal and enjoy life again.
- A defining characteristic of who you are.

Loss, hurt, grief, heartbreak . . . what's in a label?

Before we go any further, words are very important in the healing process, so I'd like to offer some clarification of some key terms that I will use frequently throughout this book.

Hurt and loss

'Hurt' and 'loss' often come together. If a life partner cheats on us, for example, it hurts us and we may lose trust in them (as well as the relationship and possibly ourselves). We feel hurt and loss when things happen that cause us significant pain. Examples range from being bullied at school to the end of an era when our grown-up children move out.

Grief

'Grief' is an umbrella term for our emotional reactions to loss and hurt caused by life events. We will be looking at grief in much more detail in Step Three of this work. For now, let's go with a working definition of grief as 'the natural emotional reaction to any significant loss or hurt'.

Heartbreak

'Heartbreak' is such a powerful word. It manages to combine both the event and our reaction. It describes what happens when we lose or are hurt by something or someone important. It also captures some of the flavour of the pain. When we are belittled or betrayed, abandoned, abused or left alone with loss and suffering, it can feel as if our heart really is breaking. Sometimes this manifests as physical pain, perhaps like the tightness and cramping I felt on the day of my breakthrough. You may have felt something similar in your own life.

It's painful stuff, but heartbreak is also an unavoidable fact of life. It can either lead us home or drive us crazy, depending on how we deal with it (or not) and what stories we tell about it. I'm here to show you that by doing your inner work you can steer away from the crazy-making, and head towards home. I will be here, guiding you every step of the way. Rest assured that you are not alone with this.

Bereavement and the false hierarchy of heartbreak

Since this is a book about facing our loss and grief, we will inevitably talk about bereavement. How could we not? It can be one of the most heartbreaking, far-reaching and complex losses many of us ever experience. As Rachel's reaction showed me, if you ask someone to say what loss means, many (if not most) people will talk about death. The two concepts are so close in our minds and our language as to be almost synonymous. And of course bereavement can be – and often is – devastating.

If an experience of bereavement is what has brought you here, you are very welcome. I am sure that you will find much to help you, even though this is not a book 'about' bereavement. You may also find it useful to consult the Resources section at the back of the book, where you can find suggestions for more specialist support.

My approach to understanding the impact of loss and hurt

is rooted in the belief that bereavement is not the only form of loss that deserves to be acknowledged and mourned and it's by no means the only form that can cause us significant emotional distress.

Neither is it the same for everyone. Sometimes bereavement can cause complex feelings, perhaps of relief as well as sadness. Sometimes we might feel very little, which may be entirely appropriate at that time. Sometimes, even when we have lost somebody very close to us, our hurt does not feel like a struggle to process. We are able to open up to our feelings. Gradually, through grieving, we begin to feel better.

Our culture talks about bereavement (evasively, awkwardly and fearfully) as if it's in a league of its own, with other 'lesser' hurts trailing afterwards in descending order. This is unhelpful to anyone dealing with any kind of loss, including the bereaved. Placing hurtful events on a scale of 'seriousness' makes it easier to dismiss some of them and harder to protect ourselves against their impact. It can also create unhelpful stories of tragedy and victimhood or anguish around 'more serious' events. If your own experience of bereavement doesn't fit this story, that can lead to feelings of anxiety, guilt or shame. All loss and pain are simply too subjective to be labelled in this way.

It is especially unhelpful to compare what has hurt us with what has hurt others. As I've said before, grief is not a competition and one person's loss does not invalidate anybody else's. In this book we will be working with a broad definition of grief and loss, one rooted in personal and subjective experience. I invite you to investigate your unique experience in the spirit of curiosity, and to be gentle with yourself as you do so.

Context is always crucial

The first heartbreak I remember in my own life occurred when I was about five years old. It's one of my earliest memories. I had been watching *Blue Peter* and – inspired by their creative gifts section – I decided to make (all by myself!) a Christmas gift for my mummy, because I wanted to show her how much I loved her. I was so excited and proud of my creation. I couldn't wait for her to open it.

When she did, on Christmas morning, she looked confused. 'What is it?' she asked.

'A jewellery box,' I replied, proudly.

Mum began to giggle. Then my dad and brother joined in and soon they were all howling with laughter.

I didn't understand what was happening. I was so confused; I felt completely crushed. These people were my family. Why would they laugh at me? In that moment, my little heart broke.

Now, on the one hand, this incident might seem a small thing. I'm pretty sure my mum didn't mean to upset me. She just got the giggles at my clumsy attempts with 'sticky-backed plastic'. (Does it still exist? Does anyone else remember it from *Blue Peter*? They loved the stuff.) But for me, that experience was *huge* because of the context in which it happened. This was my beloved mum, after all, not a stranger or even an assistant at a playgroup. I was already vulnerable because of the lack of safety in my home, so this event was devastating to my fragile sense of self. Its impact was so significant that I avoided any creative expression for decades afterwards.

My early heartbreak illustrates some useful points that might help you to think about your own losses and injuries. The most important one, to my mind, is that heartbreak is heavily dependent on context. It is deeply personal and all relative. There is a common-sense scale that shows us that your mother dying is a worse hurt than her refusing you second helpings of ice cream, but beyond that the significance of a loss or an injury depends on many interconnecting factors.

First of all, there's the emotional significance of the person who wounds us. This is a crucial factor in how much it hurts. So a parent or a spouse or a lifelong friend can potentially hurt us much more than, say, an aunt we see once a year or a casual acquaintance.

Secondly, there's the amount of understanding we have at the time when the event occurs. The fewer resources we have to make sense of our feelings and hurt, the harder it will be for us to handle them and then heal. This is why the things that hurt us in childhood are often the most consequential of all. We literally don't have the range of experience, skills, or perhaps even the language when we are aged four, or six or ten or twelve, to deal with whatever has happened to hurt us.

Taken together, the combination of young age and emotional significance explains why the first people to break our hearts are usually our parents or primary caregivers. This isn't necessarily because of any deliberate or obviously cruel action on their part; it is more that they are human and therefore fallible. No parent, however loving, can get every interaction right every time. I have made plenty of mistakes in my own parenting as my daughters could tell you, I'm sure! Parents are carrying their own (often unhealed) hurts, which, as we will see when we talk about the impact of ungrieved pain, can seriously limit their ability to have emotionally healthy relationships. And for the child, even a 'small' injury or failure to understand their needs can feel devastating, coming from their mum or dad. As children we start off believing our parents are godlike beings. They are often the first woman and man we meet, and they become our templates for what a woman and a man 'should' be. That is why we are so devastated when they 'betray' us in some way.

For all these reasons and many more, our parents can wound us significantly, even if they're doing their very best not to. We will come back to the implications of this unintentional wounding and how we can deal with and heal from it later in the book.

The sad truth is that not all parents are capable of providing a loving, safe context for their children. At one end of the spectrum are abusive parents and abusive situations, which can have devastating consequences. But even little put-downs or being laughed at can end up feeling unbearable if enough of them pile up to create a situation where a child doesn't feel safe, loved and valued.

It's not just children for whom context is crucial. An adult's resilience to injury and loss is also dependent on many things, including whether it's a one-off or repeated behaviour and whether it reminds them of a previous, possibly unconnected, event. Our reactions to heartbreak can change from one month or even one day to another, depending on what else is going on for us.

Sometimes we are surprised to feel devastated by something that previously wouldn't have troubled us that much. It's never a simple matter of cause and effect. Loss and heartbreak are too personal to fit neatly into boxes. They are also cumulative, which is an important idea that we'll be returning to shortly. For now, suffice to say that we all have a unique breaking point. If we never do our work to heal from our heartbreaks then – one day – a tiny thing might be too much to bear.

Having clarified that we are defining loss and hurt as any

event that was *significantly wounding for us*, and before we move on to thinking in more detail about how their impacts stack up in our lives, I invite you to start to think about the significant losses and emotional injuries in your own life. This is a stock-taking exercise, if you like, a preliminary checklist of possible heartbreaks for you to cross-reference with your own store.

OVER TO YOU

Begin to catalogue your heartbreaks

Here's a list of some of the ways we can experience heart-break. Please scan through and see which of them resonate with you. You might find it helpful to consider the insight of grief expert David Kessler: that grief can be provoked by 'the death of something as well as somebody'.

Spend a few minutes thinking about the losses in your own life. I suggest you make a note of what comes up for you. These notes will help when you make your timeline of heart-breaks later in the chapter. As you read on, more events or more details may occur to you. Come back and jot them down if you wish.

It's important not to judge yourself for anything. Try to steer away from editing your thoughts because you feel that you 'should' be over that bullying from your teenage years, for example. Every single thought, feeling, insight or question is welcome here.

- Loss of identity – when something fundamental about how we see ourselves changes. This can be caused by any number of significant life changes: for example, retirement, ageing, coming out, becoming a parent or our grown-up children leaving home.

- Death of a dream – the dreams we had that never came to pass. Examples include becoming a parent, getting married, following a certain career path, travelling the world.
- Moving house – leaving behind all we have known including perhaps our home, job, friends and family.
- Leaving a school or job – with the loss of security and friends that this might bring.
- End of addictions – recovering from an addiction can feel like losing a trusted and loyal (if destructive) best friend.
- Separation and divorce – the loss of our partner and the life we knew with them including in some cases a bonded family unit. Also sometimes the dreams we shared for our future together, such as growing old together or having a family.
- Major health changes – sickness, long-term health issues and the menopause can all involve loss of opportunity and freedom and shifts in our sense of self.
- Death of a beloved pet.
- Financial changes – can lead to feeling that we've lost freedom, security, self-respect, opportunity or options.
- Friendships slipping away – the loss of a close friend can leave us feeling rejected or overlooked.
- Loss of trust or faith – when we feel let down or betrayed, for example, losing our trust in the person or institution responsible.
- Loss of innocence – can occur if you had to grow up too fast, perhaps being the eldest child or because

your parent was unable to care for you, or you experienced abuse.

Heartbreaks great and small

Though it isn't useful to rate hurtful events on any supposedly objective scale of 'seriousness', I do think it's helpful to recognize that the effects of our heartbreaks can *feel more or less serious to us.* That is entirely personal and subjective, and absolutely natural.

So some of the hurts and losses you've begun to catalogue in your own life may only have bruised your heart. These 'minor' hurts often respond well to small-scale treatments. Perhaps, with acknowledgement and a good sob, we will be well on the way to healing. Other more significant losses might have split your heart almost clean in two, and some hurts are so huge that it feels as if your heart shatters into a million tiny pieces. Those are the ones that are likely to give you the most trouble. It's a bit like when you drop a glass on to a hard tiled floor – you'll be cutting yourself for years on those tiny fragments if you don't clean up thoroughly.

In Step Two, we will talk in more detail about the costs to you of not cleaning up and the consequences of various toxic coping mechanisms. For now, it might help to look at the most common strategy – which for the British especially I would say is practically our *default* strategy – for (not) dealing with our heartbreak: denial. The reason for looking at denial and repression here is that they can obscure our heartbreaks from us so effectively that they become invisible and, as we've already said, bringing awareness to our losses and hurts is the first necessary step in healing them.

Gaping wounds and the queue of heartbreaks

The thing about our emotional wounds is that, like physical ones, they need tending to. They won't get better on their own. But since most of us are not taught how to process emotional pain, we fall back on our coping mechanisms in order to function. Many of us simply close down our heart and learn to endure. This emotional repression – sort of like a stiff upper lip on steroids – can look and feel quite successful, at least for a while. Sometimes, the passing of time fools us into thinking that we've dealt with our problems.

But where do those heartbreaks go? They do not just magically disappear. It is a myth to say that time is a great healer; it's really more of a distancer. As we move further away from the event that hurt us, and lock up our broken heart in a box, we might almost be able to forget about it . . . for a while. But that's not healing and it's certainly not a permanent solution. The heartbreaks simply queue up, waiting patiently in line for us to come back to grieve them. It gets pretty crowded in that box after a while.

The cost of relying on denial and repression as our coping strategies includes becoming so emotionally disconnected that even life's positive feelings and experiences can be hard to access and enjoy. As the professor and researcher, Brené Brown says, 'We cannot selectively numb emotions. When we numb the painful emotions, we also numb the positive ones.'

Many of us use numbing agents such as drugs (including alcohol), busyness and over-work, sex, shopping or social media in order to repress our painful and unacceptable feelings. It's as if we daren't stop even for a minute in case we risk feeling something uncomfortable that we don't know what to do with. Even personal development work and spirituality can be used to avoid dealing with our emotional distress. If we go on retreat after retreat, for example, this can be a way to 'hang out in the light' while supposedly addressing the bigger questions. But if we are still avoiding that bloody locked box and all of the difficult feelings contained within it, we're not facing what we need to face. This phenomenon is known as a 'spiritual bypass' and is not at all uncommon. You can't meditate the pain away, I'm afraid. Sooner or later you have to dare to unlock that box inside you.

We all have our own 'drugs of choice', the ones that allow us to maintain our denial, but meanwhile our emotional wounds start to fester, becoming poisonous to ourselves and others. Eventually their effects become more apparent as they leak out into all aspects of our life, from our health and self-worth to our relationships and choices.

Sometimes, we are so numb that we do not even recognize that we are heartbroken. We are so deeply in denial or distanced from our emotions that we are not able to say what happened to make us feel this way. This puts us at risk of sinking into apathy, hopelessness, bitterness, depression, anxiety and other mental health issues.

So how can we begin to shake off our numbness? How can we spot the signs of heartbreak in our own lives? Have a look at the following list of signs of unacknowledged or unrecognized heartbreak. Once again, take some time to see if any of them resonate with you. I've also included a list of signs of an open and balanced heart, in case this helps. Some of us find it easier to recognize what's going on for us if we can compare and contrast two differing approaches.

Take your time to think about the way you process your feelings and react to events. See if this reflection allows you to uncover any more significant losses and hurts in your past. Please treat yourself very gently as you read this list. Remember, these are not criticisms of you personally. They are patterns of behaviour and response that *generally* point to unprocessed pain.

Signs of possible heartbreak

- I withhold affection or attention, intentionally pushing people away.
- I am overly cautious, fearful and scared of intimacy.
- I am critical, judgemental, suspicious or defensive.
- I have a tendency to cover up vulnerabilities with a harsh, steely face.
- I am secretive, scheming and have betrayed others and myself.
- I have a 'me against the world' mentality, which leads to loneliness and isolation.
- I have a tendency to feel superior, leading to a lack of empathy and self-absorption.

Signs of an open, balanced heart

- I create and attract positive experiences.
- I care for myself as much as I care for another.
- I know that I am solely responsible for my own happiness.
- I am able to easily express warmth, kindness, joy and vulnerability.
- I care for others and am aware of how I can affect them.
- I am open and approachable in my manner.
- I view myself as equal to others.

- I allow love to flow both ways, giving and receiving without ulterior motives.

Another very common side effect of not recognizing the queue of our heartbreaks (besides general emotional numbness) is displaced pain. Eventually, something happens that punctures our denial and takes us back to the pain of our past hurts and losses. We find ourselves experiencing a level of distress that is disproportionate to the current loss. For example, perhaps a new relationship comes to an end. We hadn't been together long but we are inconsolable when our partner finishes with us. Might this be linked to an earlier heartbreak? A previous time when we felt abandoned or rejected by someone? An old heartbreak still waiting patiently in the queue for its turn to be held up to the light, named, felt and released?

Our language gives us clues about what happens when hurt and loss pile up inside us rather than being released. In English, we have 'the straw that broke the camel's back'. Interestingly, this idea finds expression in numerous languages all over the world. The Spanish equivalent, for example, is 'the drop that makes the glass overflow'. We say that emotional wounds 'fester' inside us just as a physical wound can fester on our body. And the phrase 'emotional baggage' describes perfectly the idea that some of us are lugging around our old suffering, unable to set down our burden.

We have now explored what constitutes a heartbreaking loss and wound. We have acknowledged that many of us are both confused about loss and in denial about the way that we have experienced it. Having done all this preparatory work, I now invite you to think specifically and in detail about your own life and create your timeline of heartbreak.

OVER TO YOU

Create your timeline of heartbreak

The aim of this exercise is to plot out the events in your life that have caused you significant pain or hurt, in chronological order. It's best to do this when you won't be disturbed and have plenty of time so that you don't have to rush it.

Take a large piece of blank paper and draw a horizontal line from left to right, halfway down. This line represents your life, from birth to however old you are now. At the left end, write the number 0. At the right end, write your current age. Then begin to map out your timeline of heartbreaks, along the line. Refer back to your notes from the first exercise in this chapter, when you started to list your heartbreaks (see page 34). Make a mark for each event and note your age at the time. Write a brief description of what happened below the line, and connect the event to your age on the timeline, with a line or arrow. Have a look at the example on the next page, which will give you a clear image of how to do this.

Don't feel you need to dredge up every single little disappointment or hurt (otherwise your timeline will be loooooooong!). What you're looking for here are the events that caused the *significant* pain that you know, deep down, you need to confront.

Please feel free to set your own pace for completing this work. There's no rush. For some people, seeing all their heartbreaks written out in black and white can be a powerful and emotional experience. Others of you might find it relatively easy and straightforward. Either response – or any other – is very natural. It's different for everyone.

It's also very normal to find that you have very few or even

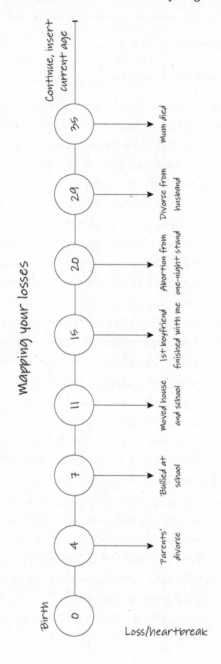

Mapping your losses

Continue, insert current age

35 — Mum died

29 — Divorce from husband

20 — Abortion from one-night stand

15 — 1st boyfriend finished with me

11 — Moved house and school

7 — Bullied at school

4 — Parents' divorce

0 — Birth

Loss/heartbreak

no memories from early childhood. Sometimes this blank is the brain's coping mechanism for dealing with traumatic or unpleasant events. Sometimes it's simply a question of forgetting. Most of us retain very few conscious memories – negative or positive – from before the age of five or six. If you're struggling to fill in your timeline, you could try thinking back to significant family occasions such as Christmases, birthdays or holidays and search for memories that way. Sometimes it helps to focus on the feelings rather than the events. So, for example, if you ask yourself, 'When did I first feel sad, lonely or scared as a child?' then you might be able to zone in on what was going on at the time for you. It's also fine to simply begin your timeline from the moment when you *do* have conscious memories. It's more helpful to get started and see what comes up than to be held back by worry over what you can or can't remember.

When you are ready, begin to plot out your heartbreaks.

Moving on from the neck-up approach

The final section of this chapter is the crucial one that consolidates your step away from denial and emotional numbness. You have now made a personal inventory of the losses and hurts that have broken your heart. I invite you to stay with any feelings this has brought up for you and begin to explore them.

This step into an emotional landscape of loss can feel very challenging to many of us. We are all on a spectrum when it comes to our comfort or lack of comfort with emotions and their expression. Some of us struggle to acknowledge that anything has ever really hurt us (that used to be me). Some of us feel consumed by our feelings about the past and find it hard to move beyond them. Others of us can tell somebody all about our past and pain in a factual way but can't begin to actually feel it.

Most of us can acknowledge our positive emotions but are much less confident with the negative ones. We have a tendency to divide emotions into 'good' and 'bad'. Happiness, excitement, satisfaction, joy and contentment are good; sadness, anger, fear, resentment and frustration are bad. But what do these labels really mean? It may be more pleasant to feel happy than sad, at least in the moment, but does that make sadness *bad*? It certainly doesn't make it any less inevitable. Surely, part of growing up is learning that we can't always have what we want when we want it. That applies to emotions just as much as ice cream!

There's a practical argument for learning to handle all our emotions, not just the ones that feel nice: it's the only approach that works over the long term because our aversion to feeling emotional pain will, ironically, keep us entrenched within it. When we reject the so-called 'bad' feelings, we don't get rid of them; we only make them stronger and increase our suffering.

When we're determined to experience only so-called positive emotions (as is the case with some of the spiritual bypass brigade), life can end up feeling very one-dimensional and lacking in depth and truth. If, on the other hand, we grasp that our feelings of sadness, anger and fear, for example, are not the enemy but in fact our teachers, we open up to real peace, joy and authentic living. We become quite literally more ourselves because we're no longer paddling in the shallows but also exploring our depths.

This is not a new idea, of course. Quite the reverse: all the world's great religions and spiritual philosophies teach it. Psychoanalysis and other forms of psychological therapy also work by investigating the depths. It's just that many of us are no longer hearing the lessons. We've been sold the lie that we can avoid life's pain at no cost to ourselves and instead buy or build the happiness we truly 'deserve'.

Some of us have fallen for the suggestion that we can analyse our way out of the depths by understanding the past intellectually, without actually having to do the messy work of expressing the painful connected emotions that lurk within. I meet lots of people like that. They acknowledge there's a problem and are trying to think their way out of it. Trouble is, they're stuck. Many of them are fluent in the language of therapy rather than emotional release. They have a very good theoretical understanding of why they are hurt but are still in tremendous amounts of emotional pain.

This is what I call the 'neck-up approach' to healing, based on an intellectual understanding of the cause and effect of pain and heartbreak in your life. It doesn't drop from your brain below the neck and into your body – most crucially, it doesn't reach your heart.

Developing this intellectual awareness is a crucial early part of the process of recovery, but on its own it's simply not enough. We need the ability to feel as well as analyse our pain. None of us is over something just because we understand what happened or can tell a story about it. We are all wounded at a level that is much deeper than our intellect can reach. In order to heal we need first to feel, and yet many of us are cut off from our emotional life. Even if we recognize that the neck-up approach isn't serving us, how do we change it? What can we do differently?

One way to begin to do this is by learning new words to

describe the landscape of our emotions. I believe that language is a crucial tool for increasing our ability to feel. This can sound counter-intuitive. Surely emotions arise spontaneously, before words? And surely we all know the difference between feeling happy and sad and can label those feelings accordingly?

The trouble is that by the time we reach adulthood, most of us have become highly skilled at managing our emotions practically out of existence. We've lost the spontaneity of childhood, the easy access to tears and laughter. So yes, the extremes we can do – if we have to – like expressing the difference between feeling over the moon and feeling really low, but we've lost the ability to feel or describe the nuance, the grey, the in-between and subtle states of emotional life. Our coping mechanism of denial has left many of us disconnected from our bodies and existing in a state of numbness.

Many people have a very limited vocabulary to describe their emotions. When I ask clients what they feel, they often say, 'I feel crap' or 'I feel upset'. But these are not feelings; they are general descriptions of a state of being. I encourage them to get more specific; so for example, 'I feel sad' or 'I feel numb' or 'I feel angry' or 'I feel hopeless'.

Language is one of the most powerful ways we have to get really specific about our inner world. It is all about nuance and capturing subtle difference. There are hundreds of ways to describe our emotional state and the more access we have to an expansive emotional language, the clearer we can become about exactly what we're feeling and why. If we can increase our vocabulary of emotions – deliberately and consciously – we can increase our ability to live more comfortably in an emotional world.

We all need to become more fluent in the language of emotion. At its simplest, that means having the words to be able to express how and what we are – or were – feeling. This matters because, unless we can name things, we can't acknowledge them fully. When it comes to healing from heartbreak, being able to name and express our emotions around loss and hurt is the first step away from living a half-life of suppressed pain, towards getting better.

Take some time to scan these lists of words to describe emotions and some of the physical sensations and signs that often accompany them. I encourage you to add to the lists with more emotional words if you have them. They are a resource for you to use when you complete the next (final) exercise for this chapter. You might find that the lists bring up certain emotional responses in you, or you might not. Either way is welcome.

Happiness	*Sadness*	*Fear*	*Anger*
Delighted	Bleak	Panicky	Furious
Excited	Empty	Frightened	Bitter
Joyful	Numb	Petrified	Outraged
Content	Low	Nervous	Frustrated
Cheerful	Distressed	Threatened	Vindictive
Serene	Miserable	Anxious	Resentful
Peaceful	Hopeless	Afraid	Annoyed
Light	Down	Tense	Irritable

OVER TO YOU

Naming your emotions

Now that you've begun to work out what happened and when by using your timeline, you can move on to the final exercise in this chapter, in which you start to explore the emotions you carry related to each event.

Return to your timeline of heartbreak and start with your earliest recollection of loss or hurt. Above the line, write a few words to describe how this experience left you feeling – at the time. For example, if your parents divorced when you were six, ask yourself, 'How did I feel, as a six-year-old, when my parents divorced?' Jot down anything that occurs to you and draw an arrow to connect the feelings to the event. (See the diagram on page 49 for guidance.)

Write as much or as little as you wish. Single words (in this case they might be sad/abandoned/angry/afraid), a few phrases or whole stories – all are welcome.

Gentleness above all is called for . . .

We've arrived at the end of the chapter. (Phew, you made it!) You've bravely ventured into the darker aspects of your past and begun to shine a torch around. It's not monsters we're looking for down there but portals: the secret doorways to a different life lodged within your own wounded heart. I know this isn't easy work, and we still have a long way to go. So, please, look after yourself. Get out for a walk or dance around the kitchen or take a long bath. Anything to shift gear and wind down after this intensive piece of work. And well done, you did it!

When we are processing a heartbreak – whether we're beginning to get a handle on what it means to us or doing the work coming up in the next chapter on toxic coping mechanisms and how they can damage us – being kind and gentle

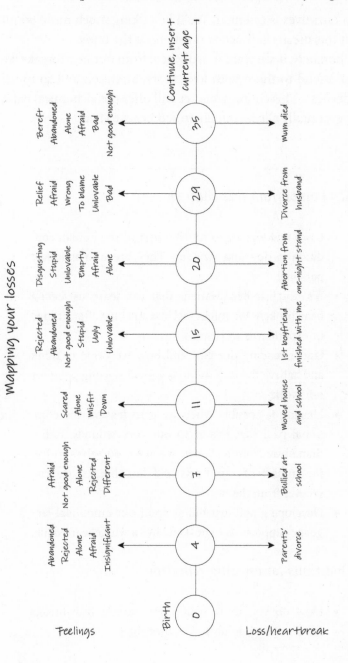

Mapping your losses

	Birth							
Feelings	0	4	7	11	15	20	29	35	Continue, insert current age

Feelings

- **4:** Abandoned, Rejected, Alone, Afraid, Insignificant
- **7:** Afraid, Not good enough, Alone, Rejected, Different
- **11:** Scared, Alone, Misfit, Down
- **15:** Rejected, Abandoned, Not good enough, Stupid, Ugly, Unlovable
- **20:** Disgusting, Stupid, Unlovable, Empty, Afraid, Alone
- **29:** Relief, Afraid, Wrong, To blame, Unlovable, Bad
- **35:** Bereft, Abandoned, Alone, Afraid, Bad, Not good enough

Loss/heartbreak

- **4:** Parents' divorce
- **7:** Bullied at school
- **11:** Moved house and school
- **15:** 1st boyfriend finished with me
- **20:** Abortion from one-night stand
- **29:** Divorce from husband
- **35:** Mum died

49

with ourselves is essential. We'll be talking much more about what this means in practice throughout the book.

Ultimately, if we want to truly heal from our heartbreaks we must attend to them with love, tears, attention and so much tenderness. This courageous act will offer the alchemical balm that eventually allows our shattered heart to heal.

Key points from this chapter

- Grief and loss are as much a part of the human condition as joy and wonder. They are also uniquely personal.
- It's not just bereavement that can leave us feeling heartbroken. We might feel loss and hurt after a range of experiences and events.
- Understanding our past and how we came to think and behave the way we do is a great starting point for our work.
- Healing is possible when we turn *towards* the emotional pain that relates to our core wounds, rather than away from it. When we allow ourselves to feel the impact of our hurts and heartbreaks, we can recover from them.
- Developing and expanding upon our emotional language supports us to heal and live a wholehearted life.

Questions for ongoing reflection

- How do you think your three earliest heartbreaks affect your adult life and relationships?

- How would you describe your relationship with your own emotions? And what about your relationship with other people's emotions? How do you express or supress your emotions?
- What new insights or learning have you gained from this chapter?
- How do you feel right now, in your body? Notice and breathe.

Step Two: Masks and Roles – the birth of the false self

Welcome to the second stepping stone on your bridge. I hope that you are beginning to see the reality of your heartbreaks with a bit more clarity, and becoming better able to name and express your emotions. I'd like to invite you to stay in detective mode a little while longer, as we begin to examine in more detail the ways that heartbreak has impacted your life.

So far, you've been reflecting on the events that hurt you, and beginning to get back in touch with how you felt when they happened. Now it's time to look at how the impacts of your heartbreak have continued to affect you over the subsequent months and years.

As we've seen, painful emotions pile up inside us if they're not dealt with. We've already talked a little about denial as a strategy for coping, and the price we pay for it in terms of emotional numbness and lack of understanding for ourselves. In this chapter we will be taking a deeper look at the physical and emotional damage caused by repression or avoidance of our heartbreaks. Basically, it's not pretty. When we don't deal with those feelings and reactions, we're not only kicking the can down the road but choosing to live a lie – and that lie has consequences.

Denial is not the only toxic coping mechanism that we need to acknowledge if we want to recover from loss and hurt. Human beings are very resilient and creative by nature, and many of us come up with our own homemade strategies for coping with our difficult feelings and the mess they can create.

When our heart gets broken, especially when it happens in childhood and we receive inadequate guidance from the often brokenhearted adults around us, we fall back on our primal need to survive. We learn to adapt in order to cover our hurt and shame. We learn what we must do to be acceptable to our families or tribe, so that we can stay connected and avoid rejection. We pack up our heartbreaks in that box with the big padlock and get on with playing a role that conceals our pain. And we wear the masks that come along with those roles, to cover the face we've come to believe is unacceptable.

Remember Rachel from the previous chapter? How she didn't believe she had anything to be sad about, and yet felt deeply sad? How she hadn't experienced what she termed 'significant heartbreaks' but had felt very abandoned and rejected by her busy, career-focused parents? Rachel is a classic example of how we can 'shape-shift' as children in order to ensure we fit in and belong. When she was growing up Rachel became 'the good girl' and the 'quiet one' in her family, so as not to make a fuss and risk further rejection. In her adult life Rachel unconsciously developed such a fear of being rejected or abandoned in her relationships that she took on the roles of 'the coper' and 'the independent one' to conceal her distress and loneliness. She wore masks of 'people-pleasing' and 'I'm fine' to try and hide her true feelings, even from herself. This sort of worked for a while, until eventually Rachel felt as if her life was one big lie and she realized that she had no clue who she really was.

The problem is that over time – as we move into adulthood – these coping strategies become more and more toxic. They don't do anything to heal our pain at its source and they have a whole host of unintended harmful consequences, some of which end up being even more destructive and agonizing than the hurt they were designed to help us cope with.

With every mask we put on and every role we play to cover up our vulnerability, our hurt or our anger, we lose connection to ourselves and to other people. Simply put, we forget who we really are. We get so busy acting out roles and wearing different masks for different occasions that our true identity becomes lost to us. The version of ourself that we show to the world is one that we've created out of desperation. It's made up of best guesses about what other people want us to be, or what we believe we need to be in order to be an OK person and belong. We mould ourselves into what we understand we *should* be and then spend our lives trying to keep up the pretence.

In therapy speak, this is known as 'the false self'. As we will see, it's perfectly natural to behave in different ways in different contexts; we all have many different aspects of who we are – parent, grandparent, professional, carer, friend, etc. An ability to be flexible and responsive in life is an asset and a sign of good health, if we are flexing appropriately to access different parts of our authentic self.

The difficulty comes when we don't know what's authentic and what's merely a defensive strategy, or a ruse to get what we want. Some of us never manage to uncover the difference. The false self becomes a prison. It may have begun as a survival strategy that allowed us to cope as a child or a young person, but if we're still acting out in this way as a mature adult we are essentially living a lie. Eventually, if our mind continues to deny that our false self has taken over, our body and soul will come to our rescue and nudge us to set about dismantling our prison.

The work in this chapter is divided up into various sections. In the first we will consider the origins of the false self. Why do we manufacture it in the first place? We will think about it as the cluster of coping strategies that we put in place, consciously and unconsciously, to protect those parts of ourselves that we now know have suffered significant heartbreaks.

We will also look at the way our beliefs about ourself, life, other people and the world end up feeding into those coping strategies. If our response to abandonment is to say to ourselves that it must have happened because we are unlovable, for example, then over time that might eventually solidify into a belief that shapes the role we play in our relationships.

Secondly, we will look in more detail at these coping strategies. I'll be inviting you to consider the many different masks and roles that people create, and to ask yourself which, if any, you have adopted in your own life. As part of this work, I'd like to take a close look at a particularly common and toxic strand of false identity: victimhood.

I will guide you to understand how these aspects of false self, which are born out of our initial reactions to painful events, then solidify over time. For example, after our parents' divorce perhaps we end up with the role of being a mini-parent to our younger siblings. What might have started as an understandable desire to offer comfort, to be useful, to be 'good' and earn praise and thanks from our family, ends up robbing us of other aspects of who we are and inhibits us in our own personal development.

Sometimes our roles and personas become such a key part of ourselves that we barely notice them any more. Our rebellious streak, for example, or our people-pleasing perfectionist side, might have begun as a coping mechanism for heartbreak or a way to hide a rejected aspect of ourself, but can end up feeling like an essential part of who we are. Eventually we come to believe that we can't manage without it.

It's not that we have 'screwed up' in adopting these strategies. They probably served us very well, for a while. We certainly don't need to berate ourselves for having done anything wrong. The problems come when we don't recognize that a coping mechanism has become toxic. If we don't at some point realize that we have *chosen* never to be alone, or never to be still or sober, for example, then we won't understand that the coping strategy has become more of a problem than the pain itself. If we don't recognize when a persona has become a label, such as 'bad boy' or 'warrior woman', defining the way we see ourselves and how others treat us, we have got stuck in a one-dimensional version of ourself. When we struggle to let go of the coping mechanisms we've put in place, we're heading for trouble.

Say hello to your wounded child

Let's begin at the beginning and consider where and when your false self was born. Remember how we talked about the radiance of babies and small children? Before major betrayals or heartbreaks, a child is happily, unselfconsciously itself. Then something happens. Flip back to your timeline of heartbreak. The first event you wrote down marks the birth of your wounded child.

The term 'wounded child' can be a bit off-putting for some people. It makes some of us defensive and others fearful. But it's not a criticism, or a diagnostic label for somebody who's unusually damaged. We all contain a wounded child. Quite possibly, we contain several.

Consider the first loss or hurt that broke your heart and left you wounded. How old were you? Four? Five? Six? And the second? Maybe you were nine, maybe you were thirteen . . . Whenever these events happened in your life, there may be a part of you that still holds your pain from those early significant heartbreaks. That part, or parts, make up your wounded child.

For example, if one of your parents left the family home when you were young, you may have felt abandoned. One of your core wounds would naturally be around abandonment. If you were unable to process the pain, either at the time or later, you might get stuck here emotionally, as a wounded child. You're suffering from a form of arrested emotional development. You grow up, of course. You look (and to a certain extent function) like an adult. But, in certain situations, whether it's at work or in an intimate relationship, if that abandonment wound gets triggered by, for example, a boyfriend breaking up with you, you might find yourself reacting like that small child again. (Sound familiar? If it makes you feel any better, that was me – for the whole of my twenties and thirties!)

When I write about 'being triggered', I'm referring to any event, comment or piece of information that plunges us back into our old hurts and painful memories. It might be a sort of emotional replay of the past but with different people taking on the roles in the present, as in the example above.

Triggers can relate to huge losses or to more minor hurts. Perhaps a friend makes a casual comment about our choice of clothes being not quite right and, even though we know they mean no harm, we're suddenly taken back to being teased relentlessly at school for having the wrong shoes or a dodgy haircut. Often we don't realize that that's what is happening at the time. Or we might recognize that our reaction feels a bit disproportionate but do not understand why we are behaving in a particular way.

A common reaction to this wounded part of ourselves is to want to shut it up. It might feel embarrassing or weak, so we might belittle it by trying to tough out the pain and push on through. We might not be willing to accept or even acknowledge that our past is affecting our adult life. But this rejection of our wounded child is a rejection of a fundamental part of ourselves. It will prevent us from thriving and feeling whole. It is the very first part of us that gets lost when we get hurt, leaving us feeling somehow broken and incomplete. It's absolutely crucial that we go back for it and all our wounded child parts.

Our wounded child is also a description of the way we can feel when we are hurt very deeply as adults. Not all significant hurts stem from childhood, of course. You might have had a very stable and happy upbringing but then experienced a huge life-shattering event as an adult, for example. This can leave you wounded and feeling very vulnerable, like a child. So when I refer to your wounded child or children, I am referring to any part of you that feels and behaves like a child who is suffering from emotional distress, no matter what or when the triggering event happened.

As with every aspect of ourselves and every element of the work in this book, we are all different. Some of us are carrying huge emotional wounds. For others, the wounds are smaller, more like bruises. In some cases, our wounded children are literally screaming out for comfort and attention; in others, our wounded child just needs a cuddle from time to time.

Which is it for you? One clue that your wounded child is alive and kicking inside you is that you are highly reactive. If people and situations trigger you easily, this can be a sign of unhealed pain. It's often the voice of the hurt child inside, waiting patiently for you to remember them. There's a great old saying which sums this up perfectly: 'If it's hysterical, it's historical.' When our reactions are disproportionate to current events, it's a big clue that we are being triggered by the past.

Take a look at the checklists of behaviours on page 60. On the left you've got a list of ways that your wounded child might act out. On the right is a list of ways that another part of you shows up to help. Here's some good news: as well as a wounded child, you also contain a wise adult. That's the part of yourself that holds the fruits of your experience and learning. The more you turn towards and settle the wounded child inside, the more your wise adult self will be able to take the lead, like a wise inner parent or elder, guiding you on your path.

Take some time to scan down the two lists and – as you did before when you were considering how loss might show up in your own life – reflect on which of these behaviours chime most with you. Jot down some notes in your notebook if that appeals. Don't worry if some of the ideas are unfamiliar. We will be coming back to all these points in due course. This is just for you to start getting a feel for which elements resonate most at this point in your life. Also (a quick 'inner critic' alert here), this is not about beating yourself up for being an emotional five-year-old. It's about approaching yourself and your past with compassion and recognizing that this information will inform your healing process.

'Wounded' child	Wise adult
Reacts to situations	Responds to situations
Makes demands	Makes requests
Expects their needs to be met	Asks for their needs to be met
Is childish	Is childlike
Is either boundary-less or barriered	Holds healthy boundaries
Blames others	Takes responsibility
Passive aggressive or aggressive in conflict	Assertive
Has a need to win/be right	Keen to find resolutions
Speaks in absolutes	Asks questions
Talks more than listens	Listens more than talks
Takes everything personally	Takes very little personally
Feels less than or better than others (inferior/grandiose)	Knows that there are no 'others'
Wants someone 'out there' to rescue them	Knows it's an inside job
Expects 100 per cent loyalty and honesty	Understands people are flawed and make mistakes
Labels and excludes	Avoids labels and includes
Looks outside of themselves for 'love'	Knows that they are love
Laughs at	Laughs with, never at
Their wounding defines them	Their wounding has shaped them

Only you can save yourself

What are the consequences of not learning how to recognize and reach out to our inner wounded child? As we've said already, the impacts of our hurts and losses really stack up over the course of a lifetime. When the first heartbreak gets buried, that reflex action can become a template for all our subsequent responses to hurt.

Besides this, there is one very specific impact of not going back to deal with our childhood wounds. It's like a kind of learned helplessness. It makes sense that we didn't know how to save or soothe ourselves back when we were children, but if we never learn to do it as adults then we will continue to look around for someone else to do it for us. Our wounded child ends up desperately seeking 'mummy' or 'daddy' everywhere and finding them nowhere. The classic example is in intimate relationships, where we are unconsciously looking for our partner to parent us in the way we needed but didn't receive when we were a child. We look for them to meet all of our unmet needs: to be seen, heard, accepted and loved unconditionally.

I've worked with many people, men and women, for whom this was the case. One particular story sticks in my mind. Nina was in her forties when I met her and had been dating men a generation older than her all her adult life. The dynamic always ended up as being that of a parent and child rather than two equal partners, with Nina in the child's role. Every time, either she or her partner would end up frustrated, with neither person getting their needs met. The relationship would inevitably end in unhappiness and blame.

It wasn't until Nina came to do her inner work that she was

able to really understand how and why this was happening. Tragically, Nina's parents were both killed in a car crash when she was only eight years old. She had always suspected that her choice of a romantic figure who was roughly the age her father would have been was significant, but when she came to really investigate, she was able to see how that massive childhood wounding was playing out in her adult choices and behaviours. It wasn't enough to identify the original wound. Nina needed to feel the pain of the original loss of her parents and then slowly begin to learn how to care for herself, meeting her own needs, which freed her to begin to relate from a more adult space in her relationships.

The wounding event doesn't need to be as tragic for it to lead to a similar dynamic playing out for people. If our caregivers were unable to look after us in a healthy way, for whatever reason, we might unconsciously carry on looking for someone to play that role throughout our lives. We might also look for a saviour, or someone to fix us. And let's face it: all the fairy stories and Hollywood romantic films reinforce this fantasy.

Many of us in such co-dependent relationships are essentially asking the other person to rescue us from our hurt and save us from having to go near that box of pain locked inside of us. We want a shortcut to feeling better and for someone else to take the pain away. We want, above everything else, not to have to do the hard work of rescuing ourselves.

This is entirely normal and simply reflects our arrested emotional development. We are emotionally still a child in certain aspects, who needs the loving guidance of a parent or carer to help us understand and work through our pain.

It may be normal but it's also doomed to failure. Speaking as someone who tried this approach for decades, having a series of relationships with versions of my dad, I can say with all sincerity that – sadly – it doesn't work! Co-dependent relationships, where one person is overly dependent on another to look after them or save them, are deeply unhealthy for both parties. The truth is that no man/woman/relationship/child/career or sum of money is going to save you. These things can act as a wonderful distraction from your wounds for a while, but only you can heal them. It's a tough lesson to hear and, believe me, I know. But no one is coming to save you. You have to do this inner work for yourself. Become your own saviour. And it is so worth it.

If you're wondering how on earth you're supposed to manage this, don't worry, we have the whole of the book to explore your healing. Your inner wise adult is going to play a key role, as you will see.

A word about vulnerability

Before you carry out the first part of this chapter's work with your inner wounded child, I'd like to offer you a few thoughts about vulnerability. Children are, by definition, very vulnerable. Beginning to address your wounded child, turning to face them and eventually opening your arms out to them, might make *you* feel very vulnerable, a bit embarrassed, upset or any number of other uncomfortable feelings.

As adults, we have all had a long training in how to make ourselves less vulnerable and how to hide the traces of vulnerability that we can't eradicate. We absorb the message that to be vulnerable is to be weak, and to be weak is to be a victim. 'Toughen up,' we are told. 'Don't let them see you are hurting; they'll just hurt you even more.' None of this training really works, though, does it? It doesn't stop us from being hurt and it certainly doesn't make our historic hurts go away.

The alternative way to approach vulnerability is to flip all that conditioning and grasp that, actually, the very opposite is true. Being vulnerable is not passive or cowardly. It is the most courageous and brave act we can make. It takes pure strength to dare to drop the pretence, along with the masks, and say and show to the world, 'I'm hurting and this is what hurt looks and feels like.'

Being vulnerable will make us even stronger, not weaker. It will in fact heal us, not hurt us more. Brené Brown has been researching the psychology of vulnerability over the course of a long and distinguished career. As she says, 'Vulnerability is the birthplace of love, belonging, joy, courage, empathy and creativity. It is the source of hope, empathy, accountability and authenticity. If we want greater clarity in our purpose or deeper and more meaningful spiritual lives, vulnerability is the path.'

Couldn't have said it better myself!

It takes practice, but allowing ourselves to be vulnerable – with other people and alone, with ourselves – can be a hugely powerful force for bringing about authentic change.

If it's hard to imagine how it might work for you, you could try thinking back to a time when someone you loved or cared about (or even a stranger), dared to show their vulnerability to you. How did you feel towards them? Perhaps a colleague burst into tears at a work meeting. Perhaps a friend admitted their fear of their partner or shared with you an experience that was deeply shameful for them. What often happens with such courageous moments of strength (yes, you read that correctly), is that they make us feel closer and more connected to the other person. We might feel inspired by their courage; maybe even dare to let ourselves be vulnerable too.

I invite you now to open up to your own vulnerability and begin to turn towards your inner wounded child.

Self-soothing for grown-ups

So many of us don't know how to comfort ourselves when we feel sad, overwhelmed or stressed. This inability to self-soothe increases the likelihood that we will become dependent on less healthy soothers, such as alcohol or our partner's immediate and unwavering attention. It can help to know how to look after ourselves in the moment, and give ourselves immediate relief and comfort. Effectively, we need to teach ourselves how to self-soothe, just as a parent teaches a small child, with affectionate touch, soft words and physical comfort.

In therapy speak, the way we treat ourselves as adults – either with nurture and love or judgement and indifference – is termed the way we 'self-parent'. This reflects the idea that until we do our healing work, we will do to ourselves what was done to us in our early life, parenting ourselves the only way we know how. So if it was a neglectful or abusive style of parenting we received, we need to learn a new, healthier way of parenting ourselves.

If you're not sure how to do this, it can be helpful to imagine what you would do for a child – your own son or daughter, niece or nephew – who came to you in distress, and then proceed to treat yourself in the same way.

What would you say and do if they came to you in pain, feeling confused and afraid?

You would pick them up, soothe and hug them. Reassure them that they are safe and that you are there for them. Get them all cosy on the sofa, wrapped up in a quilt with some yummy treats – the whole works. You would snuggle up together, listen to them and allow them to cry in your arms. You would validate their feelings. You would hold their hand and stroke their hair. This is exactly what we need to learn to do for ourselves. Catch ourselves when we fall. Hold our own hand. Be the parent that our wounded child deserves.

OVER TO YOU

Self-parenting visualization

I encourage you to spend a few moments each day doing the following self-parenting visualization. As you practise this, you are not only calming your adult self down, you are also soothing your inner wounded child.

- Find a quiet place to sit where you will not be disturbed. Allow yourself time to settle.
- Close your eyes and take some slow, deep and gentle breaths into your belly, breathing in through your nose and out through your mouth.
- When you feel ready, imagine the wounded child part of you coming to stand in front of you. Notice how old they are and how they are feeling. (Some of you might see this image in your mind's eye and others will simply sense a presence.)
- Imagine the wise adult part of you, who is sitting in the chair and gazing down at your wounded child. Take some deep breaths and really imagine looking into your child's eyes. See them there, with all of their fears, anger and sadness. Allow whatever emotions arise to do so without judgement.
- From the wise adult part of you, imagine now sending the child part of you love, compassion, acceptance

and gentle kindness from your eyes and your heart. Just as you would for any distressed child. Hold eye contact with them in your imagination as you beam love into them. Every breath you take is sending them your love.

- The next step is to imagine picking them up and holding them in your arms, like a baby (you might want to use a pillow if this helps to make the process less abstract), and start to rock them tenderly. We organically know to rock our bodies in order to soothe a baby. This is the same thing. Keep maintaining eye contact. Beaming love, compassion, acceptance and gentle kindness into their heart. Say a few words of comfort if this feels right – 'I've got you, you're safe now, I'm going to take care of you, all is well, my love.' You might even sing them a lullaby.
- Then, when the wounded child part of you begins to feel soothed and settled, slowly bring your hands up across your heart and pop this image of your child into your heart. Hold them safely there as you continue your day. If and when you need to later in the day, gently place a hand across your heart to let them know you are still there for them.

How beliefs about heartbreak shape the roles we play

What do you believe in? I don't mean do you believe in God or an afterlife, but something more personal. Do you believe that people are basically good, or that they are fundamentally not to be trusted? Do you believe that you're doing your best and that's good enough, or that you're lazy, or useless, or stupid and will never amount to anything?

All of us are carrying around in our minds a set of beliefs about how the world works, what life is all about and what sort of a person we are. We may or may not be able to put those beliefs into words, but if we take time to think about our attitudes and behaviours we will be able to see some patterns emerging.

For those of you who are starting out on personal development work, your beliefs may not yet be completely visible to you, and that's fine. The work you've been doing to uncover what you think and feel about significant events in your life will hopefully help you to start to see more clearly how your beliefs were formed.

Others of you will be more familiar with this work, and know something about belief formation already. It's a lifelong process, but one way to think about it is in terms of thoughts and language. The thoughts we have and the words we use to express those thoughts will, over time, feed into the beliefs we hold, which can be healthy or unhealthy, rooted in reality or delusional.

For the purpose of this section of the work, we're going to consider beliefs very simply and specifically, in the context of our response to heartbreak. They typically begin as unhealthy thinking patterns that we use over time to try and make sense of what happened to us. What starts off as a series of self-punishing words or phrases, if repeated often enough, will ultimately become an automatic and entrenched belief. For example, if I tell myself in my head (as I did for many years) that I am unlovable, and I repeat this to myself like a mantra, it will eventually become a firm belief: my version of 'the truth'.

Research into belief formation has demonstrated the role

of a concept called 'negativity bias', which basically means that, in general, people find it much easier to believe the bad stuff than the good about themselves and other people. This means we tend to hold on tightly to negative self-beliefs and unconsciously look for reinforcement that they are true. We will often attract relationships (with partners, friends or even bosses) with people who treat us in ways that feel familiar and confirm our beliefs. Unsurprisingly, research has shown that this pattern of behaviour and the negative belief system that sustains it are linked to the development of depression and decreased levels of self-esteem.

They are also involved in the development of our coping strategies for dealing with heartbreak. The masks and roles we end up adopting to survive our emotional distress reflect our beliefs about what happened. So to go back to the example of abandonment, if we believe that we were left by a parent or a partner because we weren't 'good enough' to make them love us enough to stick around, then that belief might feed into us playing a particular role. Perhaps we put on the mask of the tough independent person who doesn't need love and is happy alone. Or we put on the mask of the 'perfect girl' and play the role of people-pleaser, or indispensable colleague, or martyr mother.

Not all beliefs are unhealthy or disconnected from reality and everybody's sense of who they are is mediated through beliefs they have formed, consciously or unconsciously. There is nothing intrinsically wrong or unusual about the process of belief formation. But it's helpful for all kinds of personal development work to be able to understand that what we believe, even about very intimate subjects or things that actually happened to us, is not necessarily 'true' in any straightforward way. Human beings make up stories all the time to explain themselves to each other and make sense of their experiences to themselves. Sometimes, however, those stories will get us into trouble.

Masks, roles and the birth of the false self

All of us are called upon to play many different roles in life. During the course of any given day we might wear a variety of different masks to deal with different situations, from the 'professional' mask for work, to the 'competent parent' mask at the school gates and the 'I'm fine' mask for our family. Masks support us to function effectively in a particular role and sometimes, of course, we need to be able to do just that. We are all multidimensional beings and that can be a joyous part of our life. So I'm not saying that behaving in different ways in different contexts makes you inauthentic, nor am I implying that experimenting with different presentations of yourself is somehow bad or wrong.

What can get us into trouble, though, is wearing masks in order to hide (even from ourselves) the painful truths of us. When we use masks or take on roles to cover up some fundamental aspect of ourself, one that we have decided or been told is shameful, unacceptable or unwelcome, we are creating a false self. Eventually, if we wear these masks long enough, we discover we can no longer take them off. Without us really noticing, they have metaphorically merged with our face. We wake up one day and find that we have forgotten how to live without them. Our whole life feels like a big lie and we look in the mirror and have no clue who we really are. Does this resonate?

This was the case with a former client of mine called

Marcus, who eventually realized that he didn't know who he was if he wasn't playing the role of 'tough guy' wearing the masks of being 'rational' and 'unemotional'. He came to me after he recognized that he couldn't remember the last time he felt anything much at all, even with his family and friends. He was so numb and disconnected that he couldn't remember when he'd last laughed with his kids or felt loving towards his partner. That was his warning sign, and it woke him up to the fact that he'd lost all connection with the feeling part of himself.

Marcus was nothing if not a problem-solver, so he looked around for a strategy to deal with his numbness and found The Bridge Retreat. It was so moving to witness him gradually explore his emotions, and remove the roles and masks he'd adopted to handle them. 'I just can't do it any more, Donna,' he told me. 'Life's so flat. I feel dead inside. It's exhausting.'

Living as a false version of yourself as Marcus did – pretending, hiding, running – is excruciating and exhausting. If, for example, you are constantly trying to be the perfect 'dream girl sex kitten' for your boyfriend because you are terrified of being left if he sees the real 'flawed' you, then you're dooming that relationship (plus your own sanity) to failure. Your self-worth will take a battering because in your heart you will know you're living a lie and, in doing so, betraying yourself.

In my own life, I've tried out various different masks along the way. In no particular order I've been a 'good' girl/a rebel/ the angry one/the helper/the rescuer/the people-pleaser and the fighter. I could go on! Eventually, in order to survive the legacy of my childhood, where to be vulnerable was to be ridiculed, I became primarily a warrior woman. Over the years I developed a seemingly impenetrable armour, which served me very well (thank you very much!). I have overcome many life challenges with my warrior woman persona and I would not be the leader I am today without her, but over time I have come to see her limitations. What began as a means of self-defence ultimately turned into a prison.

Until well into my thirties, I faced life head on. I was a fighter and a doer for years and years until the day I just couldn't do it any more. It was utterly exhausting, and as I learned more about personal development, psychology and spirituality, I began to have serious doubts about whether it was all worth it.

If I only gave myself permission to be a fighter, what message did this send to the 'wounded child' part of me? The part of me that was hurt was getting hurt all over again every time I denied myself the possibility of feeling or being anything other than a warrior. Living like this meant there was no room for the softer emotions such as tenderness, sadness and fear. There was no innocence or capacity for me to be vulnerable. And if we can't express our vulnerabilities we can't learn, and we certainly can't heal. It's that simple (and that hard). We might feel safe, sure, but we'll stay lonely to the core.

It felt scary to begin to release my warrior woman persona, but I gradually learned that I could give her plenty of time off without losing her completely. My well-honed warrior skills can still be used when required but they no longer define me. And now I am once more a multi-faceted person, able to live my wholehearted life.

This dismantling of the false self was by far the better option for me but – a word of warning – it can be threatening for other people. As I began to change and grow, becoming more myself once again, I noticed that many people preferred the old version of me. The 'give herself away, jokey, love everyone but herself' Donna suited them much better, but it didn't suit me.

One day I woke up and looked at all the masks scattered on

my bedroom floor. I saw that they had become too heavy to wear. It was just too confusing, playing all those roles. I simply couldn't pretend for another moment to be anything other than flawed, imperfect, fabulous me. It was scary though, at first. When I took that final mask off my face and looked in the mirror, I couldn't see anything at all. It was as if I'd disappeared, which I suppose, in a way, I had. But slowly, as I lived more honestly, my face began to reappear. I took shape again, as I returned to the truth of me.

I'd like to invite you now to have a look at the following lists. The first one is of character traits that can over time begin to function as masks. The second one is of roles, which are typically played out within a family but can occur in any social group. Spend some time reflecting on which, if any, you wear and perform in your own life. Add to and expand the lists with your own experiences.

Character traits (masks)

- Confident and self-assured
- Happy-go-lucky/upbeat
- Competent and efficient
- 'I'm fine'
- In control
- Professional
- Perfect mother/daughter/partner
- People-pleaser
- Warrior/advocate
- Pretty and sweet
- Successful
- Poor me

- Confused/chaotic
- Ditzy/stupid
- Thoughtful/quiet

The masks we opt to wear are often linked to the roles we took on in our family as we were growing up. There are always a variety of roles up for grabs and we can, of course, take on more than one. For example, a 'truth-teller' can also be 'the rebel'; an 'achiever' can also be 'the special one'. Our roles can change over time, too. The 'good girl' who has had enough, for example, might morph into the 'rebel'.

When you consider your own family, can you identify which roles other people played, and why? What about you? Which roles did you try on for size in your childhood, and how did they change over time? How do these roles still show up in your life today?

When I asked a client to answer these questions recently, she said something along the lines of, 'My father was often physically absent and was always emotionally totally unavailable when I was growing up. I think he was too busy playing the role of "provider". I was a good girl and a perfectionist as a child, a rebel as a teen and then a desperate manic pixie dream girl when I was a young adult in intimate relationships. I would do anything to hold my partner's attention because if it wandered, I was sure I was no longer loved. I had to be cool, funny, perfect. I had to be adored and adorable. I still expected to be left and, sure enough, I always was . . .' Tracing her reactions to her childhood wounding, through the various roles she played, led her to see the impact of that early experience of an absent father on her adult life. She finished by describing herself as a Recovering Perfectionist, which is definitely progress!

Take a look at the list on the next page and see if you

recognize yourself in any of these descriptions. This is definitely not a definitive list but more a starting point to get you thinking. Add to the list as you wish.

Roles

- **The Good Girl/Boy** – this is the responsible, sensible child. They are often focused on other people's needs and can appear to have no needs of their own. A compulsive helper who might also mediate in the family to keep the peace. People-pleaser and nurturer.

- **The Rebel** – this person is a 'troublemaker'. Over-emotional, angry. Provokes, questions, is defiant and always in trouble. They test limits to the max and are seen to need a lot of help.

- **The Clown** – uses humour to distract from or avoid family conflicts. Denies or hides their own true feelings.

- **The Achiever** – this person is focused on perfection. They can be very logical and goal-orientated. They hold the belief that they must not fail. They can find it difficult to connect to their emotions and are often stuck in neck-up living.

- **The Truth-teller** – holds up a mirror to the whole family. Challenges the lies within the family system. Sees and points out that the 'emperor has no clothes'. Can be rejected by the family for this. (See also The Scapegoat.)

- **The Baby/The Special One** – this is usually the youngest or only child. They are treated leniently and given special treatment. They can remain an eternal child and struggle to take responsibility for their behaviour and choices. Often have issues with finances and relationships.

- **The Perfect One** – the child who does everything right and presents as 'perfect' and without any needs. Usually fiercely independent and focused on external and/or internal perfection. (See also The Achiever.)

- **The Care-taker** – this is the family member who takes care of everyone else and puts everyone else's needs above their own. Can be linked to The Good Girl/Boy. Often has issues of control and co-dependency.

- **The Independent One** – the family member who appears to have zero needs. They are self-reliant and adaptable. Rarely asks for help and appears to cope in most situations.

- **The Scapegoat** – the one who is blamed by the family for any or all of the disharmony and challenges. Often used as a way (or excuse) to avoid the deeper family issues beneath the surface. (See also The Rebel.)

- **The Stupid/Silly One** – this is the family member deemed to be somehow not intelligent enough. The one who seems to fail academically and/or who makes a lot of mistakes and errors of judgement in their life.

Victims, 'woundologists' and their unfinished business

There's one particular persona that affects a lot of people at some point in their processing of heartbreak, and can be especially toxic if we get stuck there. It's the persona of the victim. To be clear, when we are hurt or experience violence or abuse of any kind, we are often powerless and can genuinely be a victim of the circumstances and painful events of our lives. This is especially true when we are children. I am not suggesting that genuine victims of terrible events or traumas are responsible for the situation they find themselves in. The victimhood I'm referring to here relates to adults who have become overly identified with being and remaining 'the victim' of what happened to them in the past.

Victims often hold strong beliefs and tell powerful stories about the things that have happened to them, and the perpetrators. They blame the people that hurt them (and sometimes blame themselves). One of their strongest beliefs can be that whatever happened in their life was unforgivable and/or impossible to recover from.

The psychology of victimhood is extremely complex. There can be a certain power in being a victim, which makes it understandably attractive to people who have suffered loss and hurt. The problem is that, like all masks and all aspects of false self, being a victim will ultimately render you a one-dimensional version of yourself, unable to grow or develop. Some of us get completely stuck in the persona of being a victim. We construct a whole identity for ourselves solely out of our wounds.

A new client called Sheryl once shared with me in our first session that she had found out her husband was having an affair. She was understandably devastated and became very distressed as she described in detail the events that had unfolded. After a while I asked her how long ago this had happened. She replied, 'Almost twenty years.'

Over a number of weeks, we explored her need to hang on to this pain and tell this story over and again. Sheryl went on to admit that she wanted to remain a victim so she could continue to blame her ex-husband, and said she 'refused to let him off the hook' by moving on in her life. Impressively honest!

Eventually, through allowing herself to deeply grieve for the end of her marriage and the betrayal of the affair, Sheryl was ready to relinquish her need to be seen as the victim. In doing so, she reclaimed her self-respect and power and could finally move on with her life, proving to us all that it's never too late to change!

The term 'woundology' was created by author and spiritual teacher Caroline Myss to describe what happens when people (like Sheryl) don't heal from their heartbreak and instead become attached to the identity they've constructed out of their wounds. This can happen if we define ourselves solely or primarily by our past hurts, and either allow or actively use our past to determine our current life.

Those of us in the grip of woundology have a tendency to share these wounds and the related 'poor me' story with anyone and everyone who cares to listen – over and over again. We wear our pain like a badge of honour. Unconsciously or consciously, we might enjoy the attention it brings us and are reluctant to give it up. And, as with all masks, we get to the point where we have no idea who we would be without it. There is a particularly high price to pay for merging with this particular aspect of false selfhood. It can keep you stuck for ever in your painful past. And let's face it: no one likes to hang around with a woundologist for too long except others in the same boat.

Woundology feeds neatly into a blame culture, where everything is always the fault of 'the others'. It can give us a convenient excuse not to take responsibility for our lives. When we were children and we experienced hurts, trauma and abuse, we genuinely were powerless victims. We had neither the power to fight back in our own defence, nor the agency to leave.

But as adults we can change this narrative. The truth is that, unless we do, we won't heal. We won't even truly grow up. Psychotherapist and author David Richo encapsulates this in his line: 'If you're still blaming your parents for what happened in your childhood, then you haven't left home yet.' This might sound harsh (especially to those of us who haven't yet done any inner work) but its intention, I believe, is to throw down the gauntlet and demand that we all rise to the challenge. If we choose to tackle our unfinished business we *can* move forward and emotionally grow up. We can transform our inner victim into a heroine/hero and become the saviour in the story of our life. Rewrite the narrative. Reclaim our power, and finally leave home.

If you're feeling challenged about any of our work around masks and the false self, especially around victims, please remember that I'm not judging you. I've literally been there myself and bought the T-shirt! In fact, it took me three years of therapy (and thousands of pounds), to even acknowledge that I was playing the victim role in my life. But when I eventually admitted this truth, it gave me something true to work with. There comes a time for us all, if we want to heal, when it's necessary to face some painful realities and start the work of dismantling our false self.

What does it cost you to live with a false self?

Every individual's life is determined by countless intersecting factors and I'm not suggesting that heartbreak is some sort of monster that dooms us to a grisly fate. We are so much more than our pain, even if our pain is part of us. But if we don't do our inner work we run a high risk of developing problems that might block us from living a wholehearted life.

All inauthenticity is dangerous to our health, our capacity for happy healthy relationships and our ability to develop as a person. Repressed, avoided or unhealthily managed heartbreak does terrible damage to us, physically, mentally, emotionally and spiritually. It can show up in bitterness, addiction, depression, anxiety, abandoned dreams and a life that is so much smaller than it was ever meant to be.

Renowned doctor and psychoanalyst Wilhelm Reich said, 'The body is frozen history,' and that people who carry a significant burden of emotional pain are more susceptible than average to physical diseases, including gastrointestinal problems, headaches, back pain, respiratory problems, inflammatory diseases such as lupus and some cancers. Mental health is also severely affected by unprocessed emotional pain and can manifest in increased anxiety and depression.

When we deny or cover up our losses and hurts we become less resilient, more emotionally fragile, more inclined to see the world as a hostile or hopeless place. We are less open to forming new bonds and our relationships suffer because our ability to trust and to express our true feelings is diminished. We take fewer chances, even if it seems likely to others that they will bring benefits. Or, depending on our personality type, we might take part in more risky behaviours. We will use drugs, including alcohol, more frequently.

Even if we don't get ill we are likely to live less fulfilled lives. Our unreleased grief seeps out of us like toxic waste, slowly poisoning us and those who dare to love us. Festering anger can manifest in a tendency to criticize or to behave passive-aggressively in relationships. Sadness will leak out in apathy, despair, a collapse into victimhood and hopelessness. Fear might manifest as low self-worth, anxiety, panic and harsh judgement (often of ourselves). The simple truth is that hurt people hurt people. Even if that someone you're hurting is yourself.

Often, people dealing with unresolved heartbreak will justify their refusal to do their inner work by saying things like, 'The past is in the past. I'm only looking forward.' And yet you only have to look into their eyes to see that's not true. If you look closely you will see every heartbreak they've ever denied, staring back at you. The colour of their eyes is pain.

Then take a look at their body, frozen in time as it faithfully holds on to the past in the tightness of their jaw, the tension in their shoulders, the aching pain in their lower back, the layers of defence over their battered heart. Even the way they carry themselves is a testament to the continuing presence of the past. The body never lies, you see. (That's how much it loves you.)

And then there's the way that they live. You know those people who can't say anything positive about life, or themselves or other people? That person is very probably carrying a lot of emotional pain that they have yet to process. It's the same thing with people who criticize and judge others, who moralize or lecture or gossip. Bitchy jokes and a delight in passing on painful news are like an alarm going off, signalling the presence of un-dealt-with heartbreak. The (unfinished) past has so many ways of making people live a smaller life than the one calling to them. The voices in their head masquerading as their own sound so loud and convincing, whispering shouty lies that they're no good and will amount to nothing. It's hard not to believe them. The choices they make every day highlight the fact that the past is not (yet) in the past. Until they begin to heal, it is very much still in the present.

The fallout from all this blocked emotional pain is everywhere around us. You probably experienced it growing up, either at home or at school. You might be living with it now, either because a loved one's pain is seeping out – or yours is.

We do not need to accept these damaging or hurtful behaviours, either from others or from ourselves, just because the person concerned is hurting. Quite the opposite. I want to show you that the price you are paying for not dismantling your false self and stepping into vulnerability is just too high. As spiritual teacher Richard Rohr says so eloquently, 'If you do not transform your pain, you will always transmit it.' Hear this truth – it doesn't have to be this way. There is nothing you will face in your healing journey that is more painful than living half a life. Believe me, I know . . .

OVER TO YOU

Mapping your false self

You are now going to examine your life story for evidence of the masks, roles and coping behaviours that you have adopted to manage your painful feelings. Take a look at the graphic on page 83, in which your true self is represented by a whole heart surrounded by layers of the false self.

Reflect on how your false self has been built up as way to distance yourself from pain, through for example taking on particular roles or taking refuge in relationships. You might want to look back at your timeline of heartbreak to remind yourself of the events and feelings that led you to take certain

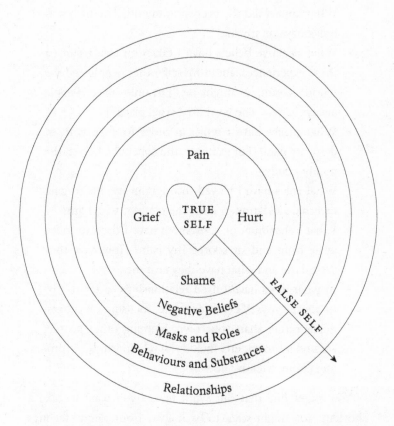

'As we move away from the pain, we move further
and further away from the truth of who we are.'

protective or soothing measures. When you're ready, reflect on the following questions. You can jot down your responses in your journal.

- What impact did the events on my timeline of heart-break have on my life?
- What negative beliefs have I taken on as a result of these experiences, about myself, other people and the world? (Examples might be: 'I'm unlovable.' 'People always leave.' 'The world is a cruel place.')
- What masks have I worn in order to cope with or deny my pain? (For example, the coper, the helper, the goody-goody.)
- What roles have I played throughout my life to gain external validation or deny the truth of who I am?
- What behaviours or substances have I used to move away from and/or soothe my pain? How have they served me and what have they cost me?
- In what ways have I used relationships to try to 'fix' or soothe myself? (For example, focusing on others' needs rather than your own, blaming other people, sex and intimacy, etc. Include all relationships – intimate, family, friends and work.)

You might find that this work makes you want to take a shortcut. You might want to back away from painful feelings and realizations and just go and eat some cake. To be honest, I don't blame you! But just get the cake *and* do the work. When we distance ourselves from our emotional pain we are also distancing ourselves from the truth of who we are. So if you're tempted to stay in the 'neck-up' approach, push yourself to move further down the body towards the heart, and use the language of emotion. Try to be as honest and detailed as possible.

This might be really painful for some of you. You might go into a survivor response – feeling numb, disconnected or devastated – as the traumatic impacts of your heartbreaks come home to you. If this is the case for you, please take it all very gently and slowly and do ask for help if you need it. On the other hand, you might find all this relatively straightforward. As always, either of these responses – or any other – is completely welcome.

'Be more Theo' – remembering your true self

So what is my reward for doing all this tough inner work, I hear you ask? Rightly so! Who will be left underneath, once the masks and roles have been dropped? Quite simply, *you* will be. Not the defended or 'broken' you of the false self, but the authentic, open-hearted truth of who you really are. Remember Theo, my four-year-old grandson, who looks in the mirror and loves what he sees. Your own version of Theo is who you will find in your mirror, staring back at you. As you step through the portal and open that pain box, you will begin to peel away all of the false layers, all the masks and roles and coping behaviours that no longer serve you. You will come to remember who you really are. You are made of the qualities that we all share: kindness, compassion, love, openness, wonder and joy. All of these qualities are your birthright. When you do your inner work, you find them waiting for you in the very same box that contained all your heartbreaks. Turns out that Pandora's box was in fact a treasure chest after all.

As the wounded child part of you begins to heal you will notice that you are becoming more childlike, which is not at all the same as childish. You start to become more creative and playful, grateful and joyous. You reclaim all of the wonderful qualities of your innocence, to set alongside the emotional maturity of an adult. You grow up.

Key points from this chapter

- Each one of us has both a wounded child and a wise adult inside of us. Our inner work is to learn to listen to, accept and embrace our wounded child so that we can be guided and supported by our wise adult self.
- Vulnerability has nothing to do with weakness. It takes immense courage to show our 'underbelly' to the world. This vulnerability is a superpower as it enhances our inner strength and resilience.
- The masks we wear and roles we play are all part of the false self. Initially we use them to protect ourselves from our emotional pain, but eventually they lead us further and further away from the truth of who we are.
- 'Woundology' refers to over-identification with our emotional wounds. It describes the way that some of us become so attached to our 'victim' story that we are unable to heal.

Questions for ongoing reflection

- What does it mean to you to show your vulnerability? What feelings come up for you when you do?

- In what ways and in which situations do you assume a 'false self' persona? What does this cost you?
- How connected are you to the 'wounded child' and 'wise adult' parts of yourself? How could you become more compassionate towards your wounds and more trusting of your own wisdom?
- What new insights or learning have you gained from this chapter?
- How do you feel right now in your body? Notice . . . and breathe.

Step Three: Grief and Loss – essential parts of the human condition

Everything I have learned about grief began with heartbreak. As I sobbed on that bathroom floor, my heart was breaking open to let grief flow out and truth flood in. I was amazed at how much I needed to cry: *me*, who hadn't cried for years. My rational mind was still fighting for control but – luckily – my body came to the rescue and gave me no option but to stop and pay attention to my emotional reality.

Yes, it hurt – but it was also the beginning of a new phase of my life. I didn't know it at the time but within a few weeks I could look back and see myself lying on the toilet floor as if that Donna were on the other side of a portal. I wanted to reach out to my old wounded self and take her hand, guide her through the doorway that was being created out of my poor broken heart.

My new life wasn't easier than the old one, at least not immediately. I was off work for months. For the first couple of weeks I believed the doctors when they said I was having a nervous breakdown. Then I began to sense that something good was happening, something that didn't fit with that terrifying label. I felt awful but I also felt more honest and more myself than I'd felt in a very long time. Whatever was happening to me was painful but it also felt true. Necessary. The journey back to integrated, wholehearted living would take several years for me, but almost from its first steps it brought some much-needed relief and rewards as well as struggle.

My message for you, as we reach the third stepping stone on your journey, is to take courage. This step is likely to be turbulent. It has to be, by necessity, because without feeling our grief we cannot heal from it.

Your pain is now pointing the way you must go in order to move forward in your one precious life. There is no way back to a time before you got hurt. If you don't move forward, your only alternative is to stay stuck – and that's no alternative at all. Dealing with bottled-up grief may be painful, but not as painful as the long, slow death of living with it.

I know this might feel daunting. Even once we understand that we must grieve our heartbreaks, and even if we long for the freedom that grieving can offer us, we are likely to feel unsure of how to do it and scared at what it will mean for us. Resistance and denial may well come up, big time. You might find yourself thinking, 'My life's not that bad, maybe I'll skip this chapter and get to the "happy bit" at the end.' This is all very natural. But if our understanding doesn't translate into urgent and practical action, our grief remains static and becomes toxic rather than being transformed and released by the active process of grieving.

It also gets harder and harder to do, the longer we leave it. We de-skill ourselves when we don't learn how to handle and process emotional pain. We weaken our resilience and end up having to lean into our addictive distractions more and more. Our wounded child never learns how to grow up into true adulthood. So I invite you to steady your nerves if you're feeling them, dig deep for faith in yourself and prepare to take the next step across your bridge.

Having recognized our heartbreaks and begun to dismantle

the coping mechanisms that trap us in a false self's version of reality, we are now turning towards the full force of our unprocessed grief. The work now is all about your emotional reaction to loss and hurt. It's time to let yourself feel every-thing safely, step by step – all the pain you've had locked up in that box – and, by slowly releasing it, start to truly heal.

Firstly, I will invite you to reflect on what grief feels like and how we ensure that we are releasing all its components and not just the bits we are more comfortable with. I will be inviting you to recognize each element of your grief: all the anger, sadness, fear, doubt, confusion, blame and shame – whatever it is that comes up for you.

Then we'll look at the practical and emotional strategies for tapping into, processing and releasing grief. I'll be show-ing you some tools and inviting you to explore which ones feel best to you. They include ways to work with your body, your heart and your soul. My approach draws heavily on rit-ual and is informed as much by spiritual practices as Western psychology.

What does grief mean to you?

As we've already seen, heartbreak is more of an everyday occurrence than we might realize until we begin our inner work. It's the same with grief. It's a heavy word because for most of us it is so strongly associated with death, devastating loss and hurt. It sounds like a potentially overwhelming experi-ence that might suck us under or shatter us into tiny pieces. Many of us believe, often without ever having really thought about it, that grief is horrific but fortunately rare. With luck we will only have to deal with it a few times in our life. The best we can hope for is to endure it until we are somehow ready to 'move on'.

I believe this approach to grief does us a tragic disservice. It leaves us scared and powerless in the face of an essential part of our human condition. It fails to equip us emotionally or spiritually to cope with and even to grow from unavoidable life events. This attitude implies that we're weak for not managing the pain that our life losses naturally produce, even though most of us have not been shown any coping mechanisms – except perhaps alcohol and Instagram – and received no consolation except the cliché that 'time is a great healer'. Yeah, right.

Remember that we are working with a very different definition of grief, as a 'natural emotional reaction to significant loss or change'. It's not a sign of weakness or failure. It's simply what we can expect to feel when we lose or are hurt by something or somebody we value, or our life takes a different path from the one we were expecting. Just as loss does not equal death, grief does not equal a once-in-a-lifetime catastrophic falling apart.

Grief is much more ambiguous than many of us realize, and sometimes turns up in emotionally complex situations where we are both losing and gaining something valuable. I once worked with a woman called Anna, who came to see me when she was feeling down some months after the birth of her first child. Anna had struggled to conceive for years and was overjoyed when she finally got pregnant and gave birth to a healthy baby boy. She was grateful for her good fortune and loved her son intensely but she was also feeling very unhappy and confused. She was wondering whether she had post-natal depression. Over a number of sessions, Anna was able to recognize the impact of the life-changing shift in identity that motherhood had brought her. It wasn't only the exhaustion of parenting a small baby, it was also the immense responsibility and related anxiety of caring for a tiny new life. 'These huge waves of grief would wash over me as it dawned on me that my old life was completely over,' Anna told me. 'My whole identity and the freedom I had known were gone, and things would never be the same again. I also felt incredibly guilty because I knew how lucky I was, when so many others had not been able to conceive.'

I'm sure many parents can connect with Anna's story and the conflicting emotions of her grief. I know I can.

It was only by acknowledging to herself the complexity of how she felt, and then allowing the conflicting emotions, including her guilt, to flow along with her tears as she grieved and honoured the loss of her old life, that Anna was able to fully inhabit her new identity as a mum without debilitating sadness or regret.

For me, grief is always a messenger. It has something to tell us. Sometimes that is simply to express the love we feel for those we have lost. At other times it reminds us of the pain of our past that we can't ignore and the changes we need to make in order to move forward. At first grief whispers its truths, but – guess what – most of us ignore them. Generously, grief will try again. Many of us, brought up to believe that we shouldn't make a fuss and terrified of the so-called 'negative' emotions, fear that if we let ourselves actually feel this pain, we will fall apart. So we continue to ignore the messages. We put on a brave face and tell ourselves that time cures all hurts, eventually. Sooner or later, though, grief will demand our full attention. It will grow frustrated at being treated like the enemy when it only wants to help. If we continue to ignore it, eventually our poor wounded heart cracks right open, as mine did.

What does grief feel like?

Our usual understanding is that the main emotional content of grief is overwhelming sadness. That is certainly an important element, but there are typically many other emotions at play when we're grieving. When we lose (or are hurt by) something or somebody important to us, we might feel sad, abandoned, angry, confused, rejected, fearful, regretful, hopeless, guilty or ashamed. (And many other feelings besides. This is not a complete list!)

Renowned psychotherapist and author David Richo suggests that the core emotions of grief are essentially anger, sadness and fear:

- Sadness – at what or who has gone away. Our heart hurts so much. We feel alone with our despair.
- Fear – that things will always feel or be this way. We will never recover. This pain will never end and life will never be the same again.
- Anger – at the unfairness, injustice, betrayal. Somebody or something important has left or betrayed us or been taken from us, and that makes us furious.

How do you feel about this description of grief? Do you recognize these three core emotional elements in your own experience? Take a moment to see what comes up for you as you think about them in relation to one or more of the losses you identified in Step One. Feel free to look at your timeline of heartbreaks. Can you begin to assess your emotional reactions at the time in terms of sadness, anger and fear?

Sometimes people struggle to see anger and fear as core

parts of grief, especially if they are still working with an understanding of loss as being equivalent to bereavement. This may or may not be the case for you, but let's investigate, using the example of the end of an intimate relationship, to see how the three core emotions of sadness, anger and fear might come up and how other diverse reactions might also contribute to grieving.

First off, we might feel natural sadness that this relationship has come to an end, even if we were the one to call it a day. Perhaps we feel sad that yet again our dreams have come to nothing and we are once again alone. We feel hurt at how things turned out between us.

Then comes fear. We might fear that we are going to be alone for ever, unable to find the love that we long for. We might fear that our sadness will never end and our broken heart will not heal. That when all is said and done, we might never be able to trust again, nor be able to move on from this painful place.

Finally there's the anger. Perhaps we are mad at the way we have been treated. We feel furious about the betrayal and at the person who has hurt us. Or maybe we are not angry at anyone in particular but simply at the unfairness of it all. How come everyone else seems to find it easy to meet someone great and keep a loving relationship?! From this angry place we might want to blame and rage at someone who stands in for the person who has left us, or even at anyone who resembles them.

There are likely to be other emotions swirling around in the mix as well. We might feel that we have brought the situation on ourselves in some way, because of our own personal failings. If so, that is likely to bring up feelings of shame, regret or guilt. It's also possible that part of us might feel relief at being out of the situation if it was making us unhappy. Grief is ambivalent like that.

Grief is so deeply personal and everybody grieves first and foremost as an individual. It's also true that our individuality is made up of numerous intersecting roles and identities, and each individual grieves within their cultural context. One particularly significant component of this, in terms of grief, is gender. People who have been socialized as female throughout their lives can sometimes get stuck in the sadness and fear dimensions of grief without accessing the anger. People who have been socialized as male, however, can get stuck in their anger and never go near their sadness and fears. After all, many little boys are told that 'big boys don't cry' and to 'man up', while their angry or aggressive outbursts are indulged as 'boisterousness'. Little girls, on the other hand, are encouraged not to shout or be loud and to diffuse any conflict or angry feelings with a nice sweet smile. After all, it's very 'unfeminine' to be furious.

The problem with this approach to grieving is that women can get stuck in a state of internal collapse, feeling only sadness and fears about their losses and perhaps some anxiety when anything remotely like anger bubbles up inside of them. (And I'm sure many of you have heard the old expression that 'depression is anger turned inwards'.) Men, on the other hand, can get blocked in their grief through feeling angry all the time. If they are raging away without being able to access the 'softer' emotions of their sadness and fears, they are missing out on the feelings that would actually heal them.

It would, of course, be wrong to generalize that 'men access their grief through anger' and 'women through sadness', but I have observed that there is a *tendency* for it to be that way. Our emotional life is very much constrained by what emotions we are told are acceptable. And the truth is we need to be able to access the full emotional landscape of our grief in order to move through it and emerge on the other side.

Most of us, regardless of our gender, have no idea how to express healthy anger as opposed to being passive aggressive – or simply showing good old-fashioned aggression. There is a lot of confusion about the difference between them. I believe that healthy anger, when expressed safely, is an energetic force that can be used positively for healing and transformation. Anger is a very natural emotion. It is also a close cousin of passion. How do we know what our boundaries are without anger? If we don't get angry about what is happening in our world, how will we find the motivational fuel to campaign for change? Would Greta Thunberg have even looked up from her schoolbooks if she wasn't full of righteous indignation? Healthy anger reminds us that we care and shows others that we are alive. We need it to create change and take action in the world.

Healthy anger is not the same thing as toxic unprocessed anger manifesting as aggression, abuse or destruction. It is not a chaotic force. It is not, above all, the same as violence. When anger is misunderstood as something unacceptable (which for many of us is how it was modelled to us in childhood), we are more likely to repress it. This only makes it more explosive and more likely to leak out of us in precisely the aggression or violence that we were trying to avoid, if only to ourselves.

I appreciate that some people are frightened of anger precisely because of the confusion that surrounds it. We don't want to admit to being angry (especially as women) because that would mean admitting to something 'ugly' or 'hostile'. We don't want to be around angry people, because who wants to be close to violence or abuse? I also understand the dread of being *seen* as 'angry'. For some groups of people, such as Black women, anger is habitually used as a label to dismiss their emotional experience and to deny and undermine their truth.

All these misunderstandings have so many negative consequences. If only more people were angry, because healthy anger is our truth and our birthright. If only more people could see how their 'de-pressed' rage sits inside them, causing physical illness and mental and spiritual despair. If only more people could trust that anger contains alchemical magic within it. Safe release of anger, and the pain and hurt that inevitably sit just underneath it, can lead us to discover what lies on the other side. Our passion, our mojo, our very life force! We will be exploring a simple exercise to support you to release your anger safely later in the chapter.

The bottom line is that grief is more complex than we often allow. My opinion is that because it is so challenging, we instinctively want to minimize it by making it smaller, simpler, rarer and less urgent than it really is. Trust me, that never ends well.

How can we work with our grief?

Luckily, there is a remedy for the pain of unprocessed grief and it's highly effective. That remedy is the process of doing our grief work.

'Grief work' is an umbrella term commonly used in therapy for the activities that allow us to identify, feel and then express the three core emotions (sadness, fear and anger) fully and safely. In my experience, there's a lot of crossover between feeling and expressing our grief, so in effect the more you open up to feeling it, the more you are able to express it, and vice versa.

'Grief work' captures the difference between grieving (which I might describe as 'the feeling of intense emotions after losing something/somebody important') and this other thing that we're discussing here, which is more like 'a conscious process of accessing and releasing trapped emotional pain'. I also refer to this process as 'soul work' because, as you return to heal those heartbroken aspects of yourself, you are essentially honouring your own soul.

Some people dislike the term 'grief work'. It can sound like hard labour, which is off-putting and scary. It can sound a bit 'therapy'. And do we really need to turn our emotions into a job, into *work*? I understand these reactions but I still use the term because it's so useful. It precisely describes the practicalities of what we're exploring in this book.

Your grieving *needs* to be done. It is an active process and, in that sense, it is a bit like work. But this is not a task you carry out to benefit somebody else: you are the person who stands to gain by far the most from it (although the ripple effects in your family will be huge). You will not be paid in money but in a different kind of riches: greater peace and more contentment.

At its simplest, this grief work is a four-part process that looks something like this:

1. To know and understand (as far as possible) your emotional truth of what happened to break your heart. This is not about factual details but about how it felt to experience it. Sometimes we do not have a narrative attached to our feelings (especially if we were wounded before we were able to speak), but we can give a voice to the truth of how it felt. For example, 'I was born carrying the belief that I did not belong in the world,' which is common for those who were 'a mistake' or 'an unwanted pregnancy'.
2. To share your story with benevolent witnesses. We will be talking more about this later in the chapter. A

benevolent witness is someone who will listen without judgement or without trying to 'fix' or take away your pain. We all need to feel seen, heard and understood. We all need our broken hearts and our experiences to be validated. This allows us to heal, let go and begin to move forward in our lives.

3. To access and feel all of the emotions of our grief (sadness, fear and anger) related to the original source of the wound or heartbreak. To release them through our body. With our voice, our movement, our tears, our screams, we allow them to safely surface and pass through us.

4. When we feel ready, to begin to write a new narrative for our life. Once we fully grieve the past events and have them honoured, we can choose to move forward holding them a little more lightly inside of us. As we travel through the portal and begin to heal, we can start to piece together the gifts from the experience. When we're ready we might even (not always) move into forgiveness and compassion, with gratitude for what the experience taught us. In this way we transform a painful experience into something of worth and meaning.

The reality, of course, is usually less linear and more complex and messier than this makes it sound but I do believe that grieving is something we can learn to do well rather than badly (or not at all). Grief work is partly about learning a new skill set.

Grief work is love in action

As well as work, I also talk about grieving and grief in terms of 'love' and 'soul'. I have heard it said that grief is the price we pay for love. The implication seems to be that if we love someone (or something), we have to accept the inevitable cost of losing them. In my opinion there's a fundamental misunderstanding here. For me, grief is emphatically not the price we pay for love. In fact, it is another form that love takes and its role is to save us – and our loved ones – from the long, slow death of ungrieved hurt, loss and heartbreak.

Grieving is both an act of love and an essential rite of passage. I'm in complete agreement with the spiritual teacher and West African tribal leader Sobonfu Somé, who wrote that, 'Grieving is a soul cleansing and a way to recover our spirit.' When you set out to heal the heartbroken aspects of yourself, you are returning for shards of your essential being. You are putting your heart and soul back together, like a spiritual jigsaw puzzle.

When we consciously interact with our old emotional pain, even if it's years after we were hurt, we are turning away from the inertia of blocked grief and towards the dynamic process of *grieving*. Grieving and grief work become one and the same, a beautiful hybrid of soul work and skill set: both spiritual and deeply practical.

Learning how to grieve in this way is first and foremost a process of healing and recovery. It brings relief from suffering and a return to full vitality. It takes you away from all those negative outcomes we discussed in the previous chapters, from the headaches, the anxiety, the loneliness and the conflicted relationships. Grief work is medicine for both the heart and soul. In time the wounds in our heart will heal over and become a precious and beautiful scar. As our scar eventually fades, we get stronger and more resilient. We put out the fires that are burning in our life. Gradually, we have more capacity to get on with rebuilding, of living and loving with and through our whole beautiful heart.

Eventually, learning to grieve empowers us to redefine our heartbreaks and rewrite our own story. When we grieve fully, we grow exponentially. David Kessler, grief expert and author of *Finding Meaning*, calls it 'post-traumatic growth'. Our resilience, empathy and wisdom develop into superpowers. They allow us to find meaning in even our most agonizing heartbreaks. That's not to say that we wouldn't, of course, have preferred people not to die, hurt or leave us, but rather to say that this loss did not happen in vain. A precious gift was left behind in its wake and it is heartfelt grieving that helps us to find it.

In a minute, we will move into the practicalities of grief work. Before we do, I want to offer you a thought that I hope you will find useful. It's about being brave but also about finding pleasure and value as we do our work. Because bravery may be essential but none of us can be brave all the time. Fortunately, you don't have to be.

Grieving is like surfing. It takes guts to get on the board in the first place and lots of persistence to scramble back on every time you fall off. You can't learn to surf by lying on the beach and watching, or by gobbling down dozens of YouTube videos. You have to get in the water and have a go. It looks and feels impossible until you've tried over and over again. Even when you've cracked the basics, you might dread the fall into the tumbling surf. Will I drown? Will I ever resurface? Eventually, though, you will reach a point in your 'grief surfing' at which you can appreciate the view underwater just as much as you enjoy the incredible views of the beach when you're cresting a wave. After all, pearls are only ever to be found at the bottom of the ocean . . .

Sometimes we will feel on top of the world (or wave). These moments are golden, precious and temporary, like everything in life. As we tumble beneath the surface of our 'negative' emotions, we see things upside down and topsy-turvy for a while. We are experiencing our humanness from a different perspective. If we can allow this to simply *be*, and surrender to the depths, maybe pick something up while we're down there, we will soon be back up on that board, surfing the waves of life once again.

The 'how' of grieving – release and relief

This section is designed to give you an overview of how you might approach *your* grieving. Grief work, like heartbreak, is intensely personal. There is no right or wrong way to do it, as long as it involves both your heart and your body.

There are two different and complementary types of activity for dealing with our grief as it begins to emerge from us, and it's important to use both of them. One is what I call 'grief release' and the other is 'grief relief'.

Release is what happens when we face and process our grief. We will be looking at this in much more detail later, but examples of grief release include crying, or moving our body to help shake the painful feelings up and out.

Relief is what happens when we make a conscious and temporary move into soothing or distracting ourselves. We are not denying our grief in these moments; we are holding it, and ourselves, in a safe place so that we can recover our equilibrium. An example might be the decision to watch a favourite funny film after a crying session, and relieve our grief by laughing our head off. We will look at relief in more detail, too.

For now, please note that grief relief must be something you *decide to do* and then decide to *stop* doing, as in the example of watching the film. Otherwise there's a risk that short-term comfort tips into ongoing grief avoidance or suppression. If we soothe ourselves constantly without doing the work of release we are no longer grieving, we're just ignoring our festering wounds.

Grieving in a healthy way by alternating the two approaches builds resilience. There's an analogy with physical fitness training. Short bursts of intense activity interspersed with rest build muscle strength, boost your cardiac health and increase your powers of endurance. Same thing with grieving. Your grief muscle strengthens with every training session but you need to soothe and rest in between.

Have a look at the following list of suggestions and see if there are any you're already using or would like to explore. We will be returning to look at some of them in more detail later in the chapter, and incorporating them into exercises you can try for yourself.

Grief release

- **Crying** – give yourself permission to have a good old sob. Watch a sad film, listen to a melancholic piece of music, write about your pain, whatever it takes to support your emotional tears to flow and be released.

- **Shaking your body** – literally shaking out some of your pain and emotional blocks can support your body to release stuck energy and bring the system back into balance. There's more on this in the section on bodywork, coming up.

- **Dancing** – along similar lines to the shaking, focused dancing with specific music can help the body to grieve. There's an exercise later in the chapter to guide you to do this.

- **Singing, speaking and chanting** – some people prefer to use their voice to express themselves and it's an important part of the physical healing process. So allowing yourself to speak, sing or chant your grief are all incredibly powerful.

- **Drawing and painting** – another great way to move beyond the mind and allow our intuitive wisdom to take over. Paint your grief or draw your pain.

- **Writing** – many of you will know that journalling about our emotional world has been proven to support the healing process. It's very powerful to write down how you are feeling and the details of your heartbreak. Give yourself permission to express your pain through the written word. Writing by hand has been shown to have far more positive effects than typing.

- **Sharing** – speaking your grief is an essential part of the grieving process. Try to find the words you need to say and dare to speak them to a benevolent witness. With time, this process of sharing comes to feel easier and you can do it more frequently.

- **Focused exercise** – walking, swimming, running and boxing are all great ways to access and release your grief but it's important to exercise with mindful intention. Using physical activity to numb or distract has a place in grief relief but that's a different thing. For grief release, take your grief with you as you walk or run or swim. Every step you take or stroke you make, you are consciously focusing on your emotional distress, visualizing it flowing through you.

- **Breathwork** – there is a wide range of free resources available online to support people to learn various breathing techniques and exercises that can help relieve stress, release emotions and calm the nervous system. Check out transformational breathing, which is a great technique, or any form of yogic breathwork.

Some of these tools might feel a bit 'out there' for some of you. That's absolutely fine, but I would encourage you to notice and acknowledge any feelings of discomfort and then make a choice to give some of them a go anyway. Some will work for you and others might not but you'll never know unless you try.

Grief relief

Grief relief is to adults as self-soothing is to babies: we all need ways to comfort ourselves when we are hurting. Just as a parent or carer patiently teaches a baby how to calm down after a crying fit and how to fall back to sleep after waking, so too must adults be taught how to calm down after their grief release work. (Babies are great at grief release by the way – all that yelling and crying comes very naturally to them!)

When we discharge our grief we are healing ourselves deeply, but we will often feel drained afterwards as our sympathetic nervous system has been activated. We need comfort and soothing to calm and recalibrate, accessing our parasympathetic nervous system, which is responsible for us returning to a restful state. We need reassurance and even sometimes a little healthy distraction. It's not good to live our lives at a continuously high pitch. We need to be able to calm ourselves down and bring our bodies back into balance. Sometimes we just need a break from it all!

That need is real and understandable. It's not weak or childish to need to switch off from our grief from time to time. In fact, it's essential, so that we do not become overwhelmed or lose sight of why we are doing this work. The methods we choose for grief relief are important, though, as we've seen. If we can't learn to self-soothe in healthy ways, we're liable to end up self-medicating with alcohol, drugs, busyness, etc., which tips us back into avoidance.

Here are a few examples to get you started on finding the grief relief strategies that work for you:

- **Physical comforts** – warm baths, cosy relaxation on the sofa, a little nap – these are all practical ways we can relieve our bodies after all the hard grief work.

- **Safe touch** – nurturing touch is a human need. We all need to be held or stroked without a sexual agenda. Hugs from friends can make all the difference to our energy and emotions. Massage, reflexology and facials are lovely if you have the resources to pay for them, or a friend or partner who's happy to provide! The exercise for touch that you can give yourself on page 178 is a great resource.

- **Giggles** – there's nothing like a good giggle to support the body and soul to return to balance. Watching a comedy you enjoy or contacting a friend and talking about happy or funny memories can all help calm our systems.

- **Gentle exercise** – any gentle physical activity can support us to settle and feel more grounded (especially after doing grief release work). Examples might be

Hatha yoga, walking, stretching, cycling, dancing or swimming. The main thing is that the pace needs to be slow here, so no ten-mile fast runs!

- **Meditations/visualizations** – these are a great way to bring yourself relief and there are many free resources available online. Any visualizations that focus on calming and centring the body are likely to be a good starting point. Yoga Nidra can be particularly helpful for this. Or even simply sitting under a tree, eyes closed and focusing on your breathing, might be enough.

- **Creative expression** – trying new and old ways to express yourself creatively. Be that singing, knitting, colouring, drawing, painting, pottery or poetry. Whatever fills your cup!

- **Connection** – phone a friend, head out for a walk or arrange a coffee with a mate.

- **Healthy and focused distraction** – watch a film, read a book, listen to music, do a jigsaw puzzle.

- **Focus on others rather than yourself** – develop a project that interests you and allows you to switch off from your inner world and focus on the wider world.

Go to the original source of your grief

In a moment I'm going to invite you to do an exercise that may challenge you but will definitely build your grief muscle. You're going to write a letter, as if from the part of you that experienced deep heartbreak, to the person who hurt or abandoned you. This tool is a powerful way to get in touch with and release old pain. (And before you have a heart attack, you will *not* be sending this letter. It's just for you and your work here.)

For many of you this first letter (and there may be several you need to write over the course of your inner work) will be addressed to the parent(s) of your childhood. This is especially relevant for those readers who know that they carry 'unfinished business' from that time.

If your first thought is to write about a more recent hurt or betrayal, I invite you to refer back to your timeline of heartbreak and remind yourself about what you discovered when you 'followed the trail' of hurt and loss. As we saw in Step One, if you have experienced a recent relationship split, for example, and are left feeling abandoned and rejected, it can be helpful to check in and see when and where you first had feelings of being abandoned and rejected. In order to heal it's important that we grieve the original source of our core wounds, but the work to determine whether our current hurts have a historical thread can be a lengthy process. We may need to return to it many times.

For those of you who already feel complete with your parents from a childhood perspective, or for those who do not believe they carry any significant childhood parental wounding, this tool also offers a way to complete with parents from an adult space. Perhaps they have died, for example, and you never got to say goodbye or tell them what they meant to you. Or perhaps the relationship has become difficult or fractured in recent times. Writing to them offers the opportunity for your adult self to complete with your parents where necessary, so that you can reconnect with them on a deeper level.

And for those of you who have done your parental work and have more recent hurts to address, this letter can be just as powerful and healing. Please use it in the way that feels most appropriate for you.

OVER TO YOU

Writing a letter for emotional completion

Choose one major loss or hurt to focus on. Identify the person or people that broke your heart. That might be a parent, a partner, or something more abstract such as fate or the universe if the loss is, for example, of a miscarried child.

Remember that you will not actually send this letter, so this is an opportunity to 'say the unsayable' without censoring your words. It's important that the letter is framed in a way that supports you to access the memories and related feelings that you need to grieve, so we're going use a series of sentence stems to guide you.

For those of you who have limited childhood memories, please know that this is very common. It's perfectly OK to focus your writing on more general impressions of how you *felt* as a child growing up in your family, rather than details of specific dates and events. For example, you might simply recall how lonely you often felt, in which case you write about that. Often people find that once they start to write they are surprised by the memories and visual images that do come back to them. If you have access to old family photos, this can help to jog your memory about how it was for you on family holidays or birthdays, Christmas and other important occasions. The priority here is that you use the sentence stems as guidance (though there's no need to stick to them rigidly), and to give a voice to the 'wounded child' part of you.

Set aside at least two hours and do this work in a place where you feel safe and will not be disturbed. It's important to nurture yourself as you write. I like to wrap myself up in a blanket with a hot-water bottle and a cup of tea. Whatever helps you to feel cosy and safe.

Write a letter expressing all your emotions about the heart-break and the person who caused it, using the sentence stems below as your guide. Numbers six and seven, which are about regret and forgiveness, will not be appropriate for all heart-breaks but do try to include all the other steps, if you can.

If you can, please write by hand rather than on a computer. Experiments have shown that when we write by hand our mind slows down and we find it easier to access feelings. There are also greater benefits for our autoimmune system.

There is no limit on how much you write. This is your opportunity to say unsaid things in order to complete your unfinished business.

Think back to how you experienced the loss or heartbreak at the time. What did you feel?

Writing the letter may or may not be emotional so it's best to try to prepare for either possibility. Don't do this exercise just before you have an exam or a big presentation at work, for example, in case your emotions are very stirred up. Before you start, you might want to pick a 'grief relief' exercise from the list on page 103 so that you have some clear ideas for what you will do afterwards to calm down and self-soothe.

Stay open to your own unique experience.

Sentence Stems*

1. *My experience of you/us/the situation was . . .*

Write about what you remember of the events that hurt you. Give your perspective without filter. This is an opportunity for you to blame and accuse if you need to. Don't hold back. What did they do to you?

2. *What I needed from you and didn't get was . . .*

Now you write about what you needed or wanted them to do, and how they let you down or made things worse by, for example, not recognizing their responsibility.

3. *And how I felt/still feel . . .*

Then you describe your feelings at the time about what happened, and any current feelings remaining (if still relevant). Again, be as emotional as you like. Use as many as possible of the emotionally specific words that we saw in Step One (see page 47).

4. *What I need you to know is . . .*

Tell the person how their choices, words and actions harmed you and how this has impacted your life.

5. *What I wish I could have said or done is . . .*

This is your chance to rewrite your story in your own words. What would you have done differently if you could go back in time? Take back your power.

6. *What I need to, or can, or can't forgive you for is . . .*

Recognize whether you can or can't forgive them. This is very much a personal choice and there is no obligation. We will be returning to this theme in the next step of our work, so there's no rush here.

7. *What I need to apologize for is . . .*

Check whether there is anything you feel you need to apologize for or anything about your own behaviour that you regret. This is not relevant for everyone.

8. *And one more thing . . .*

Is there anything else you wish to say, that has not been covered?

9. *Goodbye . . .*

Complete your letter. This is not about saying goodbye literally to the person, but to how you have held on to them and this phase of your life. It is a symbolic way of marking the moment you choose to let this go and move forward.

Now use your chosen self-soothing activity that will help you to calm down. Nurture and support yourself to recover from the deep work you have been doing.

* *These sentence stems are based on the Grief Recovery Method created by the Grief Recovery Institute and included in* The Grief Recovery Handbook.

The healing power of being witnessed

We all need to feel that we matter, especially when we are in pain or feeling vulnerable. We also need to feel that we can make sense of our emotions. If we don't feel valuable and can't regulate our emotional life then our grief work is going to be that much harder. In this section of the chapter we will be talking about how we can release painful feelings and grieve them in the presence of a witness, which is a tremendously powerful tool for healing.

The healing power of being witnessed comes partly from being seen and from being accepted. This makes us feel validated and understood. Small children look to their parents or primary caregivers to feel validated and understood. A parent's role is to help a child make sense of their experiences and develop an emotional language to describe them. So if a child is upset because they can't have something they want, their parent might respond by saying, 'I can see that you're feeling angry because you want ice cream instead of your dinner.' These words combine with the parent's attention, tone of voice and facial expressions as they name the emotion, so that the child can attach the label (anger, in this example) to the physical sensations and feelings they're experiencing. The parent is also validating the child's experience by seeing, hearing and acknowledging it.

This process of naming and validating is known as 'mirroring' and it plays a critical role in a child's development. It's how we develop our sense of self and of empathy, belonging and security. When children are healthily mirrored in this way they go on to develop trust in themselves and their feelings, as well as an ability to express those feelings in everyday life. When they are not adequately mirrored they can find it challenging to identify and regulate their emotional world, trust their feelings and express them in healthy ways to others. This impacts their sense of self-worth, confidence and ability to relate in social and intimate settings.

Whether or not we were mirrored in early life, we can all experience a form of mirroring through being witnessed. This can happen in a small and private setting, with just one person whom we have chosen to see, hear and validate our experience through their presence, attention and energy. It can also happen in a group, in a therapeutic setting or among absolutely trusted friends.

The next part of your grief work involves you choosing a witness and reading the letter that you wrote previously out loud in their presence. This is a powerful way to release grief and have it acknowledged. Before we move on to the practical aspect of that work, let's take a look at what we mean by witnessing and how to choose your witness.

For the purposes of your work, a witness is someone who will compassionately and lovingly listen to you, without interruption or any need to 'fix' or take care of you and your emotions. They are someone who will hold space for you, and listen to your story with all of its emotional truth. Someone who will show you, through their presence, their loving eyes, their attention and energy that they see and hear you and that you and your story are important and make sense to them. In this way they are silently mirroring you in the way that you needed but may not have received as a young child.

It is important that you choose your witness(es) wisely. For some of you, your letter might include secrets and shame which you will be sharing for the very first time. It takes a huge amount of courage and vulnerability to do this work, so the wounded part of you whose words are going to be heard needs to feel very safe and secure. Make sure your witness is someone you trust and who you know will hold your words in the utmost confidence: a trusted friend, therapist, coach or figure from your place of worship.

Witnessing is not about a mate agreeing with you when you share your recent heartbreak: 'Oh, the bastard! I never trusted him!' Neither is it a dialogue in which you share and then they do: 'Oh, me too, I had a similar experience when . . .'

A witness is not the person that you have written the letter to.

A witness is not someone who has their own agenda, or a vested interest in your experiences. It's not usually a suitable role for a family member, for example, who might hold a very different memory of the events that you experienced. Family members can have strong reactions to what they hear, which could be very unhelpful and painful for you. The last thing you need as you courageously speak your truth is somebody judging you or invalidating your experience.

A witness does not need to be someone who has had direct experience of what you share.

Choose somebody who you can talk to honestly beforehand, and explain what you're looking for. You need to ask them not to comment, interrupt, touch or question you for more details. You need somebody who is not going to over-react with, for example, a look of sheer horror on their face as you share about your childhood abuse. You're looking for somebody who will not over-sympathize or become overwhelmed by their own emotions of distress, which might overtake your experience. Somebody who understands the difference between having tears of sympathy in their eyes as they listen, and hijacking your experience through their own emotional release.

OVER TO YOU

Witnessing your grief

Ask a trusted person to hold space for you, explaining what is required of them. Arrange a date and time that works for you both. Allow at least an hour and a half so as not to feel rushed.

Find a suitable place to read your letter in front of your witness. It needs to be somewhere you feel safe and will not be interrupted. This might be in your own home or might be somewhere else, if that feels more neutral. You will need a chair, tissues, drinking water and perhaps a comforter such as a cosy blanket or hot-water bottle. A photo of yourself as a child and/or of the person your letter is written to can also be very helpful. Looking at the photos as you prepare to read can make it easier to connect to how you felt at the time of the incident.

It can be helpful to stand to read, while your witness sits in front of you. This can support your wounded aspects to feel more empowered. It's also important to take your time to read slowly and clearly, to allow the words to land as you hear yourself speak them, and for your witness to hear and absorb them.

Making regular eye contact with your witness is also essential so that you can stay in connection with them and see that the person looking back at you is listening without judgement to your story. Even though it might feel difficult to do this, it's so important to allow yourself to be seen in your vulnerability.

When you're ready, take some deep breaths and then begin.

During the experience some of you might feel very emotional and of course your tears are welcome. Do allow them to flow and then simply return to reading when you are ready. Others of you may feel very detached and disconnected from the words you are reading, and this is also fine. Remember, there's no 'right' way to do this work or 'right' way to feel. Trust yourself and trust the process. Some of you (especially if you are sharing significant life events for the first time) might have major physical sensations, or reactions, as your body releases your grief. Shaking, shivering and jiggling limbs are all a very natural part of somatic healing. Allow your body to do what it needs to without any need to judge. And, of course, if you need to pause to catch your breath or even take a break, then do so. Self-care is key here.

When you've finished, thank your witness and invite them to leave you to complete the work alone. It's important not to chit-chat with your witness straight away or to immediately talk about what you read out and what just happened. You can of course check in with them later, but sometimes it's better to allow yourself to process what occurred without talking it all away.

It's important to support your body to release and unblock so as soon as possible after finishing your reading, put on some music from your grief playlist and shake, dance, stomp your feelings through your body.

When that process feels complete, take some quiet time to look after yourself in whatever way feels most nurturing. A walk or bath can be very grounding. You might want to prepare and eat some delicious healthy food. Rest, watch a film. Relax. Any of these options can be a lovely way to complete your grief work by turning to grief relief.

Grieving is a mind–body experience

When it comes to grief and grief work, every part of you is going to have a role to play. Your memories, your rational mind, your heart, soul and body are all on the same team of healers. In the letter-writing exercise, for example, you were drawing on memory and using the power of mind–body connection, through the movement of your hand, to express yourself in words. Unconscious associations or feelings might have come up along the way.

As we saw in Step Two when we were looking at the impacts of coping mechanisms and the false self, the emotions attached to hurt and loss are often unconscious, and they reside not only in our memories but also in our bodies. They are linked to and partially caused by chemical changes in our entire organism. Any stressful or traumatic experience causes the body to release huge amounts of stress hormones to support us in dealing with a dangerous situation. This is our fight, flight or freeze survival response kicking in. If we suppress these instinctive reactions and do not actively release this excess energy, over time our systems can become overwhelmed.

When we deny or repress sadness, fear and anger (and all the other components of our particular grief), our body can become more rigid, closed and tight. It can feel almost as if we are holding our breath underwater. We ignore our feelings, and our body, and disconnect from both. Eventually, if we don't acknowledge these emotions and their related physical reactions, they will manifest in the body in the form of tension, pain and 'dis-ease'.

Just as our heartbreak speaks through our body – in our posture and facial expressions, in the deadness or lost sparkle of our eyes – so too must our grieving. This might sound a bit abstract, but if we can practise tuning into the wisdom of our body, we will discover that it knows what to do with heartbreak. Crying, for example, is a very natural human response to hurt and loss. A study conducted in 2014 highlighted that emotional tears (as opposed to the tears you might cry when you stub your toe really hard) contain certain stress hormones and toxins. They also trigger the release of oxytocin and other endorphins associated with increased positivity. So as we cry we are literally cleansing and calming our emotional system, reducing our emotional pain and inducing a sense of wellbeing. I love a good sob, I do!

There are all sorts of ways we can recruit our body to help with our healing process. Any focused physical activity such as beating pillows, practising martial arts, dancing to intense music, therapeutic shaking or certain yoga moves, for example, can all help to free trapped energy and allow the related emotions to surface. This sort of bodywork is often referred to as somatic healing because it depends on movement.

Therapeutic shaking, for example, is based on the work of Dr Peter Levine, who recognized the significant role of the body in the healing process. In his book *Waking the Tiger*, Dr Levine writes about how animals in the wild do not experience trauma or PTSD, thanks to their instinctive response to dangerous situations. Once the threat has passed, the animal will shake itself and breathe deeply to recalibrate its nervous system. We humans have been socially conditioned to ignore or suppress our body's natural response to stress and trauma by trying to 'grin and bear it'.

Therapeutic shaking essentially involves consciously and gently focusing on shaking the whole body to support the healing process. And we don't have to wait until we experience a life-threatening event. Even a few minutes of shaking every day can have a dramatic effect on helping the body release stress and excess energy and return to balance. Shaking is one of the simplest and easiest ways to support our body in the healing process and return us to living in the moment. You can use music if you wish, or do it in the loo for a few minutes at work. It's a great way to shake off the day's stresses and much better for you than half a bottle of wine!

Another excellent technique to try is Total Release Experience, or TRE. This is a series of easy to follow exercises that support the body to release deeply held tension by inducing its innate tremor response. The physical process can be accompanied by a profound emotional release and the technique is very effective for some people suffering from stress, anxiety and PTSD. There are lots of free online resources available (see the Resources section at the back of the book).

Bodywork also needs to include the voice, through speaking, screaming, shouting or chanting. Yoga can be accompanied by mantras. You can thump cushions and hurl abuse. The simple act of speaking your pain aloud can be extremely powerful, as we saw in the exercise for witnessing grief.

Personally, there's very little I can't release through a grief dance, accompanied by a good yell. When I feel sad, afraid or angry, I will turn on my grief playlist (yes, you did read that correctly) and dance and shake to support my body to access and release my emotions. I often end up having a good cry (still moving), and then finish off with a track or two that calm me or fill me with joy.

This is what I mean by metabolizing grief. You can't think yourself out of it; instead you need to move yourself through it. Grieving then becomes an organic, visceral process for dealing with distress by metabolizing it through our entire emotional-mental-physical system, just as food must be processed through our digestive system.

Whether it's through letter writing, crying, shaking or any other method for grief release, the goal is to reconnect to underlying emotional tension. The first layer of feelings might be the more dynamic energies of anger, frustration and resentment. Beneath them, you might tap into stiller and quieter feelings of sadness and hurt. Your grief work can support you to drop beneath all these layers, to release them and then access your original state of love, tenderness and joy – the you that existed before you were heartbroken.

If you're not sure what to do or say, ask your body and then listen. If you're not sure how to release your pain, ask your body. What's your gut instinct telling you about what to do with a particular heartbreak on your timeline? Trust it. Your body – unlike your mind – can only speak truth.

OVER TO YOU

A grief dance

This is a particularly brilliant way to release the more dynamic tensions of anger and rage but it can help with any emotion.

The basic principle is that you're shaking up and out the blocked grief you've been holding in your body.

You're first of all going to prepare a grief playlist, ahead of time. It doesn't need to be long or carefully thought out. Just three or four tracks that you associate with feelings of sadness, fear or anger, whatever you want to work with. Perhaps a bit of all of them. I've got an upbeat shouty rebellious playlist for anger and a wistful weepy one for sadness. I sometimes combine them.

When you're ready, prepare your space for privacy by closing doors and curtains, breathe deeply to centre yourself and then turn the music on. Slowly allow yourself to begin to move. It doesn't matter what you do with your body. You're not performing, so try not to imagine what you look like while you're doing this. Let the rhythm of the music be your guide.

In your mind's eye, connect to the heartbroken aspects of yourself. To that little girl or boy part of you that remains inside you. Visualize the person who hurt you and feel the fire start to ignite in your belly. Give yourself permission to express your rage, your righteous indignation, your powerlessness, your sadness and despair. Shake, dance, move your body to access all of your emotions. Wail, cry, shout (into a pillow if you have neighbours!). Grieve with your whole body. Let the music take you. Free yourself from the grip of the past. Your body intuitively knows what to do.

Your emotions may come in waves. Just keep moving. Even as you sob, dance. And eventually when you feel a shift, a softening in yourself, change the music to something calming. Lie down on the floor. Cover yourself with a blanket. Allow the gentle music to soothe you.

Place your hands over your heart. Imagine the earth beneath you, drawing out any final emotions for this session. Breathe into your core. Feel yourself fully supported and held by the earth beneath you, feel yourself fully alive in your body. Raw and yet whole.

Using rituals to process your grief

Rituals, like bodywork, provide another powerful layer to working with grief. They have been essential in my own journey and are a huge part of my approach to healing. I love them precisely because they are the opposite of the neck-up style of dealing with emotional distress by analysing it. They work in a very different way, sometimes with language but often with objects or movements and always with symbolism and intentionality. They can be highly personal, something you invent yourself and perform alone, or a communal event where thousands of people participate.

A ritual is any symbolic behaviour that we participate in to honour significant and meaningful events in our lives. They often mark transitions. Familiar examples include birthdays, where we celebrate our changing age (or not!), weddings to mark a couple's union and funerals to honour the passing of our loved ones. Rituals come in many forms and variations and are influenced by our culture, family and faith or religion.

We participate in both communal and personal rituals, sometimes without even recognizing them for what they are. The more personal ones can simply feel like everyday parts of our lives. Taking a shower and changing our clothes after work, for example, might mark the end of the working day and moving into relaxation and leisure mode. Some of us take a 'lucky' object with us for a job interview or important event.

Basketball player Michael Jordan, for example, always wore his 'lucky shorts' underneath his kit for every game he played.

Conscious intention and preparation are defining characteristics of ritual, turning an action from something we do habitually into something we do ritualistically. For example, most of us take a shower or bath each day. We don't generally think about this or prepare for it, we just do it on automatic pilot. A ritual, however, includes preparing for the experience and seeking a particular outcome. So in the bath example your preparation might include turning off your phone, lighting some candles, pouring some oils into the water, dimming the lights, playing some gentle music and laying out a warm towel and fresh clothes or nightwear to complete. The outcome you're seeking is not so much to get clean as to relax and nurture yourself, so you approach bath time with that reverence and intention. These elements transform the bath from habit to ritual.

Recent research from the University of Harvard has shown that rituals can be extremely effective in supporting people after the loss of a loved one through bereavement or the ending of a significant relationship. It has also been demonstrated that rituals are highly effective in reducing anxiety and increasing confidence before highly stressful events or tasks, such as a job interview or public speaking. I particularly love that the Harvard research shows that rituals still produce measurable relief from distress, even if the person doesn't believe in the power of rituals! I tell that to my clients all the time: that it will still work even if they roll their eyes at me!

Despite their proven benefits, many people are suspicious of rituals. They associate them with cults or certain religions. But rituals are for everyone. For me, daily rituals are a fundamental part of my life. They not only keep me on track but also allow me to make my everyday habits more enjoyable, sacred and powerful. My coffee ritual involves preparing fresh coffee with hot milk as I like it, in my favourite mug. I light a candle, wrap myself in a cosy blanket and sit in silence and stillness looking out at the beautiful view from my window. This simple ritual sets me up for the day.

West African tribal leader and spiritual teacher Sobonfu Somé, whose given name means 'keeper of the rituals', spent her life travelling the world on a mission to educate the West in the ancient practices and rituals of her tribe and her ancestors. I was fortunate enough to attend her grief ritual training, which inspired some parts of the work on The Bridge Retreat. As she says, 'Ritual is to the soul what food is to the body . . . Rituals help us to dwell in the sacred in a way that truly heals us.'

I believe that rituals can create space for something magical to happen in our lives, if we only make the time for them. They force us to slow down and become mindful, heart-full and intentional. The ritual process can trigger an alchemical reaction, transforming grief into gratitude, despair into hope and bitterness into forgiveness. That's the healing power, magic and possibility offered by ritual.

It's almost time to take the next step on your journey to leave the negative impact of your painful past behind, and what better way to mark such an important moment than with a ritual? I invite you now to burn the letter you wrote in the first stage of this chapter's work. This moment will mark your choice to continue to let go of all the painful parts of your history that have been holding you back. It will honour all the hard emotional work you have done so far and prepare you to move forward in your life, unencumbered.

OVER TO YOU

Letting go – a ritual

- You will need a fireproof container (such as an old saucepan) or access to a bonfire or small fire pit, plus some matches for burning your letter. If a small fire is not safe or practically possible for you, you could rip up your letter and bury it outside in a favourite location in nature. The main thing is not to hang on to it.

- Head outside to your garden or a safe space in nature. If it feels right for you, you might wish to read your letter through one last time.

- Now, consciously and with intention, rip up your letter and put the pieces in your fireproof container. You might wish to take a moment to say a few words. For example, 'In releasing this letter into the fire, I am choosing to let go of any attachment to my painful past and to positively move forward in my life.' Then strike a match and watch closely as the flames burn your letter. Notice how the fire transforms the letter into nothing but ash.

- Once everything has cooled down, scoop up some of the ash in a small bag or box and head out into nature (or your garden). Let yourself be drawn to a place where you can scatter or bury these ashes. Let them go. Breathe deeply.

- As you head back, see if you can find a natural object such as a leaf, feather, flower or pebble that you could pick up and take with you, without harming the natural environment. Take it into your home and keep it as a reminder of this important point on your healing journey.

- Take a shower or bath as a final act of cleansing and self-nurture. Listen to some music that you love. Drink lots of water. Eat a nutritious meal. Rest.

You've reached the end of the chapter. Phew! In many ways, this chapter contains the hardest work in the book. It's definitely the most emotionally draining. I hope you're feeling a little bit proud of yourself for having got this far. Take some time if you need it, refresh your memory about the self-parenting visualization on page 66 and remember to do it every day. Give yourself full permission to use as many supportive strategies for grief relief as you need. And then, when you're ready, let's continue.

Key points from this chapter

- Grief is a natural emotional reaction to any kind of significant loss or change.
- Grieving is a whole-body experience and involves the core emotions of sadness, fear and anger.
- Both grief release and grief relief are important aspects of healing.
- Rituals have been proven to be highly effective in the grieving process.
- Grieving builds resilience and empathy and enhances our capacity for gratitude, peace and joy.

Questions for ongoing reflection

- Which of the core emotions of grief (sadness, fear and anger) do you feel most and how do you express them safely?
- Which ones do you find the hardest to express and why might that be?
- Where in your body do you sense that you carry your unprocessed grief?
- How might you begin to do your own grief work? What first steps can you take?
- What new insights or learning have you gained from this chapter?
- How do you feel right now in your body? Notice . . . and breathe.

Step Four: Forgiveness and Compassion – the healing power of an apology

You've now come a fair way over the bridge; in fact, you will soon be arriving at the halfway point. (Whoop whoop!) Your first faltering and frightening steps are now behind you. You've done your detective work, located the pain and grief that you're carrying, and courageously let yourself begin to feel it. It may well have been hard emotional labour for some of you to get to this step, but I hope that you are also beginning to feel glimmers of the space inside that is created after releasing blocked grief.

In this chapter, our focus is on the giving and receiving of a truly heartfelt apology. We will be looking at what constitutes a heartfelt apology and why it is an important component in your grief work. We'll examine the role played by forgiveness in your healing, and dig into the reasons why so many people find it so hard to say sorry and to forgive. Our main focus is on enabling you to receive a form of apology that you need from the people who have hurt you (though perhaps not in the way that you might think). We will also touch on the idea that you too may have people to whom you would like, one day, to apologize. (Let me tell you, my list was loooooooong!)

Both saying sorry and hearing it can make us feel tremendously vulnerable, which is part of the reason many of us shy away from apologies. But as we saw in the previous chapter, vulnerability is often a sign that healing is taking place.

Other big emotional components of a heartfelt apology include empathy and compassion. In order to offer a sincere apology, we must be able to comprehend and feel that we have wronged someone. In order to accept an apology, we must be able to feel the sincerity and empathy of the person offering it. Apologies – and forgiveness – depend on a circle of mutual vulnerability and empathy for their strength.

Forgiveness is a challenge for most of us but it is a fundamental component of your healing, so we'll be spending some time on what it is and is not, who it's for, why we resist it and how to achieve it.

Finally, we'll be looking at the importance of self-forgiveness. My hope is that by the end of the book you will be able to welcome in all the rejected or previously 'unacceptable' parts of yourself. That includes all your 'wounded inner children', the aspects of your false self that you would rather set aside, and the parts of your being that might make you feel guilty or ashamed because of what you've done. Until you understand and forgive those past versions of yourself – whether it's the version that once smacked your child in a supermarket, betrayed a friend or cheated on your partner – you cannot welcome them home.

This step is a crucial one in taking you closer to peaceful and wholehearted living. So let's get started.

What is a 'heartfelt' apology?

Most of us have been taught to say sorry when we make a mistake or hurt someone. Parents and carers teach their children that it's an essential part of learning to play nicely, along with sharing and taking turns. Apologizing is one of the most basic social skills and, at the simplest and most superficial level, it's something that most of us know how to do. While this level of apology is obviously better than nothing, it isn't what I mean by a 'heartfelt' apology.

I would define a heartfelt apology in its deepest sense as a form of love. When we hurt somebody we care about, the flow of love between us can become blocked. A heartfelt apology helps the love to 'unblock' and return to flow once again. It is a way of acknowledging to another human being that you have hurt them, that what you said or did was wrong, and that you are deeply sorry. It is the recognition of your mistake(s), along with a desire to make amends. All of this requires us to bring awareness to what we have done and the impact it has had on the other person. We will need the capacity to imagine how it was for them, for which we first need to allow time for our ego to get off its high horse!

When we deeply hurt another human being, whether we intended to or not, we must have the humility to allow the words 'I'm sorry' to rise up and be released from our heart. We need to follow up on this beginning with an explanation (not a justification) of how those things that hurt the other person came to pass. It is our responsibility to speak up and where possible *show* our apology in meaningful ways. We need to commit to changing how we behave in the future.

For those of us whose heart is breaking, receiving this kind of genuine apology can be a powerful life-changing medicine. As Harriet Lerner, author of *Why Won't You Apologize?*, puts it, 'I'm sorry' are two of the most healing words in the English language.

A heartfelt apology (and the heartfelt forgiveness to match it), are, I believe, part of our true nature. From the truest part of ourselves, we want to make right what is wrong and (where possible), reconnect with the person we have harmed or been harmed by. It's often our ego that gets in the way of this natural process. (Very often it's the ego that caused it in the first place!) For our ego, it's far more important to be 'right', to 'save face' or to 'win' than it is to actually heal. Since these ego-based feelings and thoughts are often the loudest and strongest, it's all too easy to give in to them.

To be clear, a heartfelt apology does not make right what was wrong. It does not erase the truth of what happened. By the same logic, accepting such an apology does not imply that we're saying what happened was acceptable. A heartfelt apology is an acknowledgement of wrongdoing and the pain and suffering it caused. It is a form of validation but it is in no way an excuse. It may, however, offer an opportunity for healing and in some cases, even a new beginning. It does not take away the damage inflicted but, at the very least, it shows that it mattered.

What an apology is not

A bad apology can feel way worse than no apology at all. We've all had them, right? If it includes any justifications or defensiveness, it's a bad apology in my book. The classic clanger here is the, 'I'm sorry, but . . .' You just know that whatever comes after that 'but' is going to make the words that came before it, meaningless. 'I'm sorry BUT you made me so cross and that's why I shouted.' No meaningful apology ever includes the word 'but', believe me.

Some crap apologies (professional term) reverse the focus to make it all about the person supposedly offering the apology. For example, 'I'm sorry that I hurt you. I am also hurting myself, you know! I had a tough childhood too.' This so-called apology ends up being nothing to do with you, the intended recipient, and becomes everything about them. People with narcissistic tendencies love this one.

Another way that an apology is robbed of any depth or meaning is when someone *over*-apologizes. The 'Oh, I'm so so sorry . . . I'm really really sorry . . . I'm deeply sorry' brigade. Women are particularly prone to this one. When we over-apologize, it lacks substance and once again becomes all about the giver rather than the receiver. It's also incredibly irritating (or is that just me?). It can end up with the receiver trying to make the giver feel better (and stop them saying their meaningless sorrys).

One final example of a crap apology is the, 'I'm sorry you feel that way' type. This one makes me cringe just writing about it. It's a complete 'non-apology' and tends to be loved by the 'I'm so spiritual' crew. Basically, these words mean that the giver takes no responsibility for their wrongdoings whatsoever and instead offers the not-so-subtle suggestion that it is in fact the receiver that is the problem. 'It's your feelings that are the issue, not what I said or did!' This, for me, is worse than saying nothing at all. Just don't do it!

None of these examples are heartfelt apologies. Neither are they likely to end well.

The vital importance of apologies

So I ask you this, dear readers – how many of you have received a heartfelt apology like the one I defined earlier in this chapter, from the person or people who broke your heart? Not many, I imagine. If you have, how many of you completely believed and accepted this apology, and now have heartfelt forgiveness for the person who hurt you? I'm hazarding a guess that it's only a few of you – otherwise you probably wouldn't be reading this book.

Some of you are perhaps questioning the weight I'm giving to the whole business of saying sorry. It might feel to you like an impossible or unnecessary goal. Perhaps you don't speak with the person or people who broke your heart, and the very idea of trying to get an apology from them fills you with horror or fury. I hear you – and I'm about to explain a way round this. Some of you might deny that you even need an apology. 'Screw them and their sorry!' you might say. And yet you still can't quite get over it, or them, and fully move forward in your life.

One of the things that can block us from truly healing (especially around heartbreaks from childhood), is that we are unconsciously waiting for an apology from those who have wronged us. We might know rationally that the person is not capable of offering us this (they might not even be alive any more), but this makes no odds to the wounded child part of us, who is patiently waiting for those medicinal words: 'I'm so very sorry.' That part of us is still hoping that someday, the apology we deserve might arrive, like an overdue love letter delayed in the post.

'I'm sorry I hurt you.'
'I made a mistake.'
'I was wrong.'
'What can I do to try to make amends?'
'I'm so sorry and please let me show you how much . . .'

These are such simple and profound statements and yet so hard for many of us to say. If we don't, we are liable to pay a high price. Unspoken apologies can breed shame and guilt in the person who has committed the wrongdoing, leading them to close down their heart in order to cope. They can also lead to resentment and bitterness in those deserving of the 'sorry'. Once hurt has occurred, it is very hard for trust to be rebuilt and love to unblock and flow between people, without the healing of an apology.

The truth is that it takes bucketloads of courage to say sorry and really mean it. It requires us to face some unpleasant truths about our own character, and admit them: 'I was selfish', 'I wanted to hurt you', 'I was weak'. And then, where possible and when it's safe to do so, it requires us to make amends. 'What can I do to help you start to trust me again?'

When we live out our apology in this way, through our words, behaviours and choices, we both deliver and receive healing. Our life becomes healing in action.

The problem is that a fear of vulnerability and shame very often gets in the way. So many people have not done their inner work to allow their immature parts to heal and grow up. Their ego therefore runs amok, and they would rather allow their relationships to fracture or fall apart than summon the humility to say those two precious words and mean them.

This was especially true of my parents' generation, for whom saying sorry was viewed as a sign of personal weakness and – especially in the context of apologizing to your children – an admission of failure. I wonder how differently my relationship with my father might have turned out if he had only been able to say sorry. But, of course, he needed to hear it first from his parents, as they did from theirs. And so the reality is that many of us are left hanging, unconsciously waiting, feeling trapped in the pain of our past and unable to move forward, because we have never received the heartfelt apology that we deserve.

The author and activist V (formerly known as Eve Ensler) was abused by her father, first sexually, then physically and emotionally, throughout her childhood. In her incredible book *The Apology*, V writes of how she waited most of her life for her father to admit what he had done and apologize for it. He never did. Even when he had passed away, V was still waiting for those magical words to arrive, decades later. 'I did it . . . and I'm so, so sorry.'

The implications of this unhealed wound rippled far and wide into all her relationships, especially the one she had with herself. Eventually, after much suffering, V decided to take matters into her own hands and wrote a detailed and imagined apology from her father to herself. Yes, she literally wrote for him the words *she* needed to hear that he could never say, and in doing so, finally found the freedom she had been longing for her whole life.

When we receive a heartfelt apology, one that is delivered with meaning and depth, spoken from and through the heart – even if it is, as with V, from your own heart to your wounded self – we can begin to move towards forgiveness. An apology like this can be transformational. It might even set you free.

The Work

Walk a mile in their shoes . . .

I said earlier that empathy and compassion were vital components of any meaningful apology. If we are the one doing the apologizing, then unless we can recognize that what we did hurt the other person – unless we can imagine our way into what it felt like for them – we cannot hope to offer a truly heart-felt apology. By the same token, for those of us who are on the receiving end of an apology, unless we can imagine what might have contributed to the person's hurtful actions, we can neither understand nor empathize with them, much less forgive them. For both parties, on either side of the apology divide, without empathy and compassion there is limited capacity for healing.

In a little while I am going to ask you to write a letter of apology to yourself, like V did, as if from the person who hurt you. In order to prepare for that, I invite you first to try to understand their experiences and see life a little more from their perspective. One powerful way to do this is to find out as much as you can about the person who hurt you, the one you wrote to previously. What do you know of their life story? How might they have suffered in early life?

Don't worry if it is impossible for you to find out concrete information, if, for example, they were a stranger or someone you no longer have any connection to. Using your imagination is also incredibly effective. Picture the person who hurt you, as a child. Ask yourself what might have happened to them, which meant that they grew up and behaved in ways that harmed or hurt you. Dig deep in your heart and imagination and dare to see what you might find. You can journal on this theme, or even write a story about their life. And remember this is not about making excuses for their behaviour. It's about cultivating understanding, compassion and empathy.

This might feel really challenging for some of you and more safe anger release might be required, but when you're ready do please give it a go. It is a means to an end, and the end is ultimately your healing and your happiness.

What goes around comes around

As you do your inner work, you will probably be getting more and more aware of the ways in which hurt breeds more hurt. We've seen already that people who haven't grieved their own heartbreaks often leak their pain in the form of resentment, criticism, judgement and blame. These are precisely the kinds of emotional states and behaviours that lead people to inflict injury on others, perpetuating the cycle of pain. As they were hurt, so they cause hurt.

Heartbreak can be handed from one group to another or handed down through the generations. Thankfully, so can compassion. The way to break the chain of pain is to create a cycle of heartfelt apologies and forgiveness. Just as you need to hear an apology from the person who broke your heart, there will no doubt be people in your life who also deserve a heartfelt apology from you, whether that is your children, partner, ex, friend, sibling, other family member or indeed your own parents.

I'm not going to invite you to start dishing out apologies of your own just yet – so don't worry if the very thought makes you want to throw this book across the room! But apologies definitely come full circle. There is not a person alive who has not done something thoughtless, regrettable, selfish or cruel. Every single one of us is capable of behaving badly, saying or doing things that hurt others. It's all part of the human condition. Increasing our ability to recognize that 'everyone' includes us is a great way to expand our humility and build our capacity for forgiveness and self-forgiveness, and to eventually offer our own heartfelt apologies. In this particular eternal circle, all the work is win-win.

So, in that spirit, I offer you a story of my own apprentice-ship in heartfelt apologies and forgiveness. When I was a young single mother raising two children with very limited support, unsurprisingly I made a lot of mistakes. I was ill-equipped to become a parent at just 18 years old, and basically was growing up myself at the same time as trying to mother my daughters. A child raising children. I did the very best that I could with my limited parenting and nurturing skills, but I know that along the way I hurt my children deeply. I would often apologize in the moment but, if I'm honest, it was more guilt-driven than heartfelt. At the time I was in too much pain myself to offer anything more.

Later on, when I had attended to my own emotional wounds and could feel the benefits unfolding in my life, I was able to write a heartfelt apology to each of my children. I told them about my struggles, mistakes and regrets, gave them some context to events (without justifications or excuses). I let each of them know how deeply sorry I was for specific choices I had made that hurt them and told them how much I would always love them. These letters played a significant role in our own family healing. I believe that both my girls (now 36 and 32) still have their letters. That's how important those apologies were to them.

All of which leads me nicely on to the precious 'F' word . . .

Who and what is forgiveness for?

Forgiveness, like many of the concepts we're working with, is often misunderstood. Just as anger gets a bad press because we mistake it for violence or abuse, forgiveness is often confused with an excuse for the inexcusable, or passive acceptance of a profound wrongdoing. It is felt to be something that benefits the wrongdoer by letting them off the hook. It might be nice for saints and martyrs, but it's not realistic or even that desirable for the rest of us mere mortals.

Nothing could be further from the emotional truth. When you forgive, you are releasing yourself from the anger or resentment that has tied you to the energy of the experience and the person/people who hurt you. You symbolically cut those toxic ties that bind you to them and free yourself to move on. By forgiving, you are also giving up the role of the victim. You are redefining the relationship between yourself and the person who hurt you. You are taking back your power, becoming emotionally, physically, mentally and spiritually lighter.

I have seen this transformative process at work in my own life and in the lives of many others. Adam is one person who particularly comes to my mind as I write this. He wanted to work on coming to terms with his childhood, and specifically, the cruel and abusive treatment he had received at the hands of his bullying stepfather.

When we met, Adam was (understandably) furious about what this man had put him through. His 'wounded child' was very present in his life. Through the grief work we did together, he was able to safely access and release some of his anger, sadness and fears in order to return for those heartbroken parts of himself and slowly begin to heal. He was adamant, however, that forgiveness was a step too far. He felt that his stepfather did not deserve to be forgiven.

Over time, Adam came to recognize the impact and burden of the bitterness and resentment that he still carried. He had developed significant health issues and was still experiencing bursts of uncontrollable rage towards his own son. He knew that forgiveness was becoming more urgent, not for his stepfather but for himself, and his own child. When he was ready, he took steps towards exploring understanding and compassion for his stepfather, recognizing that he must have been in a lot of pain himself to behave in that way. Eventually, after lot of inner work, Adam felt able to relinquish any blame and bitterness towards him and by doing so, felt himself set free.

Yes, forgiveness challenges us, but ultimately it is for our own benefit – nobody else's. The point of your work on apologies and forgiveness is to heal yourself. Working towards forgiving those who have wronged you is not about them and what they deserve. It's about you, and what you deserve.

Secondly, forgiving is not the same as forgetting. To forgive is not to absolve somebody of blame or to say that what happened was not a big deal. It does not mean that you are changing your story about the impact of an action. It doesn't change the reality of what happened, or your pain. It certainly does not condone the injury you suffered. It's not about letting someone 'get away with it' or failing to hold them accountable. It doesn't necessarily mean you will be reconciled with the person either (although sometimes this might be possible). You can forgive them without any need to see them or re-establish a relationship.

What true, heartfelt forgiveness can offer you is the gift of finally achieving peace of mind after all the toxic rumination, blame and hatred that you might have been carrying for years or even decades. By releasing the negative feelings and judgements you have been holding towards this person, forgiveness empowers you to validate the pain and hurt you have suffered, without allowing it to define or control your life for a moment longer.

But, of course, it is very hard to move towards this freedom unless we feel that our pain has been acknowledged and validated by the person who hurt us. If whatever they did is denied, minimized, justified or ridiculed in any way, we can remain entrenched within our suffering. We are unable to move forward, to forgive or to forget. Quite simply, we get stuck with the ghosts of our past clinging on to our back, controlling our choices, robbing us of power.

I've witnessed this in many women who have been physically abused or betrayed by their partners. Despite knowing rationally that they will not receive the apology or amends that they rightfully deserve, they hang on to their blame and their resentment until it starts to fester inside them. Ultimately, they are the only one who suffers.

There is another way. It involves apologizing to ourselves, on behalf of the person who wounded us, as V did when she apologized to herself on behalf of her abusive father. By taking back ownership of the apology we know that we deserve, from the person who might never give it to us, we can begin to release ourselves from our stuck place. Once we have received the heartfelt apology that our wounded child so desperately needs to hear, and when we have allowed those words to truly land inside our battered broken hearts, we are more equipped to heal and move towards forgiveness.

You might question whether an apology of this kind actually 'counts'. All I can say is that it really does. Yes, of course we know that writing this letter is an act of imagination, but the body doesn't really know the difference. There are women in the Democratic Republic of Congo, who have had the most horrendous acts of violence and atrocities committed against them and their sisters and mothers, who use this tool; writing the letters of apology they deserve from their perpetrators. They write as many times as they need to, until they feel ready to end their inner war and let it go. So if they can, so can you.

Even if it feels challenging, the healing power of the process could work for you. I invite you to give it a go.

OVER TO YOU

Write the letter of apology that you need to receive

Your task is to write a letter to yourself in the voice of the person who hurt you, which acknowledges, explains and apologizes for the events that broke your heart. This will be the same person or people to whom you wrote your previous letter, in Step Three of your grief work. Having poured out your pain to that person, and been witnessed in your grief, it is now time to imagine a heartfelt reply from them.

So, for example, if you identified your father's decision to cut you out of his life and prioritize his second family as your key heartbreak, you will write as your father. If you identified your mother's abandonment of you as a teenager, you will write as your mother.

You will be writing sentences using the word 'I'. You might write things like, 'I know that I let you down when I chose not to see you. In fact, I know that I broke your heart.'

As you write, imagine it's the best part of that person (even if you've never met that part) talking straight to the wounded child part of yourself. These are the words that younger part of you has longed to hear.

Here are some suggestions for themes you might cover in your letter:

- Context – some context and explanation for the events or actions that hurt you. This is not about excuses.

Think back to the work you did when you made the effort to walk in their shoes. What insights did you discover about the factors that had damaged the person who damaged you? This might include what you know about their own childhood or what you imagine they might have experienced that led them to behave in the way they did. You could also include details of any influences that came from their family, social or cultural background, such as the racism or misogyny that they experienced. For example, 'I had only ever seen women in a subservient role to men within my culture and family. I had been shown that it was important to dominate them and "show them who was boss". Truth is, I was afraid of you and your power.'

- Acknowledgment – a description of what they did. By writing about what they did to you and why, the person who hurt you is acknowledging the reality of what happened and taking responsibility for their actions. Include a plain and simple statement about the event or action that broke your heart. Think about their intentions. Don't sugarcoat them. For example, you might write: 'I didn't pay you any attention or allow you any freedom when you were a teenager. The truth is I abandoned you and selfishly spent all my time with my lover. This meant I didn't even notice when you developed an eating disorder. I was too busy avoiding my own pain. I just wanted to control you and make you a good girl, someone who didn't give me any more problems.'

- Empathy – they take a walk in your shoes: They imagine how it was for you to experience what they did to you. They try to see it from your perspective, to imagine how it felt at the time and the effects it had on you later in terms of your beliefs and coping mechanisms. So for example, 'I imagine that you must have felt incredibly lonely and scared of becoming an adult without your mother around to guide you. I'm guessing it was very confusing for you and you must have wondered what you had done to make me treat you in this way. I imagine this left you feeling worthless because I treated you as if you were unimportant.'

- Wishes – they offer you the words you need to hear about the ways they let you down and failed to meet your needs. 'I wish I had been there for you. I wish I had prioritized you, got to know you, been present in your life, given you hugs, asked about your day, tried to answer your questions. I wish I had loved you in the way that you needed and deserved.'

- The apology – they apologize to your wounded child, in detail, for all their wrongdoings. This might be quite a long list or it might be one point. You might write things like, 'I'm sorry I didn't see you as your own person. I'm sorry I ignored you. I'm so sorry I broke your heart. I'm so sorry that you have paid the cost of that heartbreak in addiction, self-abuse and depression in your adult life.'

- Freedom – this is the part where they consciously and deliberately set you free by taking all the responsibility for what happened. They acknowledge that in acting in a way that broke your heart they were projecting their own pain on to you, whether it was their shame, depression or rage. Then they send you into your future without the burden of heartbreak that they created for you. So, going back to the example of a father who abandoned you, you might write, 'Speaking to you as your father, I take back any feelings of worthlessness and shame that I forced you to bear. They were never yours to carry. My wish is that you will realize that none of it was your fault, you were just a child, and that you are absolutely worthy of love and belonging. With these words I release you from the past, as only a parent can. In love and with deep humility and respect, I set you free.'

Writing this letter of heartfelt apology to yourself creates an opportunity to take back control of your life and allow the past to be part of your history without defining your future.

Once you have written the letter and when you feel ready, you will need to read it out loud and have it witnessed by a trusted other, as you did with the previous letter. This important step helps you to feel seen, heard and validated in receiving the apology that you deserve. The same guidelines for being witnessed apply as before (see page 115).

How to forgive people – a personal journey

Maybe you're muttering that if I knew what you'd suffered I wouldn't be talking about forgiveness. If that's you, please know that I do understand. I spent years, nearly two decades in fact, wrapped up in my conviction that what I had suffered was unforgivable. That was how it felt to me, for the longest time. So if you're not at the forgiveness stage (yet), you won't be getting any pushback from me.

Forgiveness is a very personal business and, like most things in life, it is not for everyone. Some people believe that the acts committed against them or against their community, and the resulting wounds, are so heinous that they are unforgivable. This is a person's individual choice. Many people take this position in relation to historic acts of aggression and prejudice such as the Atlantic slave trade, for example, or genocidal attacks on Jewish, Muslim, Christian and other minority populations throughout history. I respect this position completely. No one has the right to tell anyone else that 'they must forgive'. In fact, this can be a retraumatizing message for people who have already suffered more than enough.

For those of us who are not dealing with the huge intergenerational traumas of aggression and systemic injustice, though, I believe it's possible and desirable to work towards personal forgiveness.

If anyone had told me before I did my grief work that I would eventually reach a place of forgiveness and understanding towards both my parents, I would undoubtedly have sneered something along the lines of, 'Forgive them?! There are no excuses for what they did to me and my sister when we were children. Their behaviour was unforgivable!'

This reaction (with which your own may well resonate) was understandable given how battered and broken my poor heart still was back then. I had closed it down in order to protect the vulnerable wounded child part of me and kept it closed as a matter of survival. As an adult, my rage against my parents was what kept me warm and safe at night. But it also cost me dearly in terms of self-loathing, self-sabotage, ill health and numerous abusive relationships.

When I began to do my inner work, I explored the thorny subject of forgiveness with my therapist. Eventually, after many tears and much anger-release, I was able to reach a place where I knew I needed to forgive them; I even recognized that my forgiveness wasn't about them, but I still didn't quite know *how* to. I wasn't ready, and you simply can't rush these things.

It was only when my heart began to heal that I became ready to explore what might have happened to my parents in their own childhoods that would have led them to be such inadequate parents to my sister and me. It took a huge chunk of courage to do this, but when I did, I heard stories of my mother's own father dying when she was very young and her mother, no doubt crippled with grief, becoming detached and cold. My family shared stories with me about my mum being taken into care as a young girl, separated from her siblings, her mother and all that she knew.

My father's background was more difficult to explore because he grew up in South Africa and had come to the UK alone, but having once met his parents, who were evangelically religious and rigid in their thinking, it did not take much imagination to see how tough it must have been for him to grow up in such a restrictive and shame-filled environment.

The more time I spent considering my parents' backgrounds, the more compassion I was able to cultivate towards them. They had been two wounded children themselves, masquerading as adults and trying to be parents.

Most important of all, in the end I wanted to forgive them because I no longer wished to carry all the hurt, sadness, anger and blame inside of me. It was such a heavy burden to carry and utterly exhausting.

I reminded myself of what I now knew to be true: that forgiving does not mean forgetting or excusing. Then, when I felt ready, I held a ritual. I imagined my parents as the children they had once been, as well as the parents they went on to become.

I was able to offer them some forgiveness, which I spoke aloud to them. Immediately, I felt a burden lift from my shoulders. It was pure liberation.

The day I knew that my healing and forgiveness work had paid off and that I had officially become an emotional grown-up (yay!), was when I could see my mother and father as a woman and a man first and foremost. I could appreciate that they had had a life, love and longings way before they became my parents. I could recognize that they were each once an innocent little child (just like me) with hopes and dreams (just like me). I was able to consider their pain and suffering without comparing it to my own, recognize that they had made many mistakes because they were human (just like me). And when I finally realized what they had sacrificed for me, and the many gifts that they had passed on to me, I found freedom. I realized that there was, in fact, nothing left to forgive.

Now, this was a long and rocky emotional process. It took me considerably longer than the course of one chapter in a book, which makes sense because forgiveness, like grieving, needs to be a process in order to be effective. You cannot *decide* to forgive someone. It's not an intellectual decision that you can take, pain-free. You must work through the emotions that you need to feel, in stages, at your own pace. Sometimes this can feel like 'two steps forward, four steps back' but that's OK, so long as you can keep moving.

As with all inner work, some people really don't want to do it. They would prefer to jump on a few stages. I have heard many people say (and often believe) that they have forgiven, even though I know they haven't done their grief work. 'I understand,' they tell me. 'My parents/ex-boyfriend had a tough time, too. I know they did their best.' And yet their emotional reactions speak louder than their justifications. They find it impossible to tolerate or even be around the person who has hurt them.

This was certainly true of me with my mum. In my late twenties, feeling all 'enlightened' after a couple of therapy sessions, I declared I had forgiven my mum for the way she had treated me as a child. For all the years of neglect and abandonment and failure to protect me and my siblings. Yes, just like that. Gone! I really believed it, in my own naive way. But then I would actually see her, and all of my unprocessed emotional pain would rise to the surface and even the sound of her breathing would infuriate me! (Forgiveness, my arse.)

This is what the author M. Scott Peck describes as 'cheap forgiveness'. Cheap forgiveness is essentially an attempt to bypass the healing process. It is an intellectual exercise in which we rationalize and minimize the hurt (often to avoid feeling it), and rush towards forgiveness. This is what I call 'neck-up forgiveness' and is often well intended, with the adult empathetic part of us trying to see the best in others and understand their behaviour. The problem is, it doesn't work. Without the necessary grieving process for the wounded child part of us, for what we did not receive or how this person deeply hurt us, our forgiveness remains 'cheap'. Neck-up forgiveness can never be true forgiveness, because that resides in the heart, the very place we were wounded, which needs to be healed before it can open to the possibility of true 'heart-felt' forgiveness.

I didn't know anything about the stages of forgiveness when I was talking to my therapist, but in hindsight I can see clearly that my work followed a classic pattern of shifting beliefs. The starting point (when my heart was still so battered and closed) was my belief that 'It's unforgivable.' At that point I had barely started on my grief work, on giving voice to the broken-hearted part of myself and releasing my anger. I was burning with rage. I understood forgiveness as letting them off the hook, and I still wanted to punish them. It would have felt like admitting defeat and allowing them to 'win'.

Gradually, I came to believe the reverse. By withholding forgiveness and holding on tightly to my past pain, not only was I continuing to suffer – I was also handing them 'victory'. I remained their puppet, my strings still being pulled this way and that by ghosts from the past.

Once I had grieved, released my painful emotions, shared my story and my hurt had been witnessed, I was ready for the next stage, which was to cultivate compassion and empathy for my parents. This is what you did earlier in this chapter, when you walked a mile in the shoes of the person who hurt you.

From there, I moved on to the stage of accepting the reality of what happened and realizing that it was my choice how to react to it. I was able to accept (without excusing) that these painful things had happened, rather than wishing they hadn't. I was able to accept that I might never fully understand why they happened, so rather than spend my life searching for explanations, perhaps I could choose a different approach. I could accept that forgiveness was mine to give and that it would benefit me. Forgiveness was a choice I could make.

Once I had chosen to forgive, I held my ritual to mark the transition from unforgiving to forgiving, to honour what happened to me and mark the moment I let go of this aspect of my past.

The final stage in the process of forgiveness is to make meaning and learn from the experience, and I could see this too in my own work. Eventually, my dominant feeling towards my parents was gratitude for what they *had* been able to offer me, and the gifts my childhood experiences have brought me. (I know, right?!)

Learning to forgive yourself

If forgiveness is a gift you offer to yourself then self-forgiveness takes that idea and squares it. To forgive ourselves for the mistakes we have made and hurts we have inflicted is to offer ourselves compassion and empathy. We are all – no matter what we have done or not done – completely worthy of this empathy and compassion from and to ourselves.

This can be hard for some of us to really accept and put into practice. Depending on your personality and past experiences, you might find it easier to forgive others than yourself. You might be carrying a lot of guilt and shame, anger at yourself, disappointment or even disgust. Others of you might not have such a toxic load.

Wherever you are at, your ability to forgive yourself depends on being able to show yourself the same compassion that you would a friend. Dr Kristin Neff, a self-compassion researcher, defines it as: 'being warm and understanding toward ourselves when we suffer, fail or feel inadequate, rather than ignoring our pain or flagellating ourselves with self-criticism.'

You also need to develop a sense of being essentially worthy regardless of the mistakes you have made, rather than fundamentally flawed or rotten to your core.

These are ideas that often need a lot of practice (and we will be coming on to them in greater detail in the next chapter). I believe it's essential to start thinking about self-forgiveness at this stage, precisely because it's so vital to your healing. Without self-compassion there can be no self-forgiveness and ultimately no self-love. And that is definitely where we're headed!

Once we lift the burden of resentment towards others, we can turn our attention to forgiving ourselves for all of the many mistakes *we* have made along the way. We talked about this earlier in the chapter, when we were thinking about the eternal circle of apology and forgiveness – we all need to be able to do both bits of the process because we all hurt and are hurt.

Let's face it – to be human is to screw up. Even when we have the best intentions we make mistakes along the way, especially in our younger years when we are still learning the basics of how to 'do life'. I'm not sure I'd know how to relate to someone who has never screwed up at some level – even if such a person existed, which I doubt! Making a mess of things is what makes us all so deliciously fabulous. Our flaws, bumbles and stumbles contribute to our very humanity.

Most fundamentally, if we strive to be perfect all the time we will never take risks, never learn, never grow. We will live tiny restricted lives (and still end up hurting others and making mistakes, despite our good intentions). Some of the best people I know have screwed up big time but been able to put things right through personal reflection and humble action. They have grown exponentially and expanded their beautiful hearts as a result.

As we learn to truly forgive ourselves, our hearts become softer. We become more compassionate and more grateful for all that is good in our lives. We're less judgemental of other people's errors and lapses. We recognize that we might have made the same mistake, the same selfish decision, had we found ourselves in a similar situation. We come to recognize the common humanity in all our mistakes. Our motto might be, 'You've screwed up? Made poor choices that have hurt people you loved? Yeah, me too.'

So how exactly do we practise self-forgiveness? Smaller mistakes are usually relatively easy to forgive ourselves for (although those with a strong inner critic might disagree!). But what about those whoppers, like when we shouted at or even smacked our child in a moment of desperate exhaustion; betrayed our partner by having an affair, or spoke cruel words that destroyed a cherished friendship? How can we possibly forgive ourselves for causing those hurts?

There is no shortcut. We must move through our resistance to doing our inner work, reject the neck-up approach, just as we had to when learning to forgive others. We must return to our 'emotional detective' work and take the time to reflect upon the choices we made and their consequences. Ask ourselves challenging and truth-seeking questions to gain more clarity around what took place and why. What was happening in our lives at the time? How were we feeling, towards ourselves and others? What was our motivation? What were we thinking? Were we thinking at *all*? Asking these questions can deepen our understanding of why we behaved the way we did.

And from there we must follow the process we've already discussed: release our pain and hurt, accept the reality of what happened and recognize that we can choose how to react to it going forward. Perform the following ritual of self-forgiveness to mark the shift, and reflect on the lessons we've learned along the way and the changes we will commit to make in our lives. And then? Then we can begin to enjoy the sweet relief of no longer carrying so much self-hatred, guilt and shame.

OVER TO YOU

A meditation to support self-forgiveness

Try to find a small photograph of yourself from the time when you did whatever it was for which you want to forgive yourself. You're going to use the photo as your focus for meditation. If you do not have a photo, you can just use a small pebble or flower to represent that version of yourself.

Prepare a comfortable place to sit, somewhere you will not be disturbed. Soft music and a burning candle can help to create the right mood.

1. Sit on the floor with your photo or pebble in front of you. Take a moment to get in a comfortable sitting position, close your eyes, slow down and deepen your breath.

2. Place your hands over your heart at the centre of your chest. Consciously breathe into this space, keeping your eyes closed, and feel your hands connecting with your chest and heart. Breathe.

3. Keep the connection to your heart with your hands and your breath, and then open your eyes to focus on your photo or pebble. Think back to who you were and what was happening for you at this point in your life, when you perhaps made poor choices. Imagine yourself standing in front of you now, as you say the words 'I forgive you' slowly and repeatedly.

4. Keep your hands at your heart. Notice what happens. It's fine if you don't feel full forgiveness at this stage, just keep saying the words gently to yourself, over and over again. Notice any physical sensations that arise, and any emotions too. Try to allow them without judgement.

5. When you are ready, slowly begin to open your hands as if you're reaching out to this aspect of yourself and change your words to 'I love you' (if you feel able to). Repeat this over and over again as you look at yourself in the photograph (or in your mind's eye). If any blocks come to prevent your heart opening to yourself, gently

    use your hands in a sweeping motion over your heart as you imagine clearing the blocks away. Breathe.

6. As your hands and arms slowly open out wider, feel the energy of your heart emanating from you, towards your past self. Keep saying the words 'I forgive you' and/or 'I love you' over and again. Send yourself your love and compassion.

7. Slowly now, pick up the photograph or the pebble and hold it to your heart. As you do, continue with your words, 'I forgive you', 'I love you', as you bring the photo or pebble super slowly towards your open heart. If it feels OK, you could imagine placing that image of your past self inside your heart. Hold your heart as you allow your former self to settle back into the place from which they had been banished. When you're ready, return the photo or pebble to your lap or the floor.

8. Complete the meditation with a beautiful piece of music, some chanting, a song or a short meditation on love and forgiveness.

9. Repeat this regularly (every day if you can), until you feel a shift of emotion towards this past version of yourself.

Set yourself free

As the previous President of South Africa, Nelson Mandela, famously said on leaving prison after twenty-seven years, 'As I walked out of the door toward the gate that would lead to my freedom, I knew if I didn't leave my bitterness and hatred behind, I would still be in prison.'

These beautiful words offer us all a great example of what is possible when we truly forgive. Freedom. When we let go of all the pain, bitterness, blame and resentment held inside of us, we can finally be free. Forgiveness is about reclaiming our power and taking back control of our life.

Forgiveness for yourself and for others creates a new energy, which allows you to love yourself fully and unconditionally. It also sets you free to look for real love from other people, in all the right places.

The consequences of forgiveness – or its lack – can be seen everywhere, from our poor wounded hearts to the chaos and heartbreak of conflict out in the wider world. Every territorial dispute, every war, has unprocessed pain at its core. All armed conflict is fuelled by a sense of injustice that must be avenged. It thrives on pain that has no outlet except retaliation. The pain might be felt on behalf of a person's country, their faith, land, family or identity. The results are calamitous. When we don't forgive ourselves, others and life itself, this affects how we behave and react to individuals, our families, communities and beyond. We ignite a war inside ourselves and eventually it sets fire to the whole world.

So as you cross the bridge towards your own inner peace, know that you are also contributing to lessening what Eckhart Tolle calls 'the emotional pain body' of the world. This expression refers to the accumulation of all the negative 'unforgiving' energy and unprocessed emotional pain that exists in the world, like a dark shadow that blocks the sun. The idea of a collective pain body can be a tough one to grasp and accept, but perhaps for some of you this will resonate.

It certainly does for me. I believe that as we do to one, we do to all. When we truly forgive ourselves and others (where we can), we not only heal our own hearts, we relieve the pain burden of the entire world. That is how powerful you really are!

Key points from this chapter

- We all need to hear 'I'm sorry' from those who broke our heart.
- A heartfelt apology is medicine to the soul.
- We can offer ourselves the apology we need to hear.
- True forgiveness is not about the other person. It can set *us* free.
- Forgiving ourselves for past mistakes is an act of true compassion towards ourselves.
- Forgiveness is a very personal process; it's not for everyone and it can't be rushed.

Questions for ongoing reflection

- How might your life have been different if you had received a heartfelt apology from the person who hurt you the most?
- Who do you still need to apologize to in your own life? How and when might you do this?
- Which of your past choices still need the healing balm of your self-forgiveness? How might you take one step closer to making this possible?
- What new insights or learning have you gained from this chapter?
- How do you feel right now in your body? Notice . . . and breathe.

Step Five: True Self-love – becoming your own best friend

Welcome to the book's midway point. You're now halfway across the bridge. Some of you may still be feeling quite raw after the grief work of the previous chapters and, if so, please take heart. That feeling is a sign that you are fully engaged with your healing and that the work is working. I hope you will begin to feel lighter as we start to focus on how to make your present as warm and nurturing as possible, and lay the groundwork for a future in which you can live an authentic and wholehearted life.

In this chapter we're going to build your capacity to love and cherish yourself. We'll be exploring self-care as a radical act, and talking about how we create the foundations for true self-love (which has nothing to do with self-indulgence or self-importance by the way). If this feels in any way off-putting for some of you, please stay with me. I know it can be very cringe-worthy to talk about loving yourself – kind of absurd or embarrassing. I used to feel exactly like that.

For some of us, our sense of unworthiness is so deep that it goes beyond cringe into the realms of feeling like an impossibility. I recognize that feeling, too. If that's you, it might help to remember that accepting, liking and eventually loving ourselves is a work in progress for all of us. For now, your twin goals are simply to try to look after yourself in small healthier ways, and to treat yourself with self-compassion. The work you've been doing so far to uncover and grieve your heartbreaks has drained a lot of negative old energy but might have left *you* feeling a bit empty, too. This is a good sign. It's essential to go through this phase, and also to fill yourself up with increasing feelings of worthiness, positivity and self-respect.

We will start by exploring that nasty voice in your head known as 'the inner critic'. What it is, where it comes from, and most importantly what you can you do to make it pipe down. By the end of this chapter, you'll be ready to replace the inner critic with the inner cheerleader: a supportive voice that starts from the basis that you're fine as you are, not a failure. Self-acceptance is the first step in creating your belief that you are a completely worthy person. We will build on this acceptance, through to liking yourself and ultimately being able to love yourself. (Can you hear your inner critic right now?!)

So many of us, especially if we're women, are taught to criticize, compare and even hate ourselves by society and our culture. It starts early and it usually begins with our bodies before it spreads into our behaviours, thoughts, choices, sexuality and whole identity. We will kick off from the same place, and practise learning to accept, then like, then love our body just as it is. The pace will be gentle because this shift might feel very difficult for some of you.

It's time to discover how to move away from judgement and self-criticism towards the belief that you are fully worthy of nurture and love – your own and other people's. Quite simply, it's time to learn how to be nicer to yourself.

Why do we find it so hard to be kind to ourselves?

Before we get into the business of dismantling our inner critic, let's have a quick recap of why so many of us struggle with the idea that we're as deserving of kindness, respect, care and love as the next person.

For those of us who grew up in families where criticism or indifference were more common than love, acceptance and attention, it can feel very alien to behave kindly towards ourselves. This is really what I mean by self-love: treating ourselves with the same warmth as we would a beloved family member or dear friend. It sounds simple, but for too many people it's like a colour we have never seen or a flavour we have never tasted. What feels far more familiar (and that word 'familiar' comes from the word 'family' by the way), is to continue to do to ourselves what was done to us. If we felt rejected and abandoned as a child, for example, then we internalize this, unconsciously seeking out experiences in order to continue to reject and abandon ourselves.

Even if we grew up in a loving home, we may have absorbed the idea that we were loved *because* we were a good girl or *because* we did well at school. We might carry into adulthood the unconscious belief that we will only be loved if we are 'perfect', never cause trouble of any kind and always excel. So we end up as a chronic people-pleaser, always denying our needs in friendships and intimate relationships so as not to trigger rejection. The attention and care we are prepared to give ourselves is conditional and depends on not falling below certain standards.

These strategies of rejecting ourselves or withholding care from ourselves can sound counter-intuitive but they make sense as a self-protection mechanism. If you're used to being rejected, you can protect yourself by never putting yourself out there. If you've already rejected yourself, nobody can push you any further away. Sometimes, especially if it was a parent or a life partner who hurt us, we also have a sense that perpetuating their behaviour is a way to stay in connection with them, no matter how painful.

This was the case for a young man I worked with called Darryl, who had been abandoned in a train station toilet by his mother when he was just three days old. He was very swiftly adopted by two wonderful people and had had what he described to me as 'the perfect childhood'. He couldn't have wished for better parents. And yet throughout his adolescence and early adult life he suffered from depression and self-sabotaging behaviours. He hated his body and abused alcohol and drugs.

Until we worked together, Darryl had not felt it necessary to process his feelings about being abandoned by his birth mother. He had developed the belief that to do so would somehow be a betrayal of his adoptive parents. Eventually, when he was desperate enough to try a new approach, he began his grief work. He grieved what the little baby version of himself had needed from his birth mother and not received. Darryl was able to recognize that his abandonment by her had led him to abandon himself, over and over again. Almost as an unconscious way to remain close to her, as if he were saying, 'I will do to myself what you did to me, Mum.'

Self-abandonment is very common among those of us who felt unseen, rejected and unloved when we were young. The impulse can be so powerful that self-love feels impossible. Sometimes we find that we can be kind to ourselves in one area of our life – perhaps looking after our body in practical ways with exercise and healthy food – but then sabotage ourselves financially or in intimate relationships. Many of us consciously reject the people who hurt us and all their negative ways, but our unconscious behaviours towards ourselves tell a very different story. Until we do our grief work and commit to ongoing maintenance to protect the gains we make through our healing, we hold on to the belief that if that key person deemed us unworthy of love and care, they must have been right.

It's personal and political

Our sense of who we are is heavily shaped by our family and the specific context we grew up in, but these are not the only pressures that contribute to forming our identity. Society treats us very differently depending on aspects of our identity such as race, biological sex, gender, nationality, ethnicity, social class and religion (among many others). The experience of the world that someone has as a white middle-class woman is very different from the experience of a working-class Black man, for example. We learn who we are in the context of what society expects us to be. We also learn (sometimes harsh) lessons about what society believes we're worth. This is a hugely complex matter and is intrinsically political, touching on issues of equality, justice and – for some groups more than others – a history of systemic injustice.

As women, for example, we constantly receive the message that we are fundamentally flawed and never enough. Our bodies, our faces, our lifestyle, our very existence, are all in need of improvement. The patriarchal, consumer-capitalist system relies on us feeling inadequate and unworthy and searching for ways to improve ourselves. We're urged to buy stuff that will make us look better, feel better, *be* better. And when it doesn't work (which it's not meant to), we can be sold drink, food and drugs to consume in order to forget our sad, imperfect selves. And so it goes on. To be female in the twenty-first century, even in the so-called developed nations of the world, is still to be 'less than'.

That's the lie we've been sold, but I for one refuse to buy what they're selling any more. I refuse to believe for another single moment that I am anything less than perfect. And so are you, whoever you are and whatever groups you identify with.

The struggle to really *feel* this truth and act upon it, rather than merely understand it, means that your inner work is political as well as personal. Self-care, self-acceptance, self-compassion, self-love – these practices are not egotistical, indulgent or self-ish when the self in question has been disrespected, injured and abused as much as women, people of colour and so many other marginalized groups have been. It is essential for you to learn self-care, self-compassion and eventually self-love. Learning to truly and deeply love ourselves is one of the most radical forms of activism we will ever take.

Now that we've refreshed our understanding of why so many of us struggle with low self-worth, we need to learn how to develop our sense of worthiness, in practical and achievable ways. That means taking things slowly. It is not possible to jump straight from self-abandonment or self-loathing across to worthiness in a heartbeat. As with all the best things in life, developing a rock-steady belief that you are worthy of your own love takes time. Once we've done our grief work, we must then begin to build a new relationship with ourselves. Through consistent small practices we can start to accept ourselves, follow them up with liking ourselves and then eventually, grow to love ourselves. Really. Warts and all.

There are many different ways to do this, a few of which we're going to explore here. Some of them will feel easier for you than others, but I hope you will try all of them. The world really needs you on full beam. You deserve to live that way, and it can't be done if you're battling with inner bullies or dealing with inner demons. Speaking of which . . .

Meet your inner critic

'You moron!'
'Why did you say that?!'
'What do you look like in that dress?!'
'Shut your stupid mouth!'

These are just a few of the vicious verbal attacks that I experienced every day for years. Who was my cruel persecutor? An abusive partner, perhaps? A bullying boss? Nope. It was me, or at least it was one aspect of myself. My inner critic used words as weapons against me. Every. Single. Day. It was a relentless tirade, like having an abusive relationship with myself, with no refuge to hide in. The running commentary reinforced the message of my childhood, which boiled down to 'Donna, you are simply not good enough.' No wonder I suffered from decades of low self-worth and depression.

Most of us are familiar with the voice of the inner critic, even if we've never heard it called that. It is that voice in our head that judges, berates and criticizes us. The inner critic loves to speak in the language of shoulds and should nots, always and never. 'You should have tried harder, you idiot. You shouldn't have eaten that, you fat pig. You will always be a loser. You will never change. You're a total failure.'

For some of us it only pops up now and again; for others it is always present, so familiar that we assume it's an inevitable part of our mental and emotional landscape. Its voice ranges from the occasional whisper of negativity to a compulsive and relentless tirade of abuse.

An unchecked inner critic is a form of violence that we direct against ourselves. It is both the result and the cause of deep pain, and drives our feelings of unworthiness, guilt and shame. At its worst, it can lead to mental health issues including depression and anxiety. It may be virtually impossible to banish it completely (it's part of our own self, after all), but we can and must learn how to dial it down to a whisper.

So where does this nasty inner voice come from? Like most negative conditioning, the inner critic starts to find its voice in childhood. When we are growing up we are naturally less defended, more open and therefore more vulnerable to criticism than we are as adults, especially from those closest to us.

As we have seen, all of us are exposed to the heartbreak of childhood wounding, whether it's by a critical parent, our peers at school, a harsh teacher or another authority figure. These negative messages can devastate our fragile sense of self, even if they only happen once. If they come from somebody we love, revere or want to impress, they can lodge so deeply within our heart and mind that their message is never silenced. It takes up residence and we begin to repeat it, without even noticing that it has become part of how we talk about ourself. Left unattended, all the insults and injuries accumulate, until they evolve into the inner critic.

Every inner critic is made up of many heartbreaks, but each of us can usually identify a few key insults or judgements that have solidified into the critic's loudest rants. When I was about nine, for example, I scored badly in a maths test. I can still remember being told to stand up by my teacher and then labelled 'stupid' in front of my whole class. The burning shame of it on an impressionable and vulnerable child. The impact of this experience stayed with me for decades. I formed the belief that I was stupid to my core and, by telling myself this over and over again, I reinforced it. I sabotaged myself at school by playing truant, missing much of my education and then deciding not to bother to apply to university. 'What's the point,' I thought, 'I'm just too stupid.' I took that belief into adulthood, into my early working life and my relationships, with predictably unhelpful results.

The inner critic's power tends to grow unless we take active steps to deal with it. Like all aspects of the false self, it undermines our sense of who we are – in this case, openly and maliciously. The fact that the voice ends up sounding just like our own can make it especially difficult to root out. And all the time our inner critic's attacks erode our already fragile sense of self. Sometimes we begin to see hostility from other people that isn't really there, as our antenna for harsh judgement is so finely tuned. That can make us aggressive or 'victimy', which triggers the kind of criticism we fear and the whole cycle of judgement and defence perpetuates itself. We – you – deserve so much better.

In order to escape the relentless grip of our inner critic, we must process the heartbreaks from which it grew. We need to do our grief work because the inner critic derives its stock of insults, and its power, from unmourned loss and hurt.

You now know what this entails. You need to 'follow the trail' back to the original source. So, for example, if one of your inner critic's standard thoughts is 'I'm useless!' ask yourself when and where in your life were you first made to feel this way. Who planted the seed of this belief inside of you? Allow yourself to grieve the part of you that was made to feel like this. Express your anger, sadness and fear about what happened.

Identifying the components of the inner critic will, I hope, feel easier at this stage in your process than it would have previously, because you have been on the trail of your heartbreaks and your coping behaviours for a while now. In fact, you may already be joining up some dots as you read this, beginning to see where your tendency to tell yourself that you're fat and ugly comes from, for example. Not every heartbreak contains a sting of overt insult or criticism, but many do.

Once we've established where it comes from, we need to practise strategies for dialling it down when it pops up. The basis for doing this is to learn to question our thoughts rather than blindly believe that they're true. We need to develop the habit of pausing when we hear that familiar voice. We need to stand up to it. Fact-check it, if we can. Negative thoughts are like bullies; they hunt in packs. The leader will kick off with something like, 'Hey Sarah, you're an idiot for saying that!' And then if you don't question its validity, it heads back to the 'toxic thoughts' gang to get reinforcements. Armed with their weaponry of cruel words, the whole brutal pack descends upon you. 'You're just so stupid. This is typical of you. *And* you're ugly, etc etc . . .'

Imagining what someone else would say about a particular thought can help us to take a more objective standpoint. 'Am I really fat and ugly? Would a friend describe me like that? No. So there's an alternative way to look at this . . .'

We talked about the importance of the words we use (or don't use) when we were looking at how to process painful emotions. If we don't have the words to describe them, it makes it harder for us to analyse and release our feelings. We've also seen, in our work on the masks we put on and roles we play, how beliefs are formed out of the words we think, write and speak. Words create and reinforce our beliefs about everything, including ourself. The inner critic's vocabulary is made up of insults, negative labels and judgements. It is a classic example of how the words we use can either bring us power or steal it from us, lift us up or knock us down.

In order to keep our inner critic in retreat and build our confidence and self-worth, we must replace our toxic language with more positive, supportive words. I am a big believer in identifying all the language we use towards ourselves that is in any way derogatory or unkind, and banning it from our communications and (as much as possible) our thoughts.

Let's begin by taking an inventory of all the harsh and critical words we unthinkingly use against ourselves or others. A classic example is the way in which we think and speak about our own body. 'I'm too fat/thin. I hate my wobbly stomach, my thighs are HUGE, I'm ugly and disgusting.' How can you possibly feel good about yourself when you're under this kind of attack? Imagine if a friend or partner was saying these things. You would – I hope – recognize it as a form of abuse. But so many of us abuse ourselves like this internally all the time.

OVER TO YOU

Ban the words that feed your inner critic

Here are some examples of words and phrases that I banned from my own life. In a minute, I'm going to invite you to make a list of all the words and phrases you use that feed your inner critic while starving your self-worth. Your list might be similar or very different. Try to be as specific and personal as you can.

The 'Stop It!' list

- I'm such an idiot.
- Look at the state of me.
- I'm too fat/thin, old/young.
- I'm too much like hard work.
- I'm so stupid.
- I'm disgusting.
- I should be feeling OK.
- I should be stronger.
- I should just stop trying.
- Nothing I do is ever good enough.
- I'm so broken.
- I'm a mess.
- I'll never be able to do that.
- That's just the way I am. Useless.

Take a moment of quiet reflection before you begin, to clear your mind of what you've just read and tap into your own inner critic. What does it say when it's verbally abusing, judging or being unkind to you? Any phrase that features the word 'should' is typical of inner critics. Similarly, any phrase that begins, 'I'm *too* . . .' Whatever it is, you fill in the blank: classic inner critic. You can make a list on a piece of paper or get creative if you like, and create a collage of all the toxic words and statements your inner critic feasts upon.

When you've finished, take the blackest thickest marker you can find and put a big line through every single word. Make a commitment that you will no longer use these words about yourself (or anybody else!). Keep it as a visible reminder for a while and then, when you're ready, put this list away and don't look at it again. I recommend you bin or burn it.

Don't worry if you slip back into using old language occasionally. Just keep trying. It can help to ask a friend or partner to gently flag it up if you say any banned words aloud. For the inner monologue, you just have to practise holding yourself accountable. You could try creating a 'banned word jar' (like a swear jar). Each time you use a nasty word against yourself, you have to 'pay a fine' into the jar. The concrete action seems to embed the habit of noticing your language. This way you're enhancing your self-worth and saving for a well-deserved treat all at the same time. Win-win.

Don't expect the inner critic to vanish in a puff of smoke. It goes hand in hand with poor self-worth and has very possibly been with you for as long as you can remember. Tell yourself that it's on its way out. Now that you have grieved your core wounds, its voice will gradually become quieter – so long as you continue to do your work. Every interaction you have, every thought or feeling, is an opportunity to like and approve of yourself. Developing self-worth is a process and it can take years, but finally the day will come when the voice in your head is mainly one of kindness, compassion, encouragement and support. As if an aggressive squatter has moved out and been replaced by the housemate from heaven. From then on, even if the inner critic shows up for a visit, you'll be ready with your boundaries and your self-compassion. Rather than buying into its nonsense, you can just send it gently but firmly on its way and watch as it quietly shuffles off.

There's no such thing as an unacceptable part of you

You've just learned the essentials of dealing with your inner critic. You've created a whole load of space in your mind and heart for a more generous and loving relationship with yourself. What's next?

Before we can get on to replacing the inner critic and its insults with an inner cheerleader (who uses a whole different language) we need to pass through the next stage on your way to self-worth: self-acceptance.

Self-acceptance does not mean saying to yourself, 'I know I'm not great but I suppose I'll do.' That's still critical and judgemental talk and has nothing to do with what we're looking for.

I understand self-acceptance as the ability to stop judging yourself, stop pretending that you are what you're not, stop making excuses, stop evading responsibility or living a fantasy, and actually accept the reality of yourself just as you are, in the here and now. Self-acceptance means facing reality as it is, not as you would like it to be or wish it had been. It's about honesty without blame or judgement. It's powerful and necessary.

Now that you've grieved your heartbreaks and worked through the importance of apologies, you are ready to face what can and can't be changed and must be accepted. Principally that means accepting the reality of your past, which literally can't be undone. Whatever choices you made have brought you to where you are now and made you the person you are. You might not like some of those choices, you might want to deny others, but as you know by now denying reality is never a good idea.

When we can look at ourselves in the mirror and say, 'Yes, I made that mistake and I'm not proud of it. That was my poor choice, which I made at a very vulnerable point in my life,' and then just leave that thought there, without further rumination or recrimination . . . Now, that's acceptance. And it takes practice. We can only manage it once we've done our work on understanding and releasing our pain. But it's essential. Without it, we can't go any further over the bridge.

When my older daughter was about six years old and I was a struggling young single mother of two, I smacked her on the leg in a fit of desperation and exhaustion. For decades I literally refused to accept what I had done, much less forgive myself for it. I was full of guilt, shame and self-reproach. I punished myself in so many ways, including encouraging male partners to physically hurt me. I believed that I deserved it because I must be a terrible person for what I'd done to my own child.

Eventually I was able to understand what I had done and why, and the version of myself that did it. Not to justify or excuse my behaviour, you understand, but to accept that it had happened. It took me years to reach this point (and hundreds of pounds worth of good therapy!) but I got there, and it was liberating.

Accepting yourself doesn't mean that you give up on goals or stop taking action for change in your life, but it does mean you stop resisting the reality of what *is* – both in the past and right now in the present. You say YES to it.

So, for example, if you want to get fitter or pursue a different career, then rather than resisting your starting point in the here and now, you accept it; you say yes to it.

In a low-paid job that bores you senseless? 'I accept it.'

Bum bigger than you'd like? 'I accept it.'

Made a mistake, a huge one? Guess what? Yep. 'I accept it.'

Acceptance (of oneself and all other aspects of reality) is a conscious, moment by moment, choice and practice. The alternative is denial or resistance, both of which lead only to more suffering. The spiritual teacher Eckhart Tolle uses the example of getting stuck in a traffic jam to show how our reaction to an unpleasant but immovable fact will increase or

decrease our suffering. If we spend half an hour winding ourselves up into a frenzy about the fact that we are going to be
late, all we achieve by resisting the reality of the moment is
more stress. It's not as if our swearing will magically make the
cars disappear. As Eckhart says, we essentially go to war with
the traffic . . . and lose!

Let your body show you how to practise self-compassion

It's one thing to accept the reality of a traffic jam, but when
it comes to accepting that we're currently three stone over-
weight or that we've alienated our best friend through our
selfishness, we will probably need to dig deep into the practice
of compassion for ourselves. What are the tools for learning
how to accept without blame, how to take responsibility while
avoiding shame? How do we embed acceptance of ourselves
in our lives?

For me, there is no greater way to practise self-acceptance
and learn the practicalities of self-compassion, than by focusing on our relationship with our body. This may be a stretch
out of your comfort zone, but it's a great way to learn how to
move beyond mere acceptance and on to liking yourself, just as
you are.

So here's the deal (and your inner critic is going to love
this) . . . The true self-worth and self-love that we're aiming for
are simply not possible without learning to accept, like and – in
time – love your body.

That's such an important statement that I'm going to repeat
it. There is NO true self-worth without learning to love your
body. Let that land.

We can't have selective self-worth, where we feel worthy in

certain areas such as our intelligence but unworthy in others such as our physical appearance. True self-worth doesn't work like that. If you can't at least accept every single part of yourself, there's only so far you can go on your journey towards self-worth.

Now, I know from bitter personal experience that for most women – and increasing numbers of men – loathing is closer to how we feel about our bodies. Women are encouraged to be at war with their fat thighs and wobbly bellies virtually from childhood. Some people might escape outright hostility, but they live lives of indifference towards their body. For the very analytical among us, those who live a neck-up existence, our body can feel like a dead weight that we try to ignore, noticing it only when it lets us down by getting sick.

This is not OK. Your body is an integral part of your organism. It's an ally – the means by which you can get out of bed in the morning and walk to make a coffee. And that's before we get on to the joys of dancing, or the pleasures of good sex, or the miracle of baby-making. Awareness, acceptance and gratitude can go a long way to reshaping your relationship with your body and, ultimately, your self-worth.

It's fair to say that I spent the best part of twenty-five years (just under half my life) being utterly repulsed by my body. It didn't matter how much I weighed or how fit I was (or not): my body was the enemy. I avoided mirrors at all costs. Numerous times every day I would make negative comments, either inside my head or out loud, about how disgusting I was. One of my ex-partners once asked me to try and find one part of my body that I felt was at the very least *acceptable*. I couldn't. Not one. How sad is that?

The truth is that my body, like so many women's, has been

abused, violated, deprived, neglected, stuffed and starved. It's been judged and criticized, compared, punished and denied. Mostly by me! And yet my body has remained faithful to me and loved me enough to stay healthy and strong. How incredible is that?!

So nowadays when I look in the mirror I see it as a beautiful gift. A miracle. A body full of curves, softness, trauma scars and so much love. A body with a fabulous story to tell.

If you are unsure of how to begin to accept your body, let alone love it (!), start with some basic self-care commitments. Listen to your body with compassion. Give it what it needs. Rest it in the best bed, pillows and sheets. Exercise and stretch it daily. Dance and shake it to your favourite music. Walk in nature regularly and allow the sounds, smells and sights to fill your body up with gratitude. Breathe in the fresh air. Bask in the shade of trees. Bathe your body in long warm baths and then wrap it up in cosy pyjamas and a big soft blanket. Feed your body delicious nutritious food. Drink filtered water and green juices. Go to the dentist. Book that blood test. Self-care like this is a commitment to yourself, your health and your life. If you don't know where to start with the project of loving yourself, begin with your body.

Be warned: for as long as your inner critic is still on the scene it will try all manner of tricks to convince you not to bother (and it gets sneakier as you get wise to it). 'Who do you think you are, spending that amount of time/money on yourself? Don't bother cooking something healthy, just reach for the biscuits, you look a state anyway.' You'll notice the 'blah blah blah' of these old (and quite frankly, boring) rants, which now sound a bit like an irritating fly that buzzes at your ear. Swat them away and then carry on lacing up your gym shoes.

Building your friendship with yourself

When we are able to accept our life situation (both past and present) and ourselves just as we are, we are ready to move on to the next step. This takes us from an 'acquaintanceship' with ourselves – polite, respectful – to a true friendship with all that we are and have ever been.

Let's get warmed up by starting a new list, this time of all those aspects of yourself that you actually like. It doesn't matter if this is a very short list to start with. It will grow as you progress. Include anything you can think of, however tiny. It could be aspects of your personality, physical appearance or your skills and talents. Jot down your thoughts in your journal and add to them as you continue to read. Try to say these things out loud, to a trusted friend if you feel brave enough, or to yourself in the mirror. Practising these words is laying the groundwork for you to begin to learn a new language of self-love a little later in the chapter.

My first list of self-likes, once I'd done my self-acceptance work and got past the self-loathing stage, might have looked something like this:

I like my skin.
I like my smile.
I like my boobs.
I like my courageous spirit.
I like that I'm great at silly dancing.
I like my humour.
I like that I'm a reflective person.

It wasn't long but it was a start, and it allowed me to practise the habit of looking for the positive rather than only seeing what I had always perceived as negative.

We all need to commit to treating ourselves as we do our good friends: with open-mindedness, consideration, affection and a sense of humour. This compassionate attitude, in which we essentially try to bolster rather than attack ourselves – especially when we're stressed or struggling – is the bedrock of self-love. When we behave in this way we are reinforcing the belief that we're worthy of that support. It becomes a self-fulfilling prophecy, visible to other people as well.

As we demonstrate that we like ourselves through our behaviours and choices, we begin to tell the truth of who we are. No more lies and no more masks. God, it feels good – I promise you. Along with the relief, there grows a sense of our own worthiness that is so empowering. It's a powerful statement to say, 'I really like myself just as I am' in a world that has lot of vested interest in you undervaluing yourself. To like yourself isn't a crime, you know; in fact it's a radical and necessary part of your healing. I dare you to say 'I really like xx about myself' in your next conversation with a trusted friend!

We're going to stick with the theme of your relationship with your body as we explore the detail of how to make friends with yourself.

Let's go back to the basic self-care we talked about when we were discussing self-acceptance, and see how we can push that a little further. Beyond healthy food, enough rest, exercise that you enjoy and the softest blanket you can afford, self-care is really a day-by-day, moment-by-moment choice to prioritize your own needs as much as you do the needs of other people. It is about committing to carve out time to rest, play and nurture yourself.

This is not easy when we are all super busy, and even harder for those of us who come from a past of neglect and abandonment, but it is essential if we are to live wholehearted, authentic lives of love and service. We cannot offer our best to others if we keep nothing in reserve for ourselves.

This is not about ignoring our commitments, being self-indulgent or selfish, so if your inner critic is jumping up and down by now, just ignore it. Self-sacrifice is sometimes noble, but it can also be a weapon wielded by somebody who feels powerless, angry and full of self-loathing. The flip side of that is a person who likes themselves enough to practise self-care on the level we're describing here. That person is well on the way to opening up their heart and energies to the wider world – but from a place of abundance rather than lack.

Another huge thing for me was a safe touch exercise that I'd come across when I was working in a refuge with women who had been physically and sexually abused. These women were able to begin to reclaim and make peace with their own bodies at the same time as generating the feel-good effects of the hormone oxytocin, which is released when we have a hug.

Years later I began to use the exercise myself and I was amazed by its impact. I started off only 'accepting' my belly but as time went on, and I was able to recognize what my stretch marks and softness represented (childbirth and two incredible daughters), I came to feel very grateful to my belly. Now I really love it. And believe me, a few years ago I would have told you that was impossible!

OVER TO YOU

Safe Touch Exercise

Most of us will remember what it is like to be safely and lovingly held when we are in distress or in need of comfort. This kind of touch, through cuddles, stroking, massage and closeness, naturally stimulates the production of the hormone oxytocin, which is associated with the bonding process between parents and newborn babies as well as being in romantic love. As much as it is wonderful to receive this touch from others, we can also learn to offer it to ourselves, especially in times of stress or upset. Learning ways to self-soothe through physical touch builds resilience and allows you to practise accepting/liking/loving your body.

When you take your shower or bath, as you soap your skin, slow everything right down and really pay attention to each part of your body. Gently stroke each one, as a mother does to her baby, and say out loud, 'This is my arm and I accept/like/love my arm.' 'These are my boobs and I love my boobs.' 'This is my belly and I am learning to accept my belly.' You work your way across your whole body, stroking your skin tenderly as you wash and speak to your whole body, bit by bit. For the places that you can only accept, you use that word and for those you like/love, offer that alternative.

It was a slow process for me, but I eventually learned to see my body not as the enemy but as a war-weary warrior, battered but still standing. By speaking kindly about and to it, by feeding it well and exercising it regularly, by listening to it and allowing my body to stop and rest when it needed to, it eventually became my best friend. These days I love and accept my whole body just as it is.

The same thing is possible for you. When we do our healing work, we shift away from relating to our body as an object that we either reject or use to please others or gain attention and love. It becomes less an object that we drag around and more the vehicle for us to live our wholehearted life. When we treat it as the life-sustaining miracle that it is, everything starts to change. Everything.

Even so, there will be days (or weeks, or months) when life hits us hard and down we go. We are exhausted by life, to the point that our tank is completely empty. That's when we need *radical* self-care, which is basically self-care on steroids. When a dark night of the soul arrives, people who value themselves are willing and able to press pause on life and offer themselves some serious tender loving care. This might require daytime sleeping, good food including some treats, gentle exercise, good company or perhaps some alone time. It might well involve cancelling work or social plans, tightening boundaries or letting others be disappointed in us (yep). We might even have to ask for help (not easy for us recovering warriors). Radical self-care is ultimately about showing up for ourselves, reminding ourselves that we are worthy and loved. It is the most profound act of self-love.

The final step into self-love

When I mention self-love, people often roll their eyes and think of self-absorbed arrogant egotists (I know I used to). Really, though, it is simply a way to describe valuing yourself as much as you do those people who are most important to you – your friends, partner, kids.

The power of self-love can be transformative for you on an individual level, but also for the collective community within the wider world. For as you make yourself a priority, you create the energy, space, lightness and clarity inside of you to focus on what's really important in the world. Your life moves way beyond the small story of 'me' and 'my pain'. As you look for meaning and purpose, you find ways to love and serve more in the world. Nothing selfish or narcissistic about that!

As for what it looks like in practice, self-love is simply healthy self-worth in action. If you have a friend or a child, a sibling or a partner that you support, comfort and cherish, then you already know how to love yourself. It's simply a matter of applying those techniques and skills to yourself, one loving choice and word at a time.

Our focus in this section will be back on language. You've started taking care of yourself and practised accepting and liking your body as a way to learn how to be your own friend. Now we're going to use positive language as our key tool to push ourselves on towards self-love.

Learning the new language of self-love

We will never learn to value ourselves enough to expect the kindness and positive treatment that we are worth unless and until we can cultivate an inner cheerleader to take the place of the inner critic. That means putting the hours in to work consciously on some new language skills. You've already banned the old toxic language and have been building your capacity to be positive about yourself. Let's bring those two things together.

When I moved to live in the Canary Islands I wanted to be part of the local community so I took up Spanish lessons. Every day I would clumsily communicate with others in my basic Spanish class and get it wrong ALL the time. I still cringe when I remember telling the class, 'Mi nombre es Donna y disfruto tirarme pedos,' which for those of you who don't speak Spanish means, 'My name's Donna and I enjoy farting.' Not sure what I was trying to say but it sure wasn't that (even if it is true!). And despite these classic clangers, I kept going, kept practising every day. And guess what? Although the words felt unusual in my mouth and I blushed and bum-clenched my way through stilted conversations, ultimately I did get better at Spanish.

It's the same for all of us when we're learning a new language, or any other skill. We don't expect to pick up a guitar for the first time and sound like Jimi Hendrix (except perhaps in the privacy of a bedroom fantasy, posing in front of the mirror). We wouldn't take one driving lesson and expect to pass our test. We know that these things take consistent and regular practice. The same is true as you learn to speak in a more loving and compassionate way towards and about yourself. If you weren't brought up in an environment where that language was spoken, it's a bit like throwing yourself into a beginners' Spanish class. Expect errors, blunders and plenty of awkward silence.

The language of self-love and self-compassion is understanding and relative, unlike the black and white absolutes of the inner critic. So you won't find any shoulds or should nots here. Rather than, 'You shouldn't have had that enormous piece of cake,' or 'You're a fool for thinking he would want to date you,' your inner friend/mentor/cheerleader says things like, 'Oops, never mind. You're only human.' Or, 'You don't need his validation. You're OK whether he dates you or not.'

This is the voice of the wise part of you that has your back, that likes you and knows you're trying your best. It doesn't let you off the hook or make excuses for poor choices, but it doesn't leap on every single slip-up as proof of your uselessness, badness or worthlessness. It reminds you that other people's choices and behaviours reflect their own needs and capabilities far more than they say anything about you. The way that other people treat you and speak about you is information, not truth. If the information you're receiving suggests that he doesn't want to date you, your inner cheer-leader says, 'That's fine. Not everyone will want to date you, even though you're great. Next!'

Gradually, as you get more familiar with the language of self-compassion, you can experiment with using the word 'I' rather than 'You'. As in, 'I'm only human and I'm doing my best. I'll try again tomorrow.' Or, 'Not everyone will want to date me. I am still great.' In this way you are making a positive statement of belief in yourself. You are asserting to other people and to yourself that you won't put up with nonsense any more, that from now on you treat yourself with respect, kindness and understanding.

This might feel alien at first or even a bit fake, but try not to let that put you off. Language is one of the greatest tools for creating change in our internal and external worlds. It's powerful, as I know from my time in the Canaries. You might have cringe-worthy moments along the way but with regular practice, one day you will be fluent in the language of self-love. *Sí, es posible!*

OVER TO YOU

Teach yourself the new language of self-love

Here's a list of self-loving statements. I hope it inspires you to create your own. As you read each one, try to imagine a scenario in which you could have used it, or could use it in the future, if you practise hard enough!

- I'm learning to love that about myself.
- Sometimes I make mistakes and I'm OK with that.
- I am so grateful for my body and health.
- I'm really good at that.
- I'm feeling emotionally wobbly today.
- I have compassion for my younger self and the choices I made back then.
- I'm wounded (not broken) and healing takes time.
- I'm learning to be patient with myself.
- Oops I did it again! Hey ho, I'm only human.
- I don't know the answer to that.
- I'm feeling xx right now and that's OK.
- I don't need your validation.
- This is my boundary, don't cross it.
- I'm OK if you don't like me.
- One of my strengths is . . .
- I love myself and you can judge that all you like if you want to.
- I'm learning all the time.

Now, take your journal out and make your own list of self-loving language. Take your time and write down any and every little thing that occurs to you. Come back and do this as often as you need to, until you've filled a whole page. If all you have the first time is, 'I like my hair and I give good birthday presents,' that's a good start! Next time you might be able to expand it to, 'I'm an attractive and thoughtful person.'

Now stick your list wherever you will see it frequently and regularly: on the fridge, in the loo, on the kettle, make it your screen saver on your gadgets. Put it everywhere, just as kids do when they're revising for a spelling test.

Next, commit to using at least three of the words or statements on your list every single day. The context doesn't matter. It could be on the phone to a close friend, to your reflection in the mirror as you brush your teeth or as a mantra while exercising. Practise the art of loving yourself. Because you really are worth it! (Sorry, couldn't resist!)

Being your own best friend

The more you practise accepting and liking yourself, the stronger your skills will become. The more you use the language of self-love, the more natural it will feel to treat yourself with kindness, compassion and respect. One day you will look in the mirror and realize that you love what you see. This might still sound like a stretch to some of you, but it's a logical consequence of behaving differently. As you tell and show the truth of who you are without shame, your self-respect and self-worth will inevitably follow. You make choices that honour your body and your truth. You refuse to live the lie of unworthiness a moment longer. You start to hold your boundaries even more firmly, speaking your truth clearly and daring to show the world who you are. You can be vulnerable and recognize the strength in your vulnerability. You are growing into the person you always were but simply forgot for a while. Authentic.

Key points from this chapter

- The 'inner critic' describes the voice in our heads that judges or berates us and/or others. It stems from all the internalized negative messages we received in childhood.
- Questioning our thoughts rather than blindly believing them is a fundamental strategy in addressing the inner critic.
- Identifying and banning the toxic and violent language you use against yourself and others is also key.
- Learning to accept, like and ultimately love our bodies is an active process and absolutely possible for everyone. (Oh, yes it is!)
- Identifying a new, more loving and accepting language towards yourself is the next step towards becoming your own best friend.
- Self-care is not an optional extra. It's an essential daily practice which leads us into true self-love.

Questions for ongoing reflection

- What are some of the main messages your inner critic tells you? If you 'follow the trail', where might these have come from?
- Ask yourself 'is this really true' for each of the negative thoughts. Start to challenge and question them. Push back.
- How might you feel about yourself and your body if you started to believe a new set of more compassionate

and self-loving thoughts? How different would your life become?

- How will you commit to love, honour and cherish your body going forward?
- What ways will you speak to and treat yourself, like you do with a best friend?
- What new insights or learning have you gained from this chapter?
- How do you feel right now in your body? Notice . . . and breathe.

Step Six: Stronger Still – developing your power and resilience

How powerful are you feeling right now? I ask because many of us, especially if we've been struggling with ungrieved heartbreak for years, believe that power is for other people – not us. And yet we are far more powerful – more resilient, courageous, resourceful and persistent – than we give ourselves credit for. It's time for you to own your personal power. Take a moment to acknowledge how far you've already come in your work here, and what it has taken to reach this point. It has involved a huge amount of courage, commitment and strength on your part to keep walking across the bridge towards your future, even when the ghosts of your past try to drag you back in the opposite direction. Now that's true power!

Just to be clear: power in this context has nothing to do with the size of your muscles or your bank account and everything to do with having a strong emotional and ethical core. When you know who you are, what you want and what you believe in, and you're able to live in accordance with those values, you wield a huge amount of personal power. You trust yourself, so others trust you. You are able to rise to challenges when they inevitably come. You've got the grit to see a task through to the end and the resilience to recover from setbacks. That, my friends, is true power – and it is a glorious and beautiful thing.

For people who have traditionally been disempowered in our culture it is particularly crucial to work on developing a sense of your own strength, but for everyone who is recovering from a lifetime of heartbreak it is a necessary part of healing. We need to replace any lingering sense of ourselves as a victim, or somehow 'lesser', with the belief that we are strong, competent, able, worthy and yes, powerful.

Your healing is fully under way now. You've begun the crucial task of developing your sense that you are worthy of respect and kindness from everybody with whom you interact, including yourself. As you learn to like yourself more and more, your self-belief and esteem will blossom. You'll be ready to start thriving, not just surviving. Coming up soon are the benefits of all this hard work – contentment, peace and positive energy to replace the negative energy, fear, sadness and anger that you've been releasing. First of all, though, it's time to consolidate.

So many people tell me that they feel a flurry of anxiety when they let go of old pain and old masks. 'Who am I,' they ask themselves, 'without my old defences? And how will I manage without them? Is there anything left when I peel away the layers of the false self?'

This fear makes total sense. I remember it myself. I can tell you until I'm blue in the face that who you really are has been waiting for you all along and you have nothing to fear, but you have to find that out for yourself. Dismantling the false self, dialling down the inner critic and learning to like ourselves, just as we are, requires patience, commitment and above all a lot of faith and trust. You must be gentle with yourself as you do this work.

If you're feeling wobbly, or have doubts about whether you can keep up your journey towards wholehearted living, I'd say that's actually a really good sign you're ready for the next important step. This chapter delves into how we can protect the gains you've made so far and build on your growing self-worth to strengthen your inner resources. I hope to open your eyes to the amazing strength at your core and help you to have faith in that powerful part of yourself. By claiming our power, we integrate the belief that we can handle the heartbreaks of the future as well as heal the heartbreaks of the past. None of us can escape the challenges of life – loss, hurt, illness and death are all inevitable parts of the human journey. What we can do is build up our resilience, so that when painful events occur we're better able to cope.

The key lesson I hope you will learn in this chapter is that resilience and strength belong to you as much as to anyone else. They arise from a certain mindset, one that starts from the premise 'I've got this' and knows how to embody that belief without letting ego take over. We will cover some of the key behaviours that support you to establish your personal power, such as identifying your values so that you can set boundaries around what really matters to you. We will also look at how to communicate your values and your boundaries clearly and positively to other people, so that they can respect them – and you.

As well as doing this practical work, we also build resilience and self-confidence by changing the way we view and manage loss and hurt. We need to learn how to respond to them from a calmer, healthier aspect of ourself, rather than react from the wounded child parts of ourselves (which are hopefully not quite as wounded as they used to be). This you might call the 'wise adult' that we covered earlier, the part of us who has seen crises before and knows how to steer through the next one. It might, as we will see in the next chapter, also be our playful child, who can show us how to take a challenge less seriously and handle it creatively.

For me, the crucial context for all our work in this chapter is the need to grow into our own personal power. Our culture tends to see the powerful as those rich old white guys who run big companies or hold positions in government. That kind of high status is not what we're talking about here. Personal power for me consists in being able to steer your life in the direction you want it to go – it's partly to do with personal agency and freedom. It's also the ability to hold your boundaries, stand up for yourself and what you believe in, command respect, get things done, admit when you're wrong and be humble enough to say sorry. So it's also to do with integrity and authenticity.

True personal power is built on knowing that you're perfect, just as you are. Perfectly imperfect. It's about knowing how to be protective of yourself and your boundaries without getting defensive. How to keep working for what's important to you. How to forgive yourself for slip-ups and keep looking after yourself. How to keep on keeping on in a way that admits reality can be painful, but resists turning it into a catastrophe.

This kind of power is not something that you either have or you don't. The more we 'finish our business' from the past, get clear about our values and communicate our boundaries, the more powerful we will feel and become. Others in our life start to understand that we are not to be messed with. They see it in our eyes, in our demeanour, our posture, in the language we use and the choices we make. This kind of embodied power is priceless.

You've come a long way. Now you're strong enough to get stronger still.

Protecting the person you're becoming

This is a vulnerable moment but an exciting one: you're in the process of discovering who you are when you're not mourning old losses or covering up old pain with masks. You're beginning to get to know the truth of you, beneath all the layers of the false self. In the next chapter we will be turning our full attention to exploring who you can be when you let yourself dream, play and discover. You will be filling yourself to the brim with wonder, gratitude and joy. But before that it's important to make sure that you're feeling steady enough to let loose and enjoy that process.

How can you protect your emerging authentic self? How can you embed your new habits of loving self-acceptance, even if you're coming under pressure from other people? How can you build up your emotional resilience?

It all starts with clarifying your values. We're aiming, throughout this chapter, to develop your core emotional and ethical strength gently and honestly. In order to do that we need to identify those qualities or experiences that are most important to you. What matters to you? What or who do you value? How would you like to be remembered after you've died? Answering questions like these can help you to uncover your personal values. Values are as varied as we are, but might be, for example, being honest and trustworthy, being kind and compassionate or challenging yourself to be daring. They might also include prioritizing family life, being financially independent or giving time or money to charity.

One big reason for investigating your values is to get to know your authentic self a little better, which will put you on much firmer ground for living a wholehearted life. Another is so that you can devise strategies for protecting what you value, or bringing more of it into your life. It's not enough just to know that kindness is important to you, for example. What are you going to do practically, in the real world, to make kindness a central part of how you live your life? As always in this book, our focus is on creating positive change. So when we warm up for our first practical task in a minute, I'm not going to ask you to make a list of 'nice to haves', buzzwords, or the kind of things you think a good person 'ought' to care about. I will invite you to be as honest and authentic as you can about what motivates you and matters to you.

This might feel uncomfortable, but it's important. Our values can support us to shape our identity as we drop further into living more authentically and truthfully. And once we're living authentically, it is so much easier to bounce back from upsets, tackle difficult tasks calmly and cope with conflict. When we're authentic we can be strong because we're not wasting precious energy on denying reality or pretending to be something we're not. We know what matters to us, so it gets easier not to sweat the small stuff. And every time we make a choice that protects what's important and supports rather than undermines us, we are building our ability to trust ourselves and to get through hard times.

Resilience is a key part of personal power

Some people come through an ordeal weary but intact. They suffer but they don't fall apart and they're able to pick themselves up and get moving again relatively quickly. Others seem to crumble the moment life presents them with a challenge, and once they're down they stay down.

I am not making a value judgement here, though of course people often do. We are taught that the person who keeps a cool head in a crisis is strong, commanding, a leader. The person who panics or shuts down is hysterical, weak, a failure. But it's not enough to make these judgements solely on the basis

193

of someone's reactions in the moment. From the outside, it's hard to tell the difference between someone who is calm and someone who is disassociating from the part of themself that is experiencing stress by deploying, for example, the warrior persona. Calm is great, if it's authentic, but not if it's actually a denial of how you're really feeling.

So it's important to be clear about what we mean by resilience. In psychological terms, it is defined as 'the ability to adapt well in the face of adversity, trauma and significant stress' and 'to be able to recover and bounce back easily from misfortune and change'. Resilience is not an ability to endure suffering without complaining; neither is it the pretence that we're 'fine' about something that hurt us.

True resilience is the ability and willingness to meet life's hardships head on and work with them openly and confidently. I think of it as an unshakeable belief that, whatever is going on, we're up to the task of coming through it. It can be cultivated and practised, like strength training in the gym, and this is so worthwhile because resilience to life's inevitable painful events can be the difference between sinking and swimming. Actually, it can be the difference between sinking and surfing!

So why is it that some people seem to be more resilient than others? Studies have shown that genetics play a role in how the biology of our brain sets us up to cope with adversity. Scientists have researched how people bounce back, or don't, after childhood trauma, and have identified several genes that play a role in, for example, determining how sensitive our brain is to stress hormones such as cortisol, or the positivity-inducing serotonin.

Resilience is a massively complex behaviour and depends on numerous factors, including early life experience, good self-esteem, having a supportive network of friends and family, avoiding rumination on negative events and practising gratitude for positive ones.

Whatever our predispositions for resilience, those of us who have safe, secure and consistent childhood experiences develop a much stronger resilient core than those who face adverse childhood experiences such as being abused, bullied or neglected.

People who experience trauma sometimes go on to develop an overstressed nervous system, which means that even low-level stressors can feel overwhelming. They lack the ability to self-regulate and calm themselves down. It's as if their 'on' switch is permanently turned on. Even without trauma, life's everyday wear and tear can deplete our resilience, though it can be restocked with practice.

Like many people, Nicki had a deep fear of public speaking. Unfortunately for her, it was a big part of her job in advertising. Although she had attended training to develop her presentation skills, she still found presenting at events super stressful, and her nerves would often get the better of her. Her feelings of panic left her distressed and feeling unprofessional. They also reinforced her belief that she was rubbish at public speaking. It was a negative self-perpetuating cycle.

As Nicki and I explored her past, we talked about how shamed and ridiculed she had been by bullies at school. Nicki was able to join the dots and understand why presenting was now so challenging for her, because of the historical fear of being ridiculed, humiliated and rejected. This helped her to be more compassionate towards herself and to challenge her inner critic's bullying thoughts. The shift in approach, alongside ongoing practice, enabled Nicki to build her resilience and confidence. She can now deliver presentations with only a minor (natural) nervous reaction rather than a full-blown meltdown.

The process of building resilience through awareness and practice is precisely what you're doing right now. You are actively engaged in strengthening your resilience and building your personal power. By processing your past and working on your self-care and self-love, you are strengthening your resources to meet life's challenges as they arise.

Explore your personal values

We're now going to start our practical investigative work to uncover your values. You might have done this kind of thing before or it might be new to you. Either way, you will benefit from asking yourself these questions at this stage in your healing process.

Your values are your ethical touchstones and your emotional true north. What is really important to you? Think in terms of behaviours that you admire in other people, or aspects of your life or relationships that matter deeply to you. How passionately do you feel about each of them, and why? Can you put them in an order of priority? If you're struggling, it might help to consider whether you would be prepared to make a sacrifice for your value. This can shed light on whether it's authentic or something more superficial.

A word of caution: try to get away from black and white thinking and approach this from a more compassionate position. If you are someone who 'expects 100 per cent truth and honesty in relationships', for example, I would suggest you think carefully about this and where it stems from. Is 100 per cent realistic? Is it kind? Check whether you offer this to yourself. Are you 100 per cent trustworthy and honest with yourself? Or do you ever make mistakes and betray your own wisdom? I know I do. Are you 100 per cent honest or do you sometimes lie to yourself in order to avoid facing a painful truth? Again, me too.

I believe that expecting 100 per cent truth and honesty (or anything else) from ourselves and others is the stuff of fairy tales. It always sets us up to fail. People living in the real world are human and flawed. They make mistakes. And sometimes really good people make poor choices. So do make sure when you create your values list and practise your boundary-setting, that it is your wise adult part leading the way rather than your inner child, who still believes in Cinderella and her glass slipper. Honesty and self-compassion will serve you well in all your work on personal power.

Have a look at the list of examples below, just to get you started. Then take out your journal and jot down some ideas for yourself. Perhaps you might list them in order of importance and priority for you. You can come back and revise or add to your list as often as you need to. I find it really interesting to do this over a period of weeks. Some things come up only once but most come up over and over again. Listing your values is preparation work for your first task, on boundary-setting, which is coming up.

- Honesty
- Integrity
- Loyalty
- Trustworthiness
- Truth
- Kindness
- Open mind and open heart

- Tenderness
- Compassion
- Curiosity
- Fairness and justice
- Authenticity
- Humour
- Optimism
- Peace
- Responsibility
- Balance
- Sustainability
- Respect for the natural world
- Activism
- Work in the community
- Active listening
- Learning from mistakes
- Valuing everyone's contribution
- No hierarchies of power in the family or group
- Generosity

Setting your limits builds your power

The idea that it's important to set boundaries is nothing new to most of us, but it's still a concept that many of us struggle with. What exactly is a boundary and how on earth do we set them and stick to them? It can be confusing at the start, but boundary-setting doesn't have to be complicated and certainly isn't about aggression or defensiveness. There is a big difference between a boundary and a barrier.

Personal boundaries essentially relate to our personal limits. They let others know what is OK for us and what isn't.

A boundary is like a symbolic fence that we put up to high-light and protect our personal space, what matters to us, or what we expect in terms of our own behaviour and other people's.

The wonderful thing about a fence is that (unlike a barrier) it can have a gate, so we can choose whom we invite into (or escort out of!) our personal space. If necessary we can simply shut the gate with a very clear 'No.' A barrier, on the other hand, is more like a brick wall. Nothing gets in or out when you have a brick wall defending you. Barriers shout, 'KEEP OUT!' Boundaries state, 'Step Back.' Barriers are a defence that can keep people away and prevent love from entering or leaving. Boundaries are a form of protection, connection and clarity. They take courage to hold firm. They allow love to flow in and out, but not at any price.

There are five layers of boundaries, which act like fences around different elements of our being. Every one of them draws a line in the sand to state our position, giving us something to hold on to. They become a way to hold both ourselves and others accountable.

- Intellectual boundaries – these are about giving ourselves permission to express our own opinions, thoughts and points of view while also respecting these same rights for others.
- Emotional boundaries – here we learn to recognize, express and communicate our emotions appropriately and we respect those same rights in others.
- Physical boundaries – these include recognizing and honouring our own need for personal space as well as the needs of others for the same.
- Social boundaries – giving ourselves permission to

participate only in social activities we enjoy and that nourish us as well as choosing who we share our time with.

- Spiritual boundaries – these often come later in life for some as we establish and develop our own spiritual practices, while respecting and honouring those of others.

Before we get on to how to consciously set boundaries that reflect your key values, we need to acknowledge that all of us are operating with a boundary style already, though we may not be conscious of it. Boundaries arise inevitably as a means to manage our interactions with other people. You may have lots of boundaries or very few; you may hold them rigidly so that they are more like barriers or hold them so loosely that people regularly trample all over them, which can leave you feeling invaded and resentful. Whether we have many or none, held tightly or lightly, we all have a boundary style. The key point is to work out whether yours is working for you, or not.

Like many aspects of who we are and how we live, personal boundaries are established early in life, with the foundations being laid in childhood. How our parents did or didn't do boundaries will inevitably impact our own capacity for healthy boundary-setting. If your parents 'didn't really do emotions' and you never saw them cry, express their frustration or joy or thankfulness, then you might be similarly defensive about your own emotions or go the other way and end up with few or no boundaries around your own emotions. You might be prone to outbursts of anger or being swept away by the drama of your own feelings. You have ended up doing the opposite of what you saw and disliked as a child.

Boundaries are important. Without them, we run the risk of being overexposed to the effects of other people's agendas – or our own! Our boundaries protect our personal space and the people, groups, activities and ways of being that we have defined as important. For example, you might value openness and generosity and hold the belief that to be generous with your time is to show that you are a caring and compassionate person. There's nothing wrong with that, so long as you have learned how to put healthy boundaries around those values, to prevent you from falling into a pattern of endless giving. Unboundaried generosity will take a toll on you and is not the most effective way to show you care or make a positive difference.

So how do we set our boundaries? One way to do it, as we saw in the example above, is to start with our values. Once you have identified your personal values, you can begin to shape your boundaries in a way that both protects and honours them. So for example, you could ask yourself, 'What does kindness really mean for me? How will I ensure that I behave in ways that honour this? What will I do or say if someone is unkind in their communications with me or people I care about?' The aim is to think around your values in a real-world setting, framing them so that you can still use them as guidelines even when that proverbial shit starts flying towards the fan. Without stress-testing them in this way, the danger is that your values are an aspirational list of 'nice to haves' rather than a resource for living from your emerging, more authentic self.

Boundaries in practice

In a minute, I'm going to invite you to investigate your own boundaries. First, I thought I'd show you an example of boundary-setting in the real world. I've recently made some new friends and have been reflecting upon past friendships that came to an end. I recognize that I have previously confused and hurt people (including myself) with blurred boundaries. So I have begun to clarify friendship boundaries with new friends at the outset. This might sound odd or clinical, especially to the unboundaried among you! But I simply don't want to hurt anyone if I can help it and I'm too old to say yes and not mean it.

I started with my values in relation to friendship, and tried to expand on how they might play out. A value has to be dynamic enough to survive action in the real world. I have discussed these points with new friends but always been careful not to present them as rules. They do include promises about how I will conduct myself within our friendship, but they certainly don't demand anything from the other person.

- **Emotional honesty** – I promise to be honest with you about my feelings and if I do get triggered, I will be honest about that too. I will do my own work to ensure that I respond rather than react to any conflict or disagreements we may encounter.

- **Acceptance** – I commit to accepting all that you are and ask for the same in return. I will show you both my light and my shadow. And I will be who I am, not who you need me to be.

- **Connecting** – I commit to investing in our relationship. Connecting with you as and when it feels right for both of us. I don't 'expect' you to always be available for me nor to answer my messages or calls within an imagined 'appropriate' timescale. As an introvert,

I must be honest, less is more for me. I don't have a need to see you often but you will always be with me regardless.

- **Needs** – I promise not to have unrealistic expectations of our friendship. You are neither my mother nor my father so I do not expect you to parent me! If I do need something, I will have the courage to ask. Not easy for a 'warrior in recovery' but I will do my best.

- **Truth** – I will do my very best to tell you the truth. Sometimes, however, I might tell a white lie to protect your heart. Not pretty but true! I'll always be authentic, if not always 100 per cent truthful!

- **Disagreements** – if and when we do fall out, I promise to listen to you and hear you. I ask for the same. I will use these times to learn and grow with you and move closer towards you.

- **Apology** – I will apologize when I make a mistake and take responsibility for any clumsy actions or words on my part. I will make amends where needed.

- **Laughter** – I will laugh with you, at you and about you, playfully. Please do me the honour of offering the same! My humour will sometimes be dark but always kind. Yours doesn't have to be. As long as you're funny. If you're not, I won't laugh.

This practice can also work well in intimate relationships. It provides a useful framework for discussing boundaries with your partner and a starting point to create boundaries together, based on your particular values.

OVER TO YOU

Turning values into boundaries

Flip back and read through your list of personal values. Are you still happy with it? Is there anything you'd like to add, or remove? If you haven't already done so, pick out your top five or six values. These are the ones that you're going to work with as you practise boundary-setting.

The aim of this exercise is to imagine the choices and behaviours that you might find yourself adopting, in order to protect each value. What might you need to do to honour a value of integrity, for example? Try to think about challenges that might come up. Imagine circumstances in which you were asked to compromise. How would you respond?

Remember that we've been discussing the need to define our values and boundaries in a context of realism and compassion. Sticking with our example, integrity may be important to you but you might be able to imagine a situation in which it was challenged and you didn't uphold your standard. It's not a sin to fall short of our own standards or overstep our own boundaries, so there's no need to punish yourself, but this is exactly why it's a good idea to stress-test your boundaries before you define them. That way you aren't setting yourself (or anyone else) up for so-called failure.

You're going to end up with a sentence that expresses your commitment to protecting and honouring each of your key values. Have another quick look at my friendship boundaries on the previous pages, if you want to remind yourself of the format. For example, using the value of integrity, your boundary might read something along the lines of:

Integrity – I will do everything I can to live my life with integrity, which for me means living in accordance with my values. I will also recognize integrity in other people when I find it. I will try to avoid shaming myself or anyone else if I (they) sometimes fall short. I commit to doing my best, in the knowledge that I'm not perfect.

Let your body communicate your boundaries

What about holding or maintaining our boundaries once we have clarified them? This starts with writing them down, as you have just done, so that we are totally clear on them for ourselves. But you're probably not going to hand out a list of your boundaries to every person in your life. (Although I must confess, I am tempted to!) You need to find other ways to communicate them.

Clear and effective verbal communication is a crucial resource in your personal power tool kit and we will come on to it in more detail in due course. For now, I'll say that you can learn to get your boundaries over to people gently, as you go about your everyday interactions, just as you can learn to be assertive when people cross them, though this is not always easy. Like most things in life, setting and maintaining healthy boundaries takes practice.

By this stage in the book, I'm sure you will have noticed my trust in the body as a tool for communication. If you don't know what you need, ask your body and listen to its answer. On a similar tip, if you're not sure how to let people know about your personal limits in any situation, you could do worse than start with your body language.

The way we hold our body gives clear messages to the

world about our boundaries (among many other things). Have a think about people you know well enough to assess their style of personal boundaries. How do they carry themselves? If you have a friend with a strong but flexible boundary style, I'm willing to bet she walks tall and can shake her stuff on the dance floor! A relative with overstrong, rigid boundaries might well be stiff in their movements and mannerisms. People with weak boundaries, on the other hand, often have a collapsed, soft body posture, almost as if their body is a walking apology.

Setting aside harsh judgements (we've come too far for that nonsense!), if you recognize any of these features in yourself, it might be helpful to start some targeted bodywork. If you need support to embody strong healthy boundaries, try strength and posture training through yoga, Pilates, ballet or Alexander technique. For those with a more 'barriered' posture, the focus is to soften the body's defences while retaining the strength. Activities like Five Rhythms dance, Tai Chi, certain heart-based yoga practices and Rolfing can all help this process. (See the Resources section for more information.)

A healthy, boundaried body has a strong, upright posture, open body language and fluidity of movement. The person who embodies healthy boundaries fully inhabits their own body and is comfortable in their own skin, regardless of all the blah blah blah messages we receive about what we 'should' look like. When you embody your boundaries you convey where your limits lie with your whole presence. Your body transmits the message, 'I'm here, I'm open and I'm worthy.' A healthy embodied boundary comes from within, as if you are so 'full' inside that your worth reaches every part of your external 'shell'.

Does this sound unattainable? If so, I get it because it's like the gold standard of a healthy boundaried body! Most of us will require a bit of practice to get there, as we consciously allow our body to represent who we are and what we stand for. And it is, of course, a process. I noticed that as I gradually became more comfortable with my authentic self and more experienced at handling my own personal power, it was naturally reflected in the way I behaved, spoke, carried myself – everything. I grew into my boundaries, like a flower unfurling. This has nothing to do with aesthetics and everything to do with how clear and full you are becoming, one precious boundary at a time.

Boundaries are in essence about truth; about knowing, speaking and living our truth. This is not always easy but neither is living a series of lies. It will definitely require you to be vulnerable; but as we saw in Step Five, there is huge strength in vulnerability. The first step into vulnerability takes courage but, as we come to know and trust ourselves more and can stand up for and honour our own limits, the positive reinforcement kicks in. The more we take the risk of acting in accordance with our values and putting boundaries around our intellectual, emotional and physical space, the more we naturally enhance our feelings of self-worth and strengthen our resilience. Our capacity to cope with and recover from life's inherent challenges grows. We feed our belief that we are powerful beings, worthy of love and respect.

Not everybody will catch up with your new reality immediately. Some people will do their best to meet your new boundaried self honestly but will need a little time to adjust, just as you will yourself. But your new boundaried self will definitely upset a few (unboundaried) people along the way, especially those who have been very happy to benefit from your previous lack of boundaries. It's good to be prepared for that group of people too. Don't be surprised if you're met with judgement and blame when holding your boundaries with people who have none. Whenever I used to ask my very unboundaried mum not to constantly (negatively) comment on my appearance when I visited her as an adult, she would roll her eyes and say, 'You always were oversensitive.' It was hard for her to tolerate this new boundaried version of her daughter, so she initially reacted the only way she knew how, with judgement and 'attack'.

Ultimately, though, how other people react is not really the point. Personal boundaries are an essential part of living authentically and honouring your own worth. So take a deep breath, courageously lean into the strength of your vulnerability and practise speaking your truth.

It all comes down to communication

Having worked with individuals and couples in private therapeutic practice for many years, I would say that poor communication (unsurprisingly) is the number one reason for difficulties in people's relationships. So many of us learn the ego weapons of reactivity and defence rather than the skills of healthy communication. Boundaries versus barriers, communication and connection versus attack and defence, are a fault line in every relationship we have. We will never succeed in holding our boundaries and honouring our values unless we can communicate clearly about our needs and wishes.

Clear communication is not just about what we say and how we say it. It's multidimensional. It includes the capacity to speak our truth, to ask questions and to listen to the answers, to ask for our needs to be met, to learn to respond rather than react, and to express our true thoughts and feelings. It also includes, as we saw in the previous section, non-verbal communication such as body language and facial expressions, etc.

Now, there are plenty of great books already available on the subject of healthy communication (see Resources), but I'm going to speak specifically about communication in relation to maintaining boundaries, because it is absolutely essential.

I've found that a good starting point when we're learning about healthy communication is 'how not to do it'. It's somehow easier to identify the things that definitely aren't going to work than to define what we should be doing. So let's start with a list of unhelpful approaches to talking about boundaries. And please, you may wince, but you're not allowed to go down a rabbit hole of self-criticism if you recognize any of these from your own arsenal. Believe me, I practised this sort of 'crap communication' for many years. Most of us learned how to communicate through our families, so no surprises that if your family wasn't great at healthy communication you've picked up some less than ideal styles. No need to be harsh on yourself (see the previous section on self-compassion), just good to notice. Awareness, as you now know, is the first step to change.

Unhelpful communication styles for boundary-setting

- **Over-apologizing** – 'I'm so sorry, so so very *very* sorry.' This conveys weak boundaries and reinforces our 'less than' position in life.

- **Argumentative** – this approach can be a great way to avoid our more vulnerable feelings and also keep others at bay. It belongs in the 'barrier' rather than boundaried approach.

- **Comparisons** – if we often compare ourselves negatively to other people when we're talking, that is a reinforcement of weak boundaries and conveys to others that we are somehow 'less than' they are.

- **Blaming** – pointing the finger and making it everybody else's fault. Not taking responsibility.

- **Reactivity** – taking everything personally and not giving ourselves the time to pause, breathe and then respond.

- **Self-criticism** – when the inner critic jumps on every 'mistake' that we make and turns it into a verbal attack.

Healthy communication in boundary-setting

- **Experience** – speaking of your experience while recognizing that others have a right to a different perspective of a shared experience.

- **Feelings** – daring to talk about, and own, your feelings. 'Right now I'm feeling angry / sad . . .' Allow yourself to name and express your feelings.

- **Intuition** – checking in with your body when communicating with others and trusting what it tells you. Let the intuitive part of you lead the way.

- **Needs and wishes** – knowing what your needs and wishes are in different situations, and expressing them as simply as you can.

- **Requests** – making requests about what is important to you, which honour yourself.

- **Challenging** – making sure you challenge that pesky inner critic and avoid the banned language it speaks.

OVER TO YOU

Clear communication to support healthy boundaries

The next time you have a conversation that didn't go as you wanted (we all have them), use it as an opportunity to figure out what you were doing well and not so well. Once the dust has settled, take some time to investigate the helpful and less helpful communication styles that were at play – yours and the other person's, if you can. This will support you to process any emotional fallout as well as try different things in future.

Thinking specifically about boundaries, and channelling as much compassion as you can, you're going to write down your observations on each of the following five broad areas.

- **Experience** – write about how you experienced the other person or people, and the situation as a whole. Describe what happened, what was said and how. Try to notice any judgements you make. Ask questions to help you understand your own part. Did you react very emotionally, or quickly? Make a note of any 'stories' you're making up about the other person, their motivation or feelings. (For example, 'I know they don't love me.')
- **Feelings** – write about your feelings. Be really honest

> with yourself, without blaming or judging the other(s).
> Own your feelings by writing, for example, 'I feel . . .'
> NOT 'You made me feel . . .'
>
> - **Needs and wishes** – write about what you need or
>   needed and any wishes you have for things to have
>   been or become different.
> - **Requests** – write down any requests you might have of
>   the other person going forward. Remember that this is
>   a request, not a demand, and they have a right to say no.
> - **Accountability** – write down what you can take
>   responsibility for in terms of contributing to the dis-
>   agreement or challenging situation. Is there anything
>   you would like to have done differently or any way
>   you can commit to behaving differently in the future?

Once you have completed this work, you may or may not wish
to share it with the person involved. Regardless, it will support
you to communicate in more healthy and boundaried ways.*

> * *This exercise has been adapted from the work of M. Rosenberg on non-*
> *violent communication.*

Learn the language of boundaries

Just as actors have to learn their lines in rehearsal for the
moment when they go on stage, we can all benefit from practising the language of boundaries. As we've seen elsewhere in
the book, language – including thoughts and spoken words – is
the most powerful tool we have for (re)shaping our experience.
That's particularly true when it comes to communicating with

others about boundaries. If you can make a powerful statement of your boundary, calmly and confidently, you are embodying so much personal power.

When I'm working with people on how to hold their boundaries, I invite them to do role-play exercises using certain key phrases. Have a look at the following list. Read it aloud. Notice how you feel as you say the words. Do you recall using any of these phrases lately? Ever?

- No, thank you.
- Yes, please.
- That doesn't work for me.
- Let me think about that and get back to you.
- When you raise your voice like that, I stop listening.
- I definitely don't feel comfortable doing that.
- I haven't finished speaking, let me finish.
- That doesn't feel right for me.
- If you continue to behave that way, I will leave.
- I understand you're upset, but it's not OK for you to speak to me that way.
- I'm not ready to share that information with you yet.
- I'll let you know.
- I need some time by myself.
- I don't know the answer to that question.
- You're invading my personal space and I'm going to need you to step back.

Speaking our truth is an act of power

That might have been deeply uncomfortable for some of you. For others, it might have been exciting, like being given permission to let rip. For almost everyone I work with it's a challenge to learn to use these kinds of boundary phrases naturally and calmly in their everyday interactions. Practice literally makes 'perfect', though.

As part of building your skills at holding your personal boundaries, I'd like to focus now on one particular phrase. The shortest, the most fundamental and powerful of all: 'No.' If you want to live your authentic self and embody your personal power, you're going to need to practise the art of saying no to others. Oh yes, my lovely 'people-pleasers in recovery', that means you, too!

It's hard, I know. All work with boundaries is intrinsically connected to healthy self-worth. It requires you to admit and assert that you have needs and goals – and since you do not have unlimited time and energy to pursue them, you're going to do whatever is necessary to protect and prioritize them. This can be very challenging for those of us from marginalized groups such as women and people of colour, and doubly so if we have become very attached to identities that don't allow for us to set and hold our own boundaries.

One woman I worked with called Carla was a self-described 'good girl'. She had spent most of her life denying her own needs and focusing only on what other people needed her to be. She wore many masks to honour this role, including 'people-pleaser' and 'care-taker'. Her relationships were essentially all about trying to ensure she was loved and needed, since she had never felt that as a child. Over time, of course, Carla became exhausted and resentful about playing this role. People didn't seem to see and appreciate her in the way that she really needed.

Carla did her grief work. She grieved all the underlying reasons for playing this role and wearing these masks, and then she began to practise living more truthfully, saying no more to others and yes more to herself.

This turned out to be *the* breakthrough strategy for Carla. We worked together to embed her understanding that every time she said 'Yes' to somebody else's agenda (whether it was her daughter's last-minute requests that she would babysit, or shouldering the entire burden of the endless family admin) she was saying 'No' to herself and her own priorities. She desperately needed some personal space and enough time for self-care but never managed to get them. This made her tired, and then it made her angry, until eventually she realized that she could fix this problem by verbalizing one tiny yet powerful word. 'No.' OK, in reality it was more like six or seven but the effect was the same. 'I can't today. How about next week?' No long flowery apology or explanation, just clear, calm communication. Through being vulnerable and daring to speak her truth, Carla eventually found her way back to self-respect and worthiness.

It was terrifying for her at the beginning. Her internal monologue went something like this: 'What if they don't love me any more? What if I upset them, disappoint them or worst of all, piss them off?! Aaargh!'

The key thing with learning to say no is getting comfortable with discomfort. That can mean the discomfort of upsetting people, or the bodily discomfort that some people feel as that small but powerful word rises up from deep inside. I've heard people trying to speak this word of immense power and freedom for the first time and only managing to get a squeak out.

'No' is not just a word, it is also a political statement. It says, 'I have power and choice, I am here and you will see me and hear me. I can choose, and my choice right now is NO!' Historically, 'no' is not a word that women and other marginalized groups have had much opportunity to use. But my goodness, despite the courage it takes, once you practise – starting small with perhaps a 'No, I don't take sugar in my tea, thanks' before moving on to the bigger Nos, such as, 'No, I will not tolerate that' – you will find a liberation that your ancestors could only dream of.

I SAID NO

This morning I said No when I meant No,
In honour of – and because of – all the times
I have said Yes instead.

Did it feel empowering?
No, it did not.
It felt frightening,
Like risking it all.
It felt like finally saying the thing
That will make you not love me.

And it felt lonely and cold
And I tried to suck it back in,
Rewind the tape player,
Kill the sound of the word
With a knife.

Or paint over it with pastel colours
And make you a cup of tea –
Distract you from
What I just showed you
When no other word would come.

But she stayed there,
Defiant,

Finally freed from the
Prison made of
Pretty, acceptable,
Please-love-me
Yeses.

And I do not know what she will do next,
This bright, emboldened No.
She seems to like it here,
Out in the wild.
So I am clearing out a room
Full of things I thought I needed,
So that she can stay.

Hollie Holden

Supercharge your resilience

Everything we've done in this chapter (and throughout the book) supports you to become more resilient. Resilience is the outcome of many different skills, attitudes and beliefs combining, and it's slow and steady work to build it. But I'd like to offer you a way to supercharge your capacity for resilience and practise multidimensional communication, all at the same time.

One of the best ways I know to strengthen your sense of self and develop personal power is to ask for, and receive, feedback. Now some of you might be familiar with this in a professional context, whereby you receive feedback on your work performance, but what I'm talking about is something much more personal. I'm suggesting that you take a deep breath and ask one or two trusted friends to give you feedback on how they experience you. Gulp.

Ask them to tell you about their positive impressions of you as well as their observation of any blind spots in behaviours or choices that might be sabotaging or blocking your life. Ask them to share the positive qualities they value and admire in you first. This will help to nourish you and prepare you to receive the more 'constructive' comments.

All of us have what I think of as 'blind spots' – those behaviours and traits of which we are often only partially aware (if at all), which can be damaging to our lives. Asking for feedback means asking difficult questions, with the intention of shedding light on your blind spots. Under the right circumstances, it can be so helpful to hear from others what *they* see, that we can't.

Now, of course, we have to be mindful about whom we choose to approach. Anybody who has a strong agenda about you and your life, or very fixed opinions about you, is not the right person. It has to be somebody who understands that you're not asking them 'to tell you what's wrong with you'. That's neither helpful nor welcome in your new worthy and boundaried world! Family members are not always the best people to ask. They often have such a long and emotionally invested history with you that it's almost impossible for that not to blur their vision. A good friend whom you admire, who knows you well and has done some of their own personal developmental work might be a better choice, but there are of course always exceptions.

The difference between feedback and criticism

Let's be really clear here – feedback is NOT about criticism. Most of us are pretty good at self-criticism (or used to be!), so we don't need to go out looking for it. It is also not about being given advice on how to 'improve' yourself (there is nothing wrong with you). Nor is it an opportunity for others to 'tell' you who you are and what you need to do. (Oh, please!)

Feedback must be actively sought – it's not the same as unwanted advice. It ideally includes as much 'positive' nourishing material as it does 'constructive' comments about troubles or blocks. Above all, it must be focused on what the person asking has requested. It's about their agenda for deepening their resilience and getting to know themselves even better, rather than the needs, desires or any agenda of the person offering the observations.

For almost ten years I taught on a residential personal development programme that encouraged participants to explore their transference (reactions) to the facilitators. At the risk of doing Freud a massive disservice, transference is in essence about how we unconsciously overlay (transfer) the past on to the present, and react to people in the here and now as if they were someone from – for example – our childhoods. Basically, we get triggered by something that reminds us of our past, and we then (over)react. Transference is a very normal experience in relationships and often comes up with people we trust or whom we consider to be in positions of authority over us, such as partners or bosses. Or group facilitators on personal development programmes.

Each week, the group participants would queue up to share their transferences with us, the facilitators. And despite being clearly advised that this was about them owning their own reactivity and tracking the relevant past wounding, so many of them would (conveniently) miss that point and instead see an opportunity to tell the facilitator exactly how they were lacking, screwing up, bullying, missing the point, etc. Which definitely had nothing to do with feedback, but I can tell you that ten years of it certainly made me incredibly resilient!

Genuine feedback, however, is nothing like that and completely different. We all need it in order to grow and thrive. So seek out trusted benevolent people who will love you with their appreciation while helping you to identify your blind spots and bring your shadow side into the light.

Once you've requested feedback, your job is to stop speaking, breathe and simply listen. Listen deeply. It will take a lot of courage to dare to hear their thoughts without being overwhelmed by the urge to react, but it can be done. And the more you do it, the greater your stock of precious insight into how others perceive and experience you.

It's important to check in with yourself if something is said that doesn't feel true to you. It might be true as far as the person giving you feedback is concerned but ring false to you on some level. That's fine. Just because someone else sees you a particular way doesn't necessarily mean it's accurate, though it may still be useful. Figuring out how to assess what you're hearing and respond to it can be hard, but it's a key part of learning to trust yourself. It takes practice but, in my experience, there is no more effective way to strengthen your resilience.

I've been on both sides of this exchange many times over the years. A close friend of mine once asked for some feedback on why she seemed to find it so difficult to connect in intimate relationships. Her previous partners had often described her as aggressive and cold but she saw herself very differently, as assertive and boundaried. In our informal feedback session, I was able to offer my friend another perspective. From my more neutral position, I wondered if she was aware how dismissive she could be when she was feeling vulnerable. I had noticed interactions with her partners in which she would close down and 'harden' in her warrior woman defences when they tried to connect with her about this issue.

My friend was able to receive this feedback from me and, after some reflection, she agreed that underpinning the 'hardened shell' was her fearful and vulnerable wounded child, who was desperate not to be left. This insight allowed her to have some courageous conversations with her current partner about her defences, and how she was keen to overcome them and let herself risk vulnerability.

The exchange we had was challenging and so was my friend's with her partner, but both conversations were worth it. They were offerings of love, not judgement, and they enabled my friend to shift her behaviour in a way that massively improved her relationship with her partner.

OVER TO YOU

Ask for and listen to feedback

Ask someone you trust and like for feedback, either on a specific event or more generally about how they experience you and your behaviour. The preparation is crucial for this exercise. Firstly, do not rush the process of figuring out who is the most appropriate person to ask. It almost certainly will not be the person you think you 'should' ask, though it may well be the first person who comes to mind. Trusting your instinct is crucial to every stage of this work.

Brief the person you choose really carefully. Explain what you're asking for, and what you're not. Explain that the conversation will not be like a general chat, in which people take turns to speak and listen. You will ask them specific questions to get things rolling and then you will listen. You will not interrupt or react in any verbal or non-verbal way, until they tell you that they have finished their point. Then you will have an opportunity to respond, before either asking a follow-up question or moving on to another point.

Some possible feedback questions to get you started (please do add more as you wish):

- Can you tell me how you experience me in our friendship/relationship? Both positively and negatively?
- Do you witness any patterns in my behaviour that you believe might not serve me/us?
- Can you give me a specific example to help me understand?
- What do you believe are my blind spots in our relationship (or generally)?
- In what ways do you view me as blocked or sabotaging myself in life?
- Is there anything else you would like me to know that might help me grow?

This exercise is almost certain to make you feel very vulnerable, but it can be life-changing. It can massively expand your understanding of how others experience you, while also building up your sense of being worthy in your entirety. It's really a way of building your core resilience for life.

Afterwards, ask the person how they felt during your conversation. Listen. Be prepared to feel confused, tired or stirred up for a while and remember to use your tool of shaking your body to release emotion. Try to get plenty of rest that night.

Working with triggers to build your resilience

Triggers are especially hard to handle when we're still in the early stage of our personal development work. As we've seen, a trigger can be almost anything, from a throwaway comment to a complex relationship dynamic that feels like a rerun of the past. Whatever the trigger, the effect is the same: we are plunged back into our old hurts and painful memories. When this happens, we might find ourselves behaving in ways that come from our wounds rather than our wisdom.

I used to see this a lot with a woman I worked with called Nina, who had grown up with a bullying and controlling father and was very easily triggered by people (male or female) whom she experienced as 'pushing her around'. Unsurprisingly, Nina seemed to attract a lot of these characters into her life. It was almost as if they were there to flag up to her where healing was required. (The universe is so generous like that!)

Once she had grieved for the little girl who felt bullied and crushed by her dad, Nina's next step was to begin to treat herself in less bullying and controlling ways. Her new style of self-parenting included banning harsh language against her younger self, challenging her adult self to speak up in situations of conflict, and holding her boundaries to show others and herself that she matters. Healing in action, right there. What is especially interesting about Nina's story is that once she became the parent she needed, versions of her dad stopped showing up in her life. I love that.

Many of us have become used to thinking of our triggers as something terrifying, to be avoided. There are now trigger warnings all over the internet. The problem is, by trying to keep all triggers away from us, we never learn to work with them as opportunities to grow our resilience. And life doesn't come with a trigger warning. Sooner or later we will come up against something or someone who takes us back to our old pain. Rather than hide or run from these situations, we might be able to use them to our advantage.

To be clear, I'm not suggesting that you ever remain in a situation that feels unsafe to you *in the present*. The risks of learning in that context are way too high. But if the danger or pain is not in our present but in our past and we are merely being reminded of it, we have an opportunity to practise being strong enough to bear that memory and behave in new ways. Almost like rewriting history for a moment. Similar situation, very different outcome. This is a brilliant way to build your resilience and boost your personal power.

I use a simple model to help myself with this, which I call PEP. This is an acronym to remind me of a three-step checklist I can go through when I get triggered back into reacting from the younger, wounded parts of myself.

1. Past – which elements of my past have been triggered in this current situation or relationship? Which old wounds, limiting beliefs and related behaviours am I defaulting to?
2. Ego – how much of my reaction is coming from my ego? Do I have a need to be right, wrong, better than, less than, to compete, etc? These are all strategies that my ego uses to defend itself, but they may not be helpful.
3. Projections – what am I projecting on to the situation or person which is actually part of my own unacknowledged behaviours or beliefs? What stories am I making up based on these projections, either about myself and/or the others involved?

It takes practice to remember and use PEP at moments of heightened emotion, when we're scared or angry. It's a great reflective tool to use afterwards, to assess how we could have responded rather than reacted, and dealt with things differently. This provides really useful information for 'next time'. As you get more familiar with checking in on yourself like this you will get stronger and stronger, until one day you'll be able to catch yourself *before* you are triggered and respond in a different way in the moment: to the situation that's actually in front of you rather than the one scrolling out, like an outdated film, in your mind.

When we stay frightened of discomfort, we condemn ourselves to living smaller lives. When we open up to the immense power of vulnerability, we supercharge our resilience and step into our personal power. As author and activist Glennon Doyle wrote in her book *Untamed*, 'We can do hard things.' Too right – we can. *You* can.

Embracing the power of life's 'no'

Building on this theme of opening up to vulnerability and listening to hard lessons, I'd like to offer one more thought on the nature of personal power, before we move on in the next chapter to talking about playfulness. True power, as we've been discovering, is never about having power over other people or stoking our ego's need for praise and status. It lies in knowing our authentic self and being able to trust both our self-reliance and our deep connections with other people.

This power is not selfish or self-centred. It is not grasping or greedy. This power has learned how to say no to itself sometimes, as well as to other people. It has learned to *hear* no from others, and even from life itself, and to respond with love rather than react with temper. Because if you ask for something from another and then react badly when they say no, that wasn't a question, that was a demand! I believe that the vast majority of us could benefit from feeling the limitations of that word no.

The very privileged in this world (I definitely include myself in this group and imagine it also includes many of you), are used to getting what we want when we want it. Be it food, films, running water, information, online shopping deliveries, whatever it is, we are no longer required to delay gratification for anything. Everything we want to consume (and it's a lot), we want NOW.

I remember reading somewhere that Elvis Presley's last girlfriend, Ginger Alden, when asked what she thought killed him, replied that he died because 'Elvis didn't hear enough "No"s.' Everyone said yes to him all the time. He got what he wanted, when he wanted it . . . and look at what that ultimately cost him. I've witnessed this absence of boundaries and the deadness it drags with it in the lives of many so-called 'celebrities' and extremely wealthy people I've worked with over the years. Their ego gets inflated and they really do believe they can have it all without any consequence. Sex, drugs and rock and roll. NOW. For some of those people, going into a recovery programme to deal with their addictions provides the only 'No' that will stop (save) them.

I believe that we all need to hear more 'No's. What the Covid-19 pandemic and climate crisis have both brought upon us all, to a greater or lesser degree, is one huge global NO! *Fly whenever you want, to wherever you want?* NO! *Eat whatever food you want all year round, regardless of the cost to the planet?* NO! *Gaze at screens for hours without an impact on your mental health?*

NO! *Destroy the Earth to make more money and not lose your soul?* NOPE!

I wonder what lessons there might be for all of us within this new global NO. Boundaries contain messages. They offer information on how to interact in ways that respect and honour all the participants. It is my deepest wish that we can all learn how to speak and hold our boundaries, but also to hear them and learn from them.

Key points from this chapter

- We become more resilient through experience and practice. Processing the past supports us to strengthen our inner resources.
- Clarifying our core values helps us to get to know the truth of who we are and frame our boundaries around our values.
- Personal boundaries are an essential part of living more authentically, daring to speak and live our truth.
- Clear communication supports us to reflect, connect and hold ourselves accountable.
- Feedback enables us to continue to learn and grow.

Questions for ongoing reflection

- In what ways can you feel yourself becoming more resilient and how might you build on this?
- Where in your life do you need to say or hear no or yes more? How might you action this?

- What bodywork might support you to hold healthy boundaries rather than weak or rigid ones?
- What friendship or relationship boundaries might you need to create? Can you discuss these with a close friend or partner and come up with your own?
- What new insights or learning have you gained from this chapter?
- How do you feel right now in your body? Notice . . . and breathe.

Step Seven: Coming Home – a return to innocence, joy and wonder

Are you beginning to feel a sense of space and lightness inside yourself? I really hope so. If not, please don't lose heart. Grief work and healing take as long as they take. There's no time limit here. Progress on healing your heart is more like an upward spiral than a steady straight line. It can feel like you're going in circles sometimes, but that spiral is always moving you upwards.

We've talked already about the way that the newly emerging space inside of you might feel like a kind of emptiness at first. This feeling can be scary but it's also pretty much inevitable. At some point, if we have done our work, we will all ask this question, 'If I peel away all my defences, who on earth is left underneath?'

The simple answer to this question is: you. The truth of you – that's all. You may worry that's there's nothing to you without your defensive masks but that isn't the case. As you acquaint yourself with this new space inside you, you will begin to find a more authentic, wise, competent, strong version of yourself waiting to be rediscovered by you. You have not had a personality transplant over the course of the previous chapters, you've just cleared away some of the debris that's been blocking your ability to live in the truth of yourself. And just as you have honoured your painful past with your time, care and attention, let's now offer the truest part of you the same privileges. Let's get to really know and reconnect with who you were before your heart was broken.

In this chapter the focus is on rediscovering the innocent, joyful, curious and playful parts of yourself. You will be getting even more comfortable with your vulnerability as well as practising being daring. It's time to explore what makes you light up with positive energy. What have you always wanted to try or say or do, but been too scared to attempt? What made you excited as a child? Which activities have you put aside on the grounds that they aren't sensible, dignified, worthwhile or useful? Now that you no longer have to manage your pain all the time, what could you do instead that would fill the space inside with the healing energy of pleasing yourself?

Let's be clear here, this is not frivolous or childish (though it includes some child*like* aspects), and certainly not about gratifying the ego. We're not talking about using hedonism as a crutch. This work is about trusting your innate wisdom to tell you what you need to do in order to live in truth and positivity. It is about getting back to that sense of wonder, open-hearted curiosity and imaginative excitement that you had when you were a child.

The purpose of this return to your pre-heartbreak self is, first and foremost, to get to know them again. Wholehearted living means embracing all of you, including those deep and true elements that have been buried for years beneath the defences and masks that make up our false self. What they look like in reality will vary for each of us, although there are some common threads. When I returned to the lost and disowned parts of myself, for example, I was reclaiming the innocent, vulnerable, naive and curious versions of 'little Donna' that I had locked away in order to survive my childhood. Yours might be your tenderness, playful nature, creative expression or pure joy. Whatever you left behind or locked up in that big padlocked 'Pandora's Box' is what you reclaim in your journey back towards wholehearted living.

Another excellent reason for filling up your new internal space with something delightful is because it's fun. You've done a lot of hard emotional labour over the last few chapters. You're probably feeling ready for some light relief! And that's part of the reward of doing all this deep work. To live life more lightly and wholeheartedly.

From childlike to childish and back again

When we were small children we all looked at the world through fresh eyes. Everything was new and exciting and so we gazed, touched, smelled, tasted and listened with a sense of awe and wonder. Wow, we can waggle our fingers and toes! Oooh, those dry autumn leaves sound all crunchy beneath our feet. A shiny necklace is golden treasure to touch and pull; music is a series of magical sounds that inspires us to wiggle our little hips unselfconsciously. And as for ice-cream . . . it tastes like nectar from the gods!

All of us were like this once, encountering life moment by moment as a magical and abundant adventure. So what happened? How do we lose this innocent sense of fascination?

Much of the answer lies in wounding. As we get hurt, we retreat, defend and disconnect. Part of it is plain old growing up, which for most of us comes with responsibilities. We have a job, a mortgage, a family, bills to pay, etc. We become busy and distracted. We get tired. We trust less, laugh less and – almost without us even noticing – life becomes a serious business. We lose our 'fresh eyes' perspective and instead start to react to people and events from our wounds, which is to say from a very childish rather than childlike place. If we have a row with a loved one, for example, and it is more important for us to 'be right' and prove them 'wrong' than to reconnect and resolve the issue, that's the wounded child in us acting out. We may look like grown-ups on the outside, but if we are still carrying our ungrieved heartbreak, we remain stuck in childish patterns of behaviour that resemble the self-absorption and lack of empathy of a three-year-old.

The alternative, as we will explore in this chapter, is to give yourself permission to play, follow your curiosity, trust and explore – and in doing so, allow yourself to grow up on the inside as well as the outside.

This stage of your work won't be effective until you have grieved and released your old pain and soothed, nurtured and reassured yourself. If you unleash your inner child too early, you're more likely to end up with self-entitlement and tantrums than joy. But you're ready now. You've tackled your heartbreaks, which allows the wounded child part of you to become more settled and peaceful. You can now begin to reconnect with the childlike qualities of wonder, awe, imagination, creativity and excitement. It's time to allow the childlike part of you out to have some healthy (and long overdue) fun.

Now, for some of you, especially those who had to grow up too quickly, the idea of fun or play can feel overwhelming. Even the words might be making you cringe, or think to yourself, '*How on earth do I do that? Maybe I'll skip this chapter . . .*' Please don't. It's so important that this part of you (let's call it your 'playful child') has the space and the opportunity to express themselves.

It's important, but I understand it might also be seriously off-putting for some of you. The association between play and childhood creates a strong barrier – almost a taboo – against adults exploring anything that smacks of silliness. Our ego lacks a sense of humour and won't tolerate anything that might make it look ridiculous. Grown-ups are allowed hobbies, so long as they're self-improving or good for us, and we're permitted to indulge in potentially self-destructive hedonism from time to time so long as it doesn't get out of hand, but pure innocent play, just for its own sake? That's not for the likes of us adults. Some of us have played so little, even when we were children and it was supposedly allowed, that this challenge might involve learning to play for the very first time.

A woman called Louise who came on The Bridge retreat years ago, was somebody who had never really played. I still remember the look of horror on her face on the afternoon I announced that our session would involve letting our playful inner child choose what to explore and what to do. Poor Louise looked as if I'd invited her to go up on stage naked at the London Palladium and perform a Punch and Judy show for the audience. Her reluctance was mixed with disgust and fear. Which made sense because Louise was all about being sensible and doing the right, responsible thing. As a child, she had never had the opportunity to follow an innocent whim and see where it took her, and now she didn't know where to begin.

Louise was the eldest of five children and she grew up in the 1980s. After her father left the family when she was only nine years old, her mum found it hard to cope and suffered from severe bouts of depression and anxiety. Louise was often left to take care of her siblings, while her mother took to her bed for days or even weeks at a time. Without realizing it, Louise became a mini adult and a parent to her younger siblings. Her childhood was essentially over. These roles became the template for her adult life. Louise took on caring for others, putting their needs first and working hard, taking her responsibilities very seriously. Not a lot of fun to be had for Louise. It was only through her grief work and recovery that she was able to return for the nine-year-old version of herself. Louise grieved for her lost innocence and mourned what it had cost her. After which, she began to offer her nine-year-old self the childhood she had never had. Slowly, with her therapist's ongoing support, Louise learned how to play, to be creative and to have innocent fun again.

She explained to us that she used to feel deeply awkward around playful people, making fun of them or judging them for making a fool of themselves, when really she was jealous. Standing in the playground with her own children, Louise had watched another mother being pushed on the swing by her friend. 'I still remember how joyful and free she looked,' Louise said. 'I totally judged her at the time. I thought her behaviour was juvenile, immature, embarrassing. Now I look back and realize that those labels said more about my inability to connect to the childlike, uninhibited and free part of myself.'

I take it as a sign of Louise's recovery from heartbreak that she now regularly plays on the swings when she's at the park with her kids, much to *their* embarrassment!

The power of play

Louise's story is partly about the potential of vulnerability to show you new ways of being. Playing as a grown-up is bound up with a return to the vulnerability – and possibilities – of childhood. As you begin to reclaim your own innocence, it's crucial to find the forms of fun and play that feel right for *you*. Sometimes this requires getting vulnerable enough to try new things. You might even have to screw up your courage and allow yourself to feel a bit self-conscious or silly, without giving in to harsh self-judgement.

Some of you might already be getting excited about the idea of heading off to have fun. For some of us, all it takes is giving ourselves permission to play. For many of us, though, it's the same old problem of recognizing that a healing strategy might be helpful – in *theory* – but not having the foggiest idea how to implement it in practice.

If that's you, cast your mind back to what you liked to do for fun and play as a child. The chances are that you will still like it (or a version of it) now. So, for example, I loved to sing and dance, making up imaginary shows to perform in front of my audience of dolls. I would dress up and perform for them and could lose myself for hours in this alternative universe. I still love to sing and dance, anywhere and everywhere. I sing in the car, around my house, and dance in the kitchen at every opportunity. When I'm working, I often take mini breaks by sticking on a favourite dance track and just losing myself in movement for five minutes. It's such a great way to 'get out of my head' and back into my body. Then it's back to work I go. In these moments, I am weaving small playful activities into everyday life. I am allowing the part of me who has no worries, and can simply be, to lead me towards nourishing, uninhibited enjoyment.

If you have young children or grandchildren, or nieces and nephews, they are the very best teachers of innocent fun and play. Let them guide you. My now six-year-old grandson, Louis, has always loved to make dens. I used to feel self-conscious when he invited me to join in. It had been so long since I played like and with a child. When my own children were small I was far too defended in my warrior woman persona to indulge in playing games with them. By the time Louis came along I was ready for some fun, but it was still hard for me to cast off my adult conditioning and let myself go. Louis was my teacher. I felt grateful for this second chance to learn to play and I forced myself through the discomfort of not really knowing how. Now, when he says, 'Let's make a den, Nanny,' I lose myself in helping to create an elaborate den from quilts, blankets and pillows. Once it's finished, Louis and I eat our picnic in there and share stories of imaginary lives as explorers living in the woods. Nowadays I probably love it even more than he does!

I encourage you to find your own inner six-year-old (she's in there, believe me) and commit to letting her out to play every day, even if it's just for a few minutes. Take her dancing, let her sing loudly and off-key, paint pictures, play an instrument badly, create collages or jump in puddles, run wild and free. Do all the things a child must do in order to thrive, to become fully alive. Do all the things your heart longed for, until it was broken one too many times and you forgot how to dance a single step.

Have a look at this list of suggestions for playing with your inner child. Do any of them appeal to you? Not all of them will and, in fact, some of them might make you feel uncomfortable. Please remember that we sometimes resist that which we need the most. I hope they will at least jog your memory or get you thinking about what fun and play look like for you.

- Dancing – stick some music on and shimmy round your kitchen for the sheer hell of it.
- Singing – join a choir, sing in the shower or car, get a karaoke machine and enjoy!
- Nature – jump in puddles, climb trees, build dens, collect conkers or leaves.

- Creativity – try painting, drawing, writing poetry, making music or learn an instrument.
- Games – get out Twister, Kerplunk, Lego or Operation. Start a game of hide-and-seek or a treasure hunt. Try your hand at face painting.
- Making – baking cakes, growing vegetables, sewing, cross-stitch, weaving . . . any activity whose primary purpose is to enable you to have fun and be in the moment counts as play.

OVER TO YOU

Learning to play again

What did you love to do as a child? Climb trees? Dance? Dress up? Do it again.

Was there something you always wanted to do when you were younger but didn't get the opportunity, or that you felt too nervous to try? Guess what? It's time.

Yes, you might feel silly or nervous. *Do you have the right kit? Will people laugh at you? What if you fall flat on your bum?* If these worries sound like the fears of a child, maybe that's a sign that they come from that part of you that was, say, a scared kid who didn't get picked for sports teams or invited to join in with games, or worried too much about getting it right to give it a go. Dare to give that part of you the opportunity to play now.

Take all the pressure off yourself. You don't have to be 'good' at any of the activities you try. And really, who cares whether you're 'good' at dancing round your kitchen or swinging on a swing! It's not a competition and nobody is judging you except your (old) self.

You're going to make two lists. The first one is of all the activities you used to love as a kid. Don't censor this for 'suitability' as grown-up activities. If you loved to play with dolls, write that down. The second list is anything else you would like to try. This could be absolutely anything. Rock climbing. Ballroom dancing. Ice skating. Drumming. Going to ride roller-coasters at your local theme park. Visiting an art gallery or a flea market in search of treasure.

Spend some time thinking about how you could reintroduce elements of the things you loved as a kid, and experiment with the new activities or experiences you fancy trying. Then commit to taking your inner child out for a 'play date' at least once per week. Remember, nothing worthy or dutiful or improving. Think fun!

Acquiring the habits of playfulness and wonder

As well as looking for opportunities to play, it's also important to cultivate a general attitude of playfulness in our everyday lives. I think of playfulness as a way of being that looks for lightness rather than gloom, that forgives rather than blames, gently lets go rather than clinging on and manifests as a twinkle in your eye or a spring in your step. (You can always spot the people who have done their inner work because they have that twinkle, whether they are thirty or ninety years old.) Playfulness is having fun and looking to laugh with ourselves and with others. It's a bit of gentle teasing – the very opposite of cruel humour that attacks weakness or difference and makes people feel ridiculous or insufficient.

One of the most wonderful results of doing our inner work

is that we are able to take ourselves – and life in general – a bit less seriously. We can giggle at our blunders without attaching too much meaning to them. We don't bother with harsh self-judgement or drama. One of the greatest freedoms that comes from reconnecting to your true self is that you rarely take anything personally. What a relief! So an attitude of playfulness comes from that inner light, and can be cultivated. If we can become the compassionate, amused observer of our own behaviours as well as other people's, and giggle at our shared humanity, we are well on the way to generating that lovely twinkle. You could try chuckling at your shambolic morning appearance in the mirror rather than listening to the harsh inner judgements of old. Or giggling about your verbal bumbles or blunders in a work meeting. The other day, while I was out walking in the countryside alone after a rain-drenched few days, I fell over in a particularly boggy patch and literally lost my shoe. I had to walk some distance back to my car covered in mud with only one soggy shoe on. I cried with laughter almost all the way. It was bloody hilarious and made my week.

As you become generally more playful and curious in your life, you will notice (if you pay attention) that everywhere you look there is an opportunity for wonder and awe. It's as if you can see the world through those fresh childlike eyes once again. The more you go looking for it, the more you spot the magical, beautiful abundance that's unfolding everywhere.

Nature is a playground full of opportunities for wonder, from the flowers to the trees, to the seasons and the intricate and elaborate workings of a spider's web. What about the fact that it takes more than 200 muscles to work together just to get us up out of bed in the morning? I still find this mind-blowing. There is just so much in life to be amazed by. All that wonder requires of us is simply to pay attention, get still enough to notice. To pause on a walk and look at the incredible textures and colours of the bark on a tree, to look up in awe at the sky and to hear the birds singing and to wonder what it is they're communicating.

Whatever it is that intrigues you, when you allow yourself to follow up a train of thought and see where it takes you, you're learning more about the world and about yourself. 'Lifelong learning' has become a bit of a buzzword in corporate and education circles these days, but when it's applied to learning more about the incredible wonder that is life I can really get on board. No goals, no targets, just allowing ourselves to be filled up with a sense of appreciation for all that is amazing around us and within us.

This doesn't mean denying life's struggles and painful events, as you know. As we've said before, a Pollyanna attitude of pretending that everything's great when it isn't, is not what we're about. We need to find the sweet spot where we recognize the reality of pain and struggle without allowing that to obscure the fact that joy, beauty and magnificence are just as real. As with so many of our mental and emotional habits, cultivating playfulness and wonder is a self-reinforcing practice. The more we look for things that fill us with admiration, appreciation, curiosity and awe, the more we find them.

The opposite of wonder, of course, is indifference and detachment. People who are consumed with their emotional pain (people like me as I was, and you as you were) can become blind to the wonders of the world. 'So what?' they say, rather than, 'Wow!' And while this is understandable, it is also a fast track to disconnection and despair. When we stop appreciating the world as an incredible wonder, our heart has closed down for sure and with it our opportunity for joy. The only reason this happens is to manage or suppress pain. On the other hand, one of the many gifts awaiting us as a result of doing this work is a return to wonder, connection and joy.

The importance of being (sincerely) grateful

All this talk of wonder and appreciation leads us right on to gratitude, which we've mentioned in passing already and which I want to discuss in more detail here because it is truly one of the pillars of wholehearted living.

Gratitude is of course the quality of being thankful, but it is also a readiness to show appreciation for good things and to return kindness. It's part of the positive circle of play, exploration, wonder and awe. The more we cultivate these experiences, the better we feel and the more we appreciate those positive moments. Quite simply, curiosity and wonder lead to gratitude, and heartfelt gratitude is the fire for joy. When I stopped expecting anything and started being grateful for everything, my life got a whole lot lighter. For me, gratitude links the heart with the head and our emotions with our thoughts. It is rocket fuel for integrated and wholehearted living and it will arise spontaneously if we consistently try to notice and appreciate that which is admirable, beautiful and good.

If this sounds a little bit *wafty*, it's worth noticing that the benefits of gratitude are measurable and significant. Numerous clinical studies have demonstrated that feeling grateful triggers the release of the endorphins seratonin and dopamine, both of which are associated with better mood. Feeling grateful also dampens the release of the stress hormone cortisol, so we tend to feel less anxious when we practise gratitude. Essentially, gratitude is good for us, on every level from physical and mental wellbeing to improved relationships. But how can we practise feeling grateful, especially during those times when life feels like an assault course?

If you cast your mind back to the opening chapters of this book and your early work, when perhaps your grief and emotional pain might have felt quite intense or even overwhelming, I wonder if gratitude practice was high on your To Do list? For some of you, maybe, but for many of you it probably wasn't. And of course this is very natural. When our battered hearts are hurting, our focus tends to be on how to get through another day. (Believe me, I know. I've been there.) This is understandable but it's a shame, because gratitude works like a healing balm. It brings us respite from our pain and reconnects us with life itself. And crucially, there is always something, however tiny, to be grateful for.

During my darkest times, after the 'ladies' toilet incident' when I was off work with mental health issues, what saved me was my daily walks in nature with my dogs. Every day I would (reluctantly) drag my weary bones out into the fields near my home, to walk the two very keen dogs I had at the time. My head was fuzzy and confused and my body felt like lead, but I knew a bit about the importance of gratitude and the healing power of nature, and I was determined to bring some of my focus back to nature's abundant gifts. So I would head out with a small pad and pen in my pocket and challenge myself to look really closely at the details of the natural environment. I wrote descriptions of what I saw. I made little sketches. Anything to take me away from my negative headspace, if only for a moment.

At first, none of it seemed to touch me. I could see details in front of my eyes but couldn't feel a connection to any of it. But I persisted, and over time something began to shift. It was as if nature itself was healing me.

I can still recall the day when my gratitude for this healing and for the generosity of nature began to truly land in my heart. I was lying on my back, staring up at an azure blue sky with not a cloud to be seen, and I felt deep wonder at the miracle of it all. I can still recall the faces and sweet smells of my long deceased dogs, as they came to lick my face . . . pure bundles of love and whiffy-breathed joy, wrapped up in fur suits. I remember noticing the bees and the flowers and finding a four-leaf clover, which felt very serendipitous and which I pressed in my little notebook. All of which helped me to feel deeply and immensely grateful. I began to cry at the beauty of the natural world.

I truly believe that in some way the feelings I had on that particular day brought me back to life. They reconnected me to the land of the living. And my 'gratitude bathing', as I call it, helped to anchor these memories inside of me. It was such a powerful moment in my own healing journey that I can still recall all those details even now, some thirty years on. Gratitude practice saved me from a very dark place.

And that's another thing about gratitude: its benefits are long-lasting and feel to me cumulative. The more you practise it, the easier it is to feel genuinely grateful for all the small positive details of your life, and the more 'full up' you will feel with appreciation. I call this, 'investing in the summer of life', so that when another 'winter of life' arrives, you have this treasure chest of memories of gratitude that you can dip into. I would say that joy is most consistently found in the small details of your life, and it is gratitude that allows you to fully appreciate them. From that first exquisite cup of coffee in the morning to the sight of your child's face as they (finally) go to sleep at night, joy is definitely in the details.

Professor Brené Brown, whose work on vulnerability we

looked at earlier, spent twelve years interviewing thousands of people as part of her research. Of the hundreds of people who described their life as joyful or themselves as joyous, there was not a single one who was not actively practising gratitude. Not one. Brené found that the self-declared joyous had very tangible gratitude practices. Some of them kept a daily gratitude journal, in which they noted down three things for which they were grateful that day. Some said grace before each meal. Some made it more of a group thing than a personal practice and had family check-ins, where each person in turn offered something they had felt grateful for that day. These joyous people were not leaving gratitude to chance or paying lip service to it as a nice idea. Their gratitude was intentional and disciplined. It was the key foundation piece for their joyful living. As Brené herself says, 'There is no joy without gratitude.'

Dr Laurie Santos, a psychology professor at Yale University, takes an intriguingly counter-intuitive approach to gratitude practice. She studies the science of happiness and wellbeing and it's no surprise that heartfelt gratitude is high on her priority list. To support people to enhance and deepen their gratitude, Dr Santos prescribes weekly 'rewiring challenges', including what she calls 'a negative visualization'. She asks people to make a list of things they feel grateful for and then to imagine them being taken away. Even if the list includes loved ones, you imagine them no longer being around or becoming sick or harmed in some way.

Now this might sound somewhat dark to some of you, but Dr Santos has done the research to back it up. It's like developing a 'black belt' in gratitude this one! I've tried the negative visualization myself and it has been very powerful. My three small grandsons are – thank goodness – safe and healthy, but if I take even a moment to entertain the possibility of how different this could be, I weep with gratitude every single time! I'm a great believer in 'don't knock it till you've tried it' so perhaps you might like to give it a go.

Sometimes, of course, we all forget to recognize the riches of our life. It's easy to take for granted the abundance and comfort that surround us, as well as the thousands of examples of everyday magnificence that grace our lives. It's human nature to grow indifferent to what's under our noses, even if we know in theory that we're lucky to have it. Our brains are wired to find novelty exciting, and though there is a huge amount of variation in how much this is true of any individual, it's generally true that our brain's reward centre lights up more strongly when we encounter something that's positive and *new* rather than positive and familiar.

That's not the only factor, though. Our culture prompts us to focus on lack and scarcity, rather than abundance. The ever-present hum of 'never enough' vibrates through our bones and our brains. Consequently, your gratitude might exist in conflict with your desire for more, whether that's more time, beauty, wealth or enlightenment. This is the reality of doing personal development work within a particular cultural context. The way forward is to cultivate a heart-based practice of gratitude, by which I mean that you really allow gratitude for those things that we often take for granted to land in your heart. It's not enough to look up and say, 'I'm grateful for the sky and the trees,' or to look at your child and say, 'I'm grateful they are healthy.' If your grateful thoughts don't include an emotional impact, then they are nice but meaningless words.

This is not to be negative about anybody's efforts. Even if we're trying to be more mindful about it, weaving a deep sense of gratitude into our everyday awareness takes focused intention and discipline. It's not always easy, but like everything, it does get easier with practice. And there's no doubt that when you make gratitude part of your routine you will soon feel how it enriches your life.

OVER TO YOU

Develop a gratitude practice

Gratitude comes into its full power when it is intentional and consistent, when it's not just a fleeting feeling but is noted and reflected upon, and banked as a memory.

The first step is to cultivate more of those feelings of gratitude. Make a decision to pay more attention to the good that surrounds you. Tiny things can spark wonder if you let them. You could, for example, take a close look at what you're eating for lunch and be amazed by how it's been produced and how it's travelled to get to you.

At the same time as cultivating more grateful moments, you are going to come up with a way of fixing them in your mind and in your life. How you do this is up to you, but there is likely to be an element of ritual attached to it. You could meditate for ten minutes at the end of every day on three things that happened that made you smile, brought you joy, got you thinking or in any other way brought fascination, awe or appreciation into your life. You could write three things (or five, or ten!) down in your journal every day. You could offer up your thanks to the higher powers, however you understand them. You could try checking in with your partner or ask your kids what they're grateful for as part of their bedtime routine. Whatever you do, try to do it every day.

Once you have a regular, consistent gratitude practice up

and running, you might want to try additional exercises. For example, you could set aside time to write a letter of gratitude to someone in your life who has supported or guided you. Let them know all the ways you appreciate them and are grateful to have them in your life.

With an active gratitude practice you will become naturally more present and conscious of gratefulness welling up when you see a loved one, smell a flower, or hear a moving piece of music. You will feel gratitude as a healing balm during times of grief, anger, self-pity and loneliness. And the fuller your gratitude, the greater your capacity for joy will be. With practice, you may even find yourself able to appreciate the lessons from life's biggest teachers: all the losses, the pain and the failures that you have been grieving. You will in any case discover more and more reasons to be grateful.

Joy is a superpower

Once we have begun to shed some of the heavy burdens of our past, life – unsurprisingly – feels a whole lot lighter. Then, as we practise wonder, gratitude and playfulness, joy naturally starts to bubble up inside of us. In the aftermath of my grief work I noticed that I was starting to laugh spontaneously again. Like a child. My manner and my approach to life became more playful. I started to laugh at myself, not in the old cruel way of the inner critic, but more as a best friend would: giggling at the absurdity of something I would previously have thought a calamity. Where shame and self-flagellation might once have reared their ugly heads when I made a mistake, now my instinct for joy, fuelled by self-compassion, would automatically kick in. *Oh, Donna did you REALLY just say that?! Yep, I think you might have . . .* And I'd be off in fits of giggles.

I began to truly understand that joy is the result of a process and a conscious practice, rather than a random fleeting experience. Joy is not merely what you feel when you fall in love or are offered a great job or meet your first grandchild. (Though those things are amazing, clearly.) Joy is your emotional true north, the guiding star. Seek it and you find it. Choose it and you manifest it.

You know that warmth you feel when you are around a joyful person and their energy seems to brighten up the whole room and rub off on everyone around them? (Just as the opposite happens when we hang out with a misery guts.) For me, this feeling of positive energy radiating and becoming available for the common good encapsulates why joy is such a superpower. The more joyous you become, the more energy you have and will spread to those around you. Life will still contain its inevitable ups and downs, same as always, but your capacity to recover from the downs will increase dramatically.

Talking of misery guts, it's worth listing three more thieves of joy, as I call them. These are not so much about other (miserable) people as our own unhelpful behaviours. See if you recognize any of them . . .

1. Comparisons – *'I'm not as good as so and so . . .' 'If only I could be like X, they get it and I don't.'*
2. Expectations – *'I should have . . .' 'They should have . . .' 'Life should be . . .'*
3. Judgements – *'Who do they think they are?' 'I'm not good enough . . . and neither are you!'*

These thought processes lead us away from joy and connection with ourselves, other people and our world. Joy is what happens when we're so busy with wonder, play and adventure that we're fully in the flow. Joy is what happens when we are paying attention, fascinated by something glorious, whether that's the butterfly that's just landed on our knee or a favourite painting or a truly delicious plate of food. For joy to come through, we must keep our channels open and expand our way of being. Not close ourselves down and cut ourselves off, with these negative, ego-based approaches to life. They will only fuel our disconnection and hijack our light.

OVER TO YOU

Create your own recipe for joy

You now know about some of the key ingredients that, for many of us, combine to create that fantastic and delicious dish called joy. We are all different, though, and we all find our joy in different places. What brings it into your life?

Here I've listed some of the elements that have led me to more joyful living. Have a read and see what comes up for you. Your personal ingredients might be broadly the same as mine, or not at all.

Ingredients for Donna's delicious dish of joy

- Making time for simple activities that relax and destress me: walking, cooking, reading, meditating, being with family, friends, pets, trees and time away from screens
- Expressing myself creatively

- Seeking out opportunities for fun and play
- A dollop of belly laughs and silliness for good measure
- Investing in relationships that activate my joy
- Moving on from those who are 'past their sell-by-date'
- Being in service – supporting others and connecting meaningfully with my community
- Moving my body through shaking and dancing, to get the energy of joy to flow
- A dash of daily gratitude
- And a generous sprinkling of love, kindness and appreciation

Write out your recipe in your journal. Try to be as specific about your ingredients as possible. Add as many as you like. And then, when you're ready, stir everything together and watch your joy rise, like a perfect soufflé. Yum!

Discovering your joy

Joy is warm sunshine against a bitter wind; the healing light within the dark night. It is the long-term fuel for incredible power and resilience. When you cultivate more joy in your life – without turning away from painful realities – you are strengthening your resources while planting and watering the seeds of love and hope. Every joyous moment in our lives is an act of sheer rebellion against the darker forces. Over time, these moments add up to an enduring power. I wish you joy of your discovery of its life force!

Key points from this chapter

- Having begun to heal the wounded child aspects of ourselves, we need to learn to play once again with the innocence that was waiting for us.
- Playfulness is a way of being in the world that allows us not to take ourselves or life too seriously.
- Wonder and awe are the childlike qualities of our innocence that we reclaim through doing our inner work.
- Actively practising gratitude generates more lightness and joy in our lives.
- Joy is an internal celebration, and it's highly contagious!

Questions for ongoing reflection

- What did you love doing for fun and play as a child? How might you bring some of this back into your life?
- Where and how can you bring more playfulness and humour into your daily life?
- What can you notice about your body and its functions that taps into your wonder and awe?
- Which of the three thieves of joy do you need to be mindful of?
- What new insights or learning have you gained from this chapter?
- How do you feel right now in your body? Notice . . . and breathe.

Step Eight: Wholehearted Living – the rebirth of your true self

Let's start this chapter with another pause. I invite you to take a deep breath and cast your mind back to when you started this book. How were you feeling about yourself? What did you think about the possibility of healing from heartbreak? Were you excited, or sceptical? Were you driven by casual curiosity, or were you so fed up that you were desperate to try anything? If you can't remember clearly, flick back to the first pages of your journal and take a look at what you wrote about your state of mind and your hopes (or lack of hope) for your healing.

See if you can detect even a tiny shift in your response to these questions when you consider them now, whether that's eight or ten or twenty weeks on. How do you feel and what do you think about yourself in relation to heartbreak *now*?

I hope there has been some positive change. I very much hope that you feel even a little more peaceful and excited about your future now, than you did back then. But nevertheless the change may still seem small. None of us can heal ourselves over the course of nine steps and neither should we aspire to. All parts of you are welcome, all of you is valid, all of you *is* '*perfectly imperfect*'. If you can connect to this truth, however fleetingly, that in itself is the change we have been working towards. Do you know that if a ship sailing across the ocean changes its course by even a fraction, it will alter its landing place by thousands of miles? Well the same is true for you. Just a few small shifts in your inner and outer compass can have a major impact on how your life unfolds and where you end up.

Please take a moment to acknowledge what it has taken for you to steer your life in this new direction. Allow yourself to feel a sense of pride at your courage and commitment throughout this process. And yes, of course life's still not perfect and neither are you (thank goodness!), but you are creating real change, real expansion and real growth. Healing in action. Step by wobbly step you have continued to show up for yourself. Nobody else did it for you (nor could they). Any positive shift is all down to you.

Wherever you are in your experience of this healing process, you are without doubt returning to the truth of who you are, with every step you take. Now *that* is something worth honouring. So take a moment to do just that – honour yourself in whatever way feels most meaningful for you. Because whether you accept my congratulations or not, it's a huge achievement to have got this far.

Now our focus for the work in this chapter is on integration. How to gather up and unite all the fragmented aspects of yourself we have been working with throughout the book. Like inserting the final pieces of a jigsaw puzzle. We will be looking at what it means to integrate every aspect of our experience and personality into our conscious mind and into our open heart, including all the aspects we've previously cast out, denied or rejected. We will be exploring how to embrace these parts of ourselves, as if we were welcoming lost family members home (which we kind of are).

The concept of 'welcoming ourselves home' is one of those ideas from therapy and personal development that can sound more like jargon than something we could practically do for ourselves. So we'll be exploring what it means in real-life terms and why it is such a crucial and positive step, and most importantly how on earth to actually do it.

However we describe the process of gathering ourselves in, the outcome is the same: a sense of wholeness and completion, which in turn allows us to live authentically and wholeheartedly. The process of integration happens through learning to recognize, welcome and nurture our neglected and banished parts. It also requires taking positive risks and stretching beyond our comfort zone. Authenticity happens when we are brave enough to be vulnerable, humble, open-hearted and honest. It's nerve-racking and the outcomes are by definition uncertain, but even when it's hard I can promise you that it is absolutely worth it.

So, now that you've honoured yourself for getting this far, you are ready for the next step across your bridge.

Integration . . . or welcoming the whole of you

Wholehearted living is what I wish for you, by which I mean a gloriously multifaceted, vibrant and authentic life that reflects all that you are. That just isn't possible without welcoming every bit of you into an integrated whole.

For me, integration is a deepening of the process of consciously embracing, accepting and (eventually) learning to love all parts of yourself. It involves returning for those aspects from which you have become disconnected, or those you've actively disowned. All those elements that have been judged, either by you or by others, as in some way 'faulty' or 'unacceptable'. So that part of you that felt never good enough? You go back for her. Remember the part that felt ugly and stupid? You go back for her. And the unlovable one? Yes, her too. It's like you scoop them all up under your arms and carry them home in a loving, messy bundle.

The good news is that you have already begun the process of integration with the accept, like or love yourself process that we looked at in Step Five. Arguably, you could say that you began the process way back on page one, when you started your grief work. It's all part of the same whole. Once we have grieved our past and dismantled the inauthentic aspects of the false self, we are free to reclaim those aspects that were wounded, rejected or hidden away as the missing pieces to our own puzzle.

I understand that for some of you it might be hard to accept that the not-good-enough, the stupid, angry, inadequate, failing, fat, hysterical, needy, drunken (insert your own unacceptable element here) and just generally *unlovable* parts of you hold the key to your own freedom, but believe me, they really do. Wholehearted living requires you to acknowledge that, for example, there is still a four-year-old version of you trapped within your consciousness and waiting for you with open arms. She's nowhere near as wounded as she used to be thanks to all the healing work you've done, and she just can't wait to bring her playful giggles back into your heart. Same thing with the seven- and eleven- and twenty-three-year-old versions . . . they all belong with you. Believe me, it's very hard to feel whole without them.

For so much of my life I rejected the parts of myself that I found lacking. My warrior woman persona sent all the 'weak', 'stupid', vulnerable mini-Donnas packing. They became my emotional orphans. I disowned them because I didn't want to see myself as in any way like them. But of course they were an important part of me, and my history. They are parts of the whole jigsaw, parts of my story, and without them I was so much less myself. No wonder I felt like something was missing. It was. Meanwhile, all the time I was exhausting myself by fighting this truth, the orphaned parts of me had nowhere else to go. So they waited sadly, increasingly desperate to be invited back into my heart.

It took me a long time to realize that *they* were who I had been waiting for my whole life. I had been searching (for love, for purpose, for wholeness) in all the wrong places. Eventually, the penny dropped. I went back – or rather, inside – and found angry confused teenage Donna. (She was none too happy to have been kept waiting, I can tell you!) I apologized, gave her a hug and told her I loved her. Together, we went looking for the nine-year-old too-stupid Donna and gave her a hug and some much-needed love. Then we all went and rescued terrified four-year-old Donna. We had to coax *her* out from her lifelong hiding place under the bed. Hugs and love all round. In doing this, I unlocked the door to my battered heart and all those mini-Donnas scrambled back in. And in that moment of blissful integration I found, to my utmost surprise, that I felt completely whole. Such sweet and precious relief.

So what does it take to reclaim all these parts of ourselves? How do we actually do it? Well, as I've said, the good news is that you're well on your way. The process kicks off with grief work. It's not possible to fast-track to integration without first acknowledging and grieving your past, as you have been doing through the previous chapters. We have to be willing to grieve for what happened to us to create all those fragmented parts of ourselves in the first place. After the grief work, the next stage is to work on moving yourself from a place of self-rejection and self-abandonment towards self-acceptance, followed by liking and then ultimately loving yourself again. And you've been tackling this through offering yourself more self-compassion and understanding, using kinder language, making more loving choices for yourself and daring to start to explore new possibilities and to have fun along the way. So, as I hope you can see, you have already made huge progress towards welcoming yourself home.

Let's consolidate all this by consciously continuing to take care of your emotional orphans. In psychological terms this is known as 'self-parenting'. We've seen this idea already in the context of self-soothing and grief relief, but it's coming up again here because it is such a key aspect of your work on integration.

Self-parenting, as we've seen, refers to the idea that unless we do our work, we will treat ourselves as we were treated during our early years. That's fine if you were nurtured and noticed, held and loved, reassured and spoken to with respect by your parent(s) or carer(s), but bad news if, like many of us, you felt judged, neglected, abandoned, ignored, unseen and not good enough. That results in all the negative self-judgements and self-sabotaging choices that reinforce your belief that you're unlovable or a failure. In other words, precisely the kind of behaviours we've been examining and dismantling over the course of the book.

Another aspect of healthy self-parenting is to examine what we've inherited from our parents in terms of how they treated themselves and each other. So, for example, your mother may have treated her own body as the enemy, to be dieted into submission. She may have tried to mould herself according to what she thought your father wanted her to look like and be like. Even if she didn't tell *you* that *your* body was unacceptable, or that a woman should please a man, you will have observed her behaving in this way.

And because our parents are generally the first example of a woman and a man we meet, they teach us how to be a woman or a man. More broadly, we learn from them how to treat and interact with other people. Irrespective of our own gender or sexual identities, we all learn unconscious lessons about what it 'means' to be a woman or a man and how we 'should' relate to people. Our parents become our template, if you like, for how to do (or not do) life. And, of course, their self-talk and self-care (or lack of it) were influenced by their own wounding and rub off on us. They too were parenting in the way they were parented. So the cycle stretches back into the past. But, as we will see in this chapter and the next, it doesn't need to continue into the future. It could, if you choose, end with you.

OVER TO YOU

Learning to look after your emotional orphans

Make a list of up to six of your core wounds. (You might wish to refer back to your timeline of heartbreak for this.) Note how old you were when each of these wounds was created. Your task is to consider all the ways you might care for any child or young person of that age who had been through a difficult time, and then do those things for yourself.

So, for example, I was four when I sustained my first core wound. How would I treat a distressed four-year-old? I would give her a cuddle and let her cry. I would soothe her and encourage her to pour out her woes without telling her that everything was OK or that she needed to be brave. I would treat her with tenderness and care, offer treats and time for fun. I would reassure her when she was afraid and speak to her only with kindness and respect.

With a distressed teenager you might swap out treats and fun for dishing them up some healthy food and an even stronger emphasis on listening and gentle questions. Or whatever you think will be most beneficial for you . . .

Consistency is key here. You're aiming to get into the habit of nurturing and soothing yourself every time you get triggered into behaving like a four-year-old. (Or a thirteen-year-old, etc.) That takes awareness and practice, so don't worry if you slip back into old negative ways from time to time.

You're also going to consciously choose to bring the young parts of yourself with you, every day. If you have a photo of yourself at the age you felt most wounded, then pop it in your pocket or purse and carry it with you. The idea is to have a daily loving connection with all the inner child aspects of your being, as well as healthy resources for self-soothing as and when you need them. (See the self-parenting visualization back on page 66.)

Do not expect that your inner four-year-old will never show up again, even with months and perhaps years of compassionate care. Say to yourself as and when you need to, *'Sometimes there is a part of me that feels not good enough and that's OK. I am learning to love and accept that part of me. She's welcome here.'* This is how you continue to grow into wholehearted living: word by word, choice by choice, moment by moment and day by day. If you follow this process consistently enough, one day you will wake up and realize that your heart no longer feels broken. You will feel its wholeness (scars and all), recognizing that all parts of you are finally home and that home is your own sense of belonging inside of yourself.

Where there is light there is always shadow

As well as our emotional orphans, there is another important aspect of ourselves that we need to recognize, accept and integrate if we are to return to the wholeness of ourselves: 'the shadow self'. This concept was conceived by the psychiatrist Carl Jung, who was very interested in the role played by the darker aspects of our personality, in our life and choices.

Simply put, shadow is made up of all those elements of ourselves that we wish to keep hidden in order to fit in with our family, community and society. On one level, it's a collection of our more 'unpleasant' characteristics: those selfish, judgemental, arrogant, prejudiced, aggressive and unloving parts of us that do not fit with our ideas about who we are, or are supposed to be as a kind and decent member of society.

We are rarely able to see our shadow without help from somebody else or through training our conscious attention to seek it out. Remember we discussed blind spots in the previous chapter? Your shadow self lives in your blind spots. When we deny, reject or suppress shadow it doesn't go away; it lurks just out of sight. And sooner or later, it starts to cause trouble.

Just as our unresolved pain leaks out of us, so our unacknowledged shadow does the same. For example, I've met plenty of people who insist that they're 'not the angry type'. They go through life denying and suppressing their anger (which as we know is a natural emotional reaction to hurt or injustice). So their anger gets placed unconsciously in their 'shadow'. Then when this 'I'm not angry' person gets behind the wheel of a car, it's a case of 'Hello shadow!' Suddenly they're swearing and gesticulating furiously at other drivers and making it deeply uncomfortable to be in the car with them.

Another example might be someone who has grown up in a household where alcohol addiction created destruction and chaos for their family. As an adult this person is tee-total and harshly judgemental about people who drink heavily. Meanwhile, they secretly develop a sex and porn addiction. Their addictive shadow simply presents itself in a different form to the one they have ruled unacceptable.

The truth is we all have a shadow self. Unless we shine our light of awareness on to it, we might find ourselves unconsciously behaving in ways that we would rather not, which in turn creates the perfect breeding ground for guilt and shame. That's why getting to know these shadowy parts of ourselves is so important. To be able to say, 'Sometimes I behave in ways that are incredibly arrogant and selfish,' is to shine light on to a shadowy layer.

To be clear, this doesn't mean giving ourselves permission to behave like an arrogant arsehole unchecked. It's not that at all. We simply recognize and accept responsibility for these darker aspects that are hiding inside of us. We acknowledge that we can be a good person who also has so-called 'negative traits'. Just like everyone else. When we learn to accept both our light and dark sides as part of the rich tapestry of what it means to be human, we feel even more whole and at home inside ourselves. We remember that we have a place in the world, warts and all.

Shadow is not all 'bad', either. As well as the dark side, Jung identified a positive shadow, made up of perfectly normal instincts and reactions such as sexual desire. If we have been taught not to trust our instincts or follow our creative impulses, those aspects of ourselves remain in our shadow self but they are not negative – they are pure untapped potential.

Remember, our shadow contains all the aspects of ourselves

that we dare not allow to be seen in case they trigger rejection by our family, community or society. So your positive shadow can include your greatness, your confidence, self-worth, sexuality, creativity, intelligence – any part of yourself that you have been told or shown that you are forbidden to allow to shine. We often identify these positive shadow qualities in other people rather than accepting and owning them for ourselves. 'Oh, look at her, isn't she so amazing/funny/capable!' we say, projecting our positive shadow on to somebody else. The challenge is to claim these qualities, just as you did your negative ones. *All* parts of you are welcome. There's a great saying that sums it up: 'If you spot it, you've got it.' That which you strongly admire in another is of course also inside you. Oh yes it is.

Can you identify any elements of your shadow self that you would like to consciously try to integrate? They can be either positive or negative. In fact, most aspects of shadow could be defined either way. Very few things are so bad that they cannot be owned, though, sadly, there has always been a lot of shame and guilt attached to some aspects of human behaviour. An obvious example is around sexuality. If a gay person grows up in a family, group or culture that is openly homophobic, they may have to deny their sexuality. That element of them then gets split off and must hide in their shadow. It can become hidden and shame-filled. Bringing it out of the shadow can be terrifying, but also unleash enormous life force and massively dial down the feelings of shame and guilt that come from keeping any aspect of oneself hidden in the dark. Not easy I know, but when safe to do so, it's an essential aspect of healing and a return to wholeness.

Have a look at this list of elements of 'negative' shadow self and make a note of any that chime with you. Any kind of strong emotional reaction you have to any of them, whether it's rejection or fascination, might be a clue to some aspect of your shadow self.

- Rage
- Resentment
- Aggression
- Wildness
- Chaos
- Jealousy
- Greed
- Hatred
- Fear
- Laziness
- Cruelty
- Entitlement
- Arrogance
- Selfishness
- Narcissism
- Cynicism
- Disgust
- Vengeful
- Punitive
- Brash
- Boastful
- Lustful
- Destructive

Add your own shadow traits if they're not on the list and consider how you might begin to integrate them into your life. What can you do differently that means they don't need to exist and fester in the dark? How might you shine your light

of awareness on to them, ensuring that they don't unconsciously sabotage your life?

Wholehearted living is not for the faint-hearted

I have to level with you. Reclaiming and integrating the truth
of who you are, with all your orphans and all of your light
and darkness included, is neither easy nor quick. This is the
kind of awakening you inevitably have to work for and practise
over and again before it starts to really stick. Then – if you're
lucky – you can make do with regular maintenance. But maintenance is always going to be required because the society
most of us live in is deeply invested in us falling back to sleep.
Our developed world's intertwining structures of patriarchy,
consumerism and materialism depend on us believing in the
lies of inadequacy and lack.

Living an authentic life isn't always easy in the moment. The
day to day of wholehearted integrated living can sometimes
feel like an effort, especially if we compare it to the lives of ease
we see on Instagram. Sometimes it's just so tempting to fake
the good life or sign up for the perfect curated lifestyle, rather
than do the work to authentically live in the way we choose.
Tempting but ultimately unsatisfying and lacking nourishment
(like a chocolate éclair). The easier option, the one that avoids
vulnerability or buys a solution off the peg, always leads eventually to feelings of unhappiness and 'dis-ease'.

Whenever I work with someone who has slipped back into
a period of deep sadness or feels depressed or anxious again
for no apparent reason, one of the first questions I ask them
is, 'Where in your life are you still living a lie?' Other questions
that might also help to gently uncover what's going on include:

'What masks are you still wearing?' 'How else do you remain hidden from view?' 'Have you gone looking for your shadow self as well as your orphans?'

I believe that in the end, however, it's easier to live in truth than in lies. A fake life of lies drains us of our life force, leaving us depressed, anxious and apathetic. Far braver and more fulfilling to dare to live our multifaceted, truthful, wholehearted life. When people dare to get brutally honest about their own lies, (both the little ones and the HUGE nose growers, even if they are not yet ready to change them), something alchemical happens. Truth itself starts to emerge and heal them. And living in truth is one of the best cures for unhappiness and apathy I know.

It takes courage, and a whole lot of vulnerability

Showing our hidden side, expressing our deepest desires, asking for what we really want . . . all these things take enormous courage, but (and I know I sound like a stuck record) they get easier the more you practise them. Sometimes our courageous vulnerability leads us to the outcome we wanted. Sometimes it leads us in a completely different direction. We might end up in disappointment. We might end up with something that's great, even if it's not the thing we originally hoped for. In all these cases, by speaking our truth we can at least know that we no longer have to carry a lie, and the living out of truth will show us things we might never have imagined. Truth is like that. Transformative – in unpredictable ways. This can be both scary and exciting. It shows us that change, even painful change, can lead to growth if we are prepared to stay humble, brave, honest and curious about where we're going.

Some years ago I worked with a couple called Holly and David, who had been married for more than twenty-five years. They had been struggling to reconnect with each other since their grown-up children left home, and both felt that they were drifting apart. They had always had very different interests and now they had very different approaches to their newfound freedom. They came to work with me to find out if there was a way back for them as a couple, or whether their relationship had run its course.

I recall one particular session in which their frustrations came to a head. Both were keen to blame the unhappy situation that they now found themselves in. Both were heavily in their defences, full armour on, ready to attack. At one point Holly said to David, 'You're not interested in me, or anything I do. It's like I'm invisible to you. You're so selfish!'

I asked her to pause, close her eyes and take a few deep breaths, as if she were breathing into and out of her heart. From this more tender place, could she find a way to express herself without verbally attacking David?

Holly closed her eyes and took several slow deep breaths. I wondered what would happen next. Then she began to cry, very gently, as she was able to soften into her grief.

She opened her eyes and when she spoke, Holly's voice was soft and clear. 'The truth is, David, I'm terrified that you don't love me any more. I'm so afraid you're going to leave me and I'm just not sure I can cope with any more loss.'

In this exquisite moment of vulnerability and truth, the energy between them completely shifted. David began to cry, too. He reached for Holly's hand. 'Thank you,' he said and they simply looked at each other. No further words were required, at least not for that blessed interval of restorative peace, in which both of them were able to rest in the space Holly had created through her vulnerability.

I've never forgotten Holly's courageous act. It was as if she had unbuckled her armour, reached inside her chest and taken out her broken heart to show David. Her words were no longer an accusation. She was not speaking from woundology. She was simply and bravely speaking her truth. 'Here, look at my heart. I'm bleeding. It's broken and hurting.' It was such an incredibly beautiful, powerful and moving moment.

This is not a 'happy ever after' story, or at least not of the conventional kind. Holly and David went on to separate and then divorce, but they did it in a very loving, conscious and honest way. They recognized that those words of truth courageously shared by Holly, marked the moment that everything changed for them both.

I continued to work with Holly for a while after their separation and she was able to acknowledge the courage it had taken for her to say and do what she did in that session. Her actions had led, not to the outcome she had wanted at the time, but to something else that was, she could see, better for both her and David in the end. The process had been painful, but it had been worth it. By choosing to speak from a place of wholehearted authenticity, she had also created a layer of resilience in herself. The vulnerability and courage that led to her speaking her truth enhanced her capacity to cope with what followed. This new layer of resilience allowed her to move beyond coping and eventually into thriving in her new unplanned life.

Authentic living is about finding the beauty in the chaos of real life. Perhaps your relationship, like Holly's, is coming to an end. If so, can you let go of your need not to fail, of your need to be right, of your need to live a quiet life without pain or fuss? How can you steer more towards courageous truth? How can you bring every part of yourself to the conversations you have with your partner? The more you manage this, the more resilient you will become and better your outcomes will be in the long run.

Letting go of our need to live only from the 'acceptable' elements of our personality is frightening, but not as frightening as the alternative. When we recognize that we are all flawed, we all have shadows and are all perfectly imperfect, we are offering ourselves and others the most powerful act of compassion. We are able to connect through our very humanity. 'You've made mistakes? Me too!' 'You've made poor choices that have hurt those you love? Me too.' This is all part of 'whole-hearted' authentic living, rather than a half-hearted fake existence.

We must dare ourselves to make the courageous choices that previously we might have avoided, in order to live with and from every element of our unique being. Those choices include speaking truth to power, holding 'tough love' boundaries and living with the consequence that not everyone will like this new *true* version of ourselves. And that's OK. The more we live authentically, the less we will feel the need for external validation. Dita Von Teese said it perfectly: 'You can be the ripest, juiciest peach in the world, and there's still going to be somebody who hates peaches.'

When we dare to show ourselves in our fullness, it gives other people permission to do the same. This is especially important for the next generation. We can shine the light of authenticity, courage and truth along the path we walk, so that our children can see to follow in our footsteps.

OVER TO YOU

The Bum Clench Challenge (BCC)

One of the ways I keep myself on my toes and ensure that I don't fall back into old unhelpful behaviours, is by setting myself regular BCCs. A Bum Clench Challenge happens when we push ourselves out of our comfort zone to try something new that we might fear. So-called because I've noticed that whenever I'm doing something that makes me feel scared or nervous, I clench my bum cheeks. It's my version of the toe curl!

A BCC is deeply personal, but some issues seem to come up time and again. It might involve having a difficult conversation with a family member, one that you've avoided for years. Or standing up for yourself at work and holding a boundary there. Or daring to tell a new partner how you really feel about them (double clench). It might be apologizing to your children for the mistakes you made that you know hurt them. Perhaps it's joining a dating website or a dance class, because you've always wanted to learn to tango but have two left feet. (Enough about me.)

Whatever the BCC looks like for you, it's got to be something that makes you feel vulnerable. It could be silly or serious. Your nerves could be about allowing yourself to risk looking like a bit of a fool (tango) or about letting someone see you crying and in emotional pain (that conversation you've been putting off). Either way, you're going to have to find the courage to acknowledge your nerves, take a deep breath, clench those cheeks and take the plunge. Now, that's true authentic living in action.

So go ahead and make a list of possible Bum Clench Challenges. Trust your instincts. Pick three BCCs and commit to doing them over a period of no more than three months. One a month at the very least. I double dare you!

You can do this! The BCC is a great resource for whole-hearted living. It will enable you to continue to learn, grow and expand into the truth of who you are. It also comes with the added bonus that you get some seriously tight buns as a result. Win-win.

Redefining what it means to feel at home

The more we grow into ourselves, the more we realize that it's true what all the spiritual teachings tell us – that 'home' is not where you live or who you're with but a feeling of completion within. I used to assume that I would find the feeling of belonging through something or someone else. The discovery that it didn't depend on anybody or anything outside of myself was a revelation. I had spent so many years (slow learner) yearning to belong somewhere and to somebody. Once my own process of integrating my rejected aspects was well under way, I began to feel an inner 'fullness' and rootedness for the first time in my life. I just didn't feel as if anything were missing any more, because it wasn't. All of my mini-Donnas were safe back home. All of my disowned, shadowy, less than fabulous bits were right there too, fully acknowledged. I belonged to them and they belonged to and with me. From this place of fullness I could continue to evolve, and begin to connect with others and the wider world in a brand new way: from a place of abundance and wholeness rather than neediness and lack.

I came to feel that I wanted to celebrate my return to my true self, and all the sense of belonging and happy connection it had brought me. The more I thought about it, the more I wanted to mark my journey back to my integrated, authentic self. It had been a huge and long labour of love. It was (self) love that had healed my wounded aspects and my emotional orphans. Love that had welcomed in my shadow self. I had, after a lifetime of alienation and self-hatred, learned to stop looking for love elsewhere and instead focus on loving every aspect of myself. That freed me up to move on from old pain and into new exciting open-hearted living, in a way that I just could never have imagined when I was sobbing on that bathroom floor. At times this work had been painful, tiring, frightening and risky, but I had done it and I was proud that I had steered myself home.

So I decided that was something worth celebrating and that a ritual was in order. Obviously. So on my fiftieth birthday, I quietly got married in a church in Austria. To myself. (Yep.) I had one physical witness (my best friend Gabi), although I could feel my African ancestors' presence behind me, drumming and strutting their stuff. It was a beautiful and special day that included champagne and cake, walking, cycling and belly laughing, rivers and mountains, and taking powerful vows.

Self-marriage is of course easily dismissed as slightly crazy, and I totally get that. It makes me giggle too. But if you take away the marriage label and call it a commitment ceremony, in which I took vows to love, cherish, honour and accept all parts of myself, is that really so crazy? I got married in a church because, although I'm not religious, I love the sacredness of churches. As part of my ceremony I also spent time in the mountains and splashing in rivers, because nature is just as much a sacred space for me. In my vows I committed to stay with myself in sickness and health; for richer, for poorer; in darkness and in light, for better and for worse. I also committed to dedicate my life to love in all of its abundance. Not just the romantic fantasy, not just love for my family or those I know and like. But to embody, live, breathe and spread love towards all beings. Even spiders. In the words of the great Spiritual Guru, Queen Beyoncé, 'If you like it then you shoulda put a ring on it.' I do and so I did.

Celebrate your own labour of love

So I'd like to challenge you to consider a commitment ritual of some kind to mark your own loving journey back to yourself. There are lots of reasons why this might feel valid for you. Firstly, it's a great way to honour your hard work. Secondly, it cements your belief in and commitment to your newly integrated and wholehearted self. Thirdly, champagne and cake are always nice. (Or tea and cake, or cheese and wine, or coffee and your treat of choice . . .)

Your ritual doesn't need to resemble mine. It doesn't need to involve churches, witnesses or anything that makes you think of weddings. Though I am going to make a strong case for vows. The centrepiece of my ritual was speaking aloud the vows of commitment I had written for myself. I still use them frequently, as a touchstone for how to live my life from a place of authentic and wholehearted love. They have become an important part of how I keep myself on track. These vows allow me to remember who I am in my true self, what's important to me and how I want to live. I try to honour them every day and, of course, I 'fail'. When that happens, I don't use them as a weapon to beat myself up. I see them more as a kind of compass. When I lose my way, they guide me back home.

I've listed a few of my vows here, as a starting point to get you thinking. Just in case you want to write some of your own . . .

1. I vow to live authentically and courageously, taking full responsibility for my own life and choices.
2. I vow to treat myself and others with kindness, love, compassion and respect, both through my words and my actions.
3. I vow to try to live a life led by love, not fear; and by spirit, not ego.
4. I vow to live with an open heart and in service to the world.
5. I vow to practise gratitude every day and recognize that even painful life experiences can bring with them gifts.
6. I vow to continue learning and growing throughout my life.

As an alternative to writing and speaking your own vows, you might consider a powerful ritual that uses stones to symbolize aspects of yourself that you have gathered in and now wish to celebrate rather than reject. We used this stone ritual on one of our retreats at The Bridge. It's called 'The Walk of Freedom'. I particularly love the fact that it gets you out into nature, walking and connecting. So if that's more your thing, this could be for you.

The idea is to collect six smooth, clean and flat-ish pebbles. You're going to write on them, so you'll need a Sharpie or other permanent marker. Head out for a walk, taking your pebbles and pen with you. This ritual is particularly lovely if you can go somewhere with a bit of privacy and calm and quiet. If you have a favourite woodland or a lake you love to visit, go there. But the park will do as well.

Once you're comfortably wandering, you're going to take out a pebble and write on it one of the six core wounds you've been working with. For example, abandoned, failure, unlovable etc. As you write, allow yourself to remember the wounding and all it has cost you since, in terms of lost relationships, years of addiction, missed opportunities, whatever it might be. Then, hide the pebble somewhere that you can return to. You'll be coming back to retrieve all your pebbles, so don't hide them too well! (You could always make yourself a little treasure map, if you like.) Having left failure behind you, wander on and do the same thing with the next pebble and the next core wound. Leave all six pebbles behind you and then, when you're done, find a place to stop/sit/lie and take a moment to pause, bask and breathe into the beauty of your natural environment and reflect on how far you have come. Take as long as you need.

When you're ready, you're going to go back for your pebbles one by one. And this time, as you gather each of them in, you're going to write on the other side of the pebble something that you want to claim for your life going forward. This may (or may not) be an opposite of the wounded aspect that you had previously banished. So for example, when you get back to your 'failure' pebble you might choose to write 'successful', or 'perfectly imperfect'. You don't have to be quite so literal, though. You might write down a quality in yourself that came as a gift or a positive outcome from the original wounding. You could choose an aspect of shadow self unconnected to the wounding that you have also chosen to gather in. Let yourself be guided by your intuition on the walk, as thoughts and feelings come up, or you can choose to plan it a little in advance, though I would recommend keeping an open heart and mind about what comes up for you as you do this form of walking meditative ritual.

At the end of your walk you will have six pebbles, each with two words written on them. Take them home with you and place them somewhere such as on a shelf, altar or in a little box. These are aspects of yourself that you are learning to love and embrace, and that you want to celebrate and cherish. Keep those pebbly reminders somewhere close to you.

OVER TO YOU

Your commitment ritual

Choose one of the two rituals I've described and then do it! No evasions, no excuses. You can do both if you like, but it's not an option to do neither (I am such a bossy boots). Welcome every aspect of yourself home and then enjoy the sense of being absolutely in the right place, with everything and everybody you need. Feel the love.

Wholehearted love creates a new legacy

Your new home is your very own heart, which through your work you have made big enough to contain every single aspect of yourself. You are becoming genuinely big-hearted. You're right at home in yourself, you belong to and with yourself, and there's so much love to go around that you are able to start to embody love for all other beings.

This is a glorious place to live from. It's a place of safety, full-ness, comfort ease and authenticity. The best springboard you could possibly have for stepping out and on into a huge, excit-ing new phase of life. We'll be exploring that in the next – and final – step.

I wanted to close this chapter with an image of love stretching back into infinity, which came to me one day not long after my commitment ceremony in which I spoke my vows to myself. Standing at my mirror one morning, I finally realized that I completely and wholeheartedly loved the person I saw in its reflection. Just as I had sensed my ancestors that day on the way to the church, now I could sense, through the eyes of love, my parents staring back at me. Not just in my face but in my whole body and demeanour; in my thoughts, beliefs and choices. Every part of me had been shaped by our shared history. It was powerful stuff (and no, I wasn't on drugs!). Then, I glimpsed their parents, standing behind them. My grandparents on both sides. And behind them, *their* parents. It was remarkable to catch a glimpse of that sense of lineage and personal history. And here I was, standing tall and free because of some of the known – and no doubt many unknown – sacrifices they had made in their lives. It was a deeply profound and healing moment for me.

Back and back it goes through the generations, you see. When we take a look from a place of secure belonging and love, we can finally see all those who came before us. These are the people, for better and for worse, who we carry within us. Our ancestors. We have respectfully discarded any poisoned arrows they unquestioningly shot into us. It is now up to us to gratefully make use of the many gifts we have also received from them. It is up to us to honour our legacy by living the life we have been blessed with. In love, service and truth.

If you travel far enough, one day you will recognise yourself coming down to meet you. And you will say – Yes.
—Marian Woodman

Key points from this chapter

- Welcoming yourself home means to consciously choose to accept and learn to love all parts of yourself, without exception.
- Belonging is an 'inside job'. We need to learn to belong to ourselves before we can fully feel that we belong anywhere outside of ourselves.
- We all have a positive and negative shadow within us and owning these parts contributes to our return to wholeness.
- Living authentically is about speaking and showing our truth. Daring to show up as we are in life, warts and all.
- It takes courage and vulnerability to dare to live in truth. Fear is a natural part of shifting outside our comfort zone.

Questions for ongoing reflection

- What parts of yourself are you ready to commit to 'welcoming home' within yourself, and how might you do this?
- What courageous and vulnerable acts can you commit to that will build on your growth?

- What parts of your shadow can you recognize? What are some of the darker aspects of your personality that you can begin to shine a light on?
- What have you learned in this chapter? Notice how you feel . . . and breathe.

Step Nine: The Spiritual Dimension – deepening into life

There is a story that we humans have been part of for millennia, even if we don't know it, that goes something like this: into every life, however peaceful or privileged, sooner or later 'trouble' will come calling. None of us can escape or avoid it. The hero(ine) of the story is called to leave behind the safety and comfort of the known and ordinary and set off on a quest of some kind, whereby they will be challenged to face this 'trouble' and prove themself by accepting the challenge rather than dodging it. Along the way they must battle demons or monsters, overcome obstacles and endure many hardships as they learn, change and grow. If they do all this, in the end they will return home – utterly transformed.

It was American academic Joseph Campbell who coined the phrase 'the hero's journey' to describe this archetypal narrative of a heroic figure who leaves the familiar world, faces a crisis and triumphs over adversity before returning with great powers. Campbell studied world mythologies and comparative religion and detected what he called this 'monomyth' in a massive variety of contexts. He wasn't the first to spot it, of course. This story has been much studied and endlessly used in various forms. It appears not just in spiritual teachings, myths and fairy tales, but in Hollywood films (think *The Wizard of Oz*, and *The Matrix* just for starters) and contemporary literature. It's also the narrative that helps to frame the story of your work in this book, and your progress through your life.

For us mere mortals, it tends not to be a messenger from the gods or a dragon from its mountain lair that comes knocking on our door. Our 'monster' might be a divorce, a separation, the death of a loved one, or reaching rock bottom with an addiction. Sometimes the calling might not be a crisis so much as an adventure, such as a need to travel, or leaving home for university, having a baby or changing career. Either way, something significant happens in your life that kicks off a process of change and deep growth. Campbell called this the 'Departure', as we are called to leave behind all that we know in our 'ordinary world'.

This phase often involves what I call 'the unravelling', which is the initial response to painful inner (and outer) chaos, and is something you just have to go through for transformation to occur. Life as you know it begins to come undone and you are metaphorically (or sometimes literally, as in my case in the loo) brought to your knees. But this moment of crisis is also a catalyst. If you heed the call and set off on your quest, you will face challenges and adversity along the way. You will encounter dark messengers (depression, anxiety, illness, eating disorders, addiction . . .) and do battle with them. This is what Campbell called the 'Initiation' phase. Sometimes you might try to resist the new direction of your life or try to outrun the messengers and monsters, and your suffering only increases. Eventually, having faced and slain some of your demons, you will begin your long journey home, carrying hard-won gifts such as a reconnection to a much wiser, more compassionate and heroic version of yourself. (This phase is called 'The Return.')

Does any of this resonate for you? Can you see yourself in this story? I do hope so because this story is all of ours. I hope that the reflections you've been making and the work you've been carrying out throughout this book have enabled you to see that you too have been on your own hero's journey. Perhaps many times. There will have been periods of your life that were relatively calm, safe and comfortable, followed by a calling to adventure or the challenge of painful life events. Every call is a portal: an opening into a new way of being that you choose either to crawl through, or not. Your grief work is the bridge that supports you to pass through and receive the healing medicine contained within.

Your whole life is one long hero's journey, you see. And since reading this book, you have chosen to become the hero(ine) of your own story. You have returned to save yourself. By doing this work, all of your emotional orphans have been (or soon will be) rescued. And although there's no 'happy ever after' ending offered here, there is something way better: the 'authentically ever after' ending, which is the truest and most beautiful kind. I hope you feel like the hero(ine) that you truly are at this point in the book and in your life's journey!

In this final chapter, I want to do two things. Firstly, contextualize all this work you've been doing in a less psychological and more spiritual framework. I'll be introducing you to the idea that life can be understood in terms of before and after awakening. In phase one, before life issues its call, you might live with a certain conditioned and limited mindset. Once you've completed your quest (or done your work, however you prefer to think of it) you start to wake up and see yourself, others and the world very differently. It's as if the blinkers have been removed and you can see and understand the deeper meaning of what you've been through. Each life event – no matter how painful – had some invaluable lessons wrapped within it.

Having explored this idea of a shift into the more spiritual dimension, I want to briefly highlight some of the benefits of stepping firmly into that second unblinkered phase of life.

They are freedom, peace, authentic wholehearted living – all the things we've been talking about – and also purpose, faith, connection to others and to a source of inspiration that's bigger than you. This final chapter in the book is my invitation to you, to commit to living on the other side of the portal(s) you have found in your past. I'd like to show you a little of the sort of future you could have, if you decide to continue to rewrite your story with yourself as its hero.

Before and after your awakening

In his brilliant book *Falling Upward*, the author and Anglican priest Richard Rohr offers us a simple model of the two halves of life, which equate to before and after the hero's challenge. Rohr calls that challenge 'necessary suffering'. The chaos and adversity that we experience as a result of upheaval are not only unavoidable but also necessary in order for us to grow spiritually and to deepen into life. He suggests that, as creatures of comfort, humans require these periods of emotional and sometimes physical suffering in order to avoid stagnation. We need that push of uncertainty or discomfort to continue to learn, soften and grow into life. Without this suffering and the gifts contained within it, we cannot pass from the first to the second half of life.

I love Rohr's approach, which I have tweaked to incorporate into my work for people who are ready for it. (People like you, I hope.) I call the stages of life 'phase one and phase two' as, in my experience, they have less to do with chronological age and more to do with maturity and readiness. Some (unhealed) people are four-year-olds living in a sixty-year-old's body, and others (the old soul kind), are 1000-year-olds living in a twenty-year-old's body. I think of the crisis that propels us to change as a form of death and rebirth. The old version of ourselves (our false self) must die before we can reconnect to and rebirth the truth of ourselves and begin to fully live again.

Rohr describes the purpose of the first phase of life as building a strong container, and of the second phase as rediscovering the contents that the (empty) container was always meant to hold. I love the idea that everything we face and overcome in phase one prepares us for a different kind of richness, which will fill us up in phase two. I love that the effort of dealing with what we encounter will never be wasted (unless we refuse to properly face it, in which case, yes, the energy we expend in struggle will all go down the drain).

The work you have been doing so far has primarily been about processing, understanding and integrating your phase-one experiences of life, in order to prepare you for phase two. And I'm so excited for you! Phase two is when we 'deepen into life'. It can only be experienced once you've worked your way, via the hero's journey, out of phase one. In the second phase you will move beyond paddling in the shallows of false-self existence and learn to dive deep, swim and even breathe under water. That's not to say we can't resurface for a paddle in the shallows now and then. I mean, who doesn't love a new pair of shoes? (Or whatever frivolous but fun distraction does it for you.) But it does mean that money, material comfort, status, being cool, staying young and beautiful – whatever our previous markers of success – no longer define us. We stop kidding ourselves that they will fill us up or make us whole. We simply enjoy paddling for a while in the shallow waters, while remaining aware of and connected to the hidden depths and beauty below the surface.

I'd like to explore the characteristics of the different phases of life in a little more detail, so that you can think about your own personal development in relation to this model. The aim here is not to imply that you 'should' already have passed from phase one to two, either by doing the work in this book or any other mechanism. You are not 'failing' if you sense that you're still in phase one. Honesty, self-compassion and understanding are key. Much better to know that you still have some work to do than to kid yourself that you've practically attained enlightenment when your friends might tell a very different story! So resist any temptation to rewrite your story too quickly. Coming up is the overview for you to consider, before you carry out the exercises in this final chapter.

Phase One – the small story of 'me'

This phase stretches from birth through childhood, adolescence and into adulthood. We learn and grow, passing through the various stages of our development and the shaping of our identity. We face challenges, joys and heartbreaks. Most of us encounter romantic love and deal with the loss and pain that this can bring.

During phase one our ego development is necessarily strong, driving us forward to learn, plan, achieve, acquire and overcome. We have an 'outside in' approach to life, looking for the person, job, house, car, money (or shoes!) that will somehow complete the identity we are working hard to create for ourselves.

This approach to life is all about us as an individual. There is often an emphasis on how we compare to our peers. Are we succeeding or falling behind? Are we having enough fun? Earning enough money? It can be thrilling and exciting, terrifying and overwhelming, a rollercoaster of ups and downs.

It also comes with an inevitable sense (illusion) of separation, an inner restlessness, insecurities and fears. We tend to place limits and conditions on our expressions of love, sharing our hearts only with those we consider part of our 'tribe': friends, family, lovers or partners and pets.

We spend a lot of our time in this first phase admiring and protecting what we've acquired and aspiring to achieve and 'be' more. 'Maybe when I'm richer, thinner, head of the department, when I have my own business, when I'm no longer broken . . .' The ego loves a 'maybe when . . .' Our life tends to be more future-focused and bound up with obligations and responsibilities. We measure ourselves against others and against social and cultural norms. We fret over what we 'should have' done or acquired before we can learn to lean back, surf life's delicious waves and simply enjoy the view. There's very little living in the moment in this phase and a lot of 'could do better' and 'if only'.

And of course there is the inevitable wounding, picked up along the way. We may become more reactive, defensive and blaming. The false self builds layer upon layer of armour to protect all that we have fought so hard for and to keep others away from the hurts underneath. All of this is perfectly natural and, in fact, necessary. Our 'container' is formed by everything that happens in phase one, readying itself to be filled up with mysterious gifts and unexpected insights once we've navigated the breakthrough that will lead us into phase two.

Breaking down to breaking through

As you know, sooner or later each one of us will face a moment of reckoning. The life we have created for ourselves starts to come crumbling down or simply no longer works for us on a fundamental level. We experience some form of 'breakdown' and we start to ask ourselves phase-two type questions. 'What's it all about? There must be more to life than this, surely?'

For some of us, this necessary stage of restlessness and suffering can feel like facing death. It's that big and that hard. And in a way it is a death, but only of our false self. It is incredibly difficult and painful but we can, with guidance, get a sense of the movement occurring within the chaos and begin to connect to our deep yearning for something else.

For others of us, the transition is not so much triggered by a crisis as provoked by a sense of discomfort with where we've ended up. As we start to question the meaning of our lives, beyond careers and consumption, family and relationships, we turn towards our yearning for the 'something more'. And I don't mean more shoes! Even if we have no idea what that means (at least on an intellectual level), we begin to hear life's call to us to deepen and go beyond the surface layers of phase one. If we are ready we will listen, and in that moment of true listening phase two begins.

Some people refuse the call, as we know. They will have the breakdown without the break*through*. They refuse to do their inner work, preferring to remain a victim of their past and focus their energy on blaming others. (That's woundology, right there.) Sadly, further suffering for them is inevitable. So great are their fears of change and of vulnerability that they prefer to remain in phase one, however painful that is. Many 'phase-two resisters', as I affectionately call them, have to acquire addictive strategies to cope with the stagnation. They suffer a kind of spiritual death and remain an empty vessel with nothing to fill it. Painful indeed.

However, for those courageous enough to do their inner

work – those like you, reading this book – the breakdown can and will become a breakthrough. Even if you can't see it that way at first, or for a while. The portal opens as the life challenge brings you to your knees, and you bravely crawl through.

Phase Two – the BIG story of 'we'

Once we are through the portal of healing and out the other side, once our wounds are healing into scars, our focus naturally begins to shift. We now have the capacity to take a step back, like an observer getting some distance, in order to view our suffering as part of what I call 'the small story of me'. We recognize that there is a much bigger and more expansive 'story of we' that perhaps – until now – has escaped us.

But not any more. We are now ready to become more aware of the collective experience of life. We start to view our personal story within the much broader context of what it means to be human. We recognize that we all struggle, that we all lose our way, stumbling and bumbling along, making the mistakes and the poor choices that lead us to the necessary suffering of the first phase. We are all just trying to find out which direction we need to take, who we are and what we are made of.

Some face far greater struggles than you or I will ever know, and having recognized this, we start to feel deeply grateful for what we have been spared. We become acutely aware of the wounded child dimension to every adult we meet. We can't help it. We see the child in their eyes, looking back at us. Our sense of compassion and our awareness of the interconnectedness of all beings grows beyond measure. We know that when we look closely, we are more alike than not. We all need each other: plants, animals, ecosystems, the planet. When all is said and done, we really are one.

We begin to refocus our attention from 'outside in' to 'inside out' living, as we recognize that everything we really need is inside of us. We know that nothing and no one else can 'fix' us or fill us up. We start to trust our decisions and rely on ourselves. Our confidence returns and we become clearer about who we are at our very core. And as we remember the truth of who we are, toxic relationships begin to fall away or are reshaped and renewed. Our old interests, comforts and careers are changed. Default behaviours, beliefs and habits are gradually addressed, to make room for new ones.

We no longer buy into our ego's nonsense. We learn to giggle at ourselves when ego pops up to inflate our sense of importance ('Don't you know who I am!') or when it deflates, and takes with it our sense of worthiness ('Who do you think you are?'). We just stop taking ourselves and our thoughts so seriously. Life becomes so much lighter and brighter.

As we deepen into this phase, we discover that there is more than enough room in our ever-expanding heart to love ourselves and others, even those we don't know. We have the capacity to give love so generously now that we are no longer held back and limited by our own pain and suffering. We start to see that love is not something that needs to be rationed but is the underlying source of everything, so we can spread it far and wide. We receive and give love, knowing that it has to be a two-way process.

We begin to think of love as kindness in action and to remember that we have an abundance of it. There are so many ways we can love others unknown to us – through our kindness, compassion, attention, service, warmth or simply a smile that reaches our eyes. As we head deeper into phase two, we develop a strong need to live simply, treading more gently on the Earth, taking only what we need and giving back as much as we can. All of this is what I refer to as 'Love beyond love.' Love with a capital L. It's a more expansive way to think about it than the traditional romantic and familial model we have been used to in phase one. For me, this kind of Love is what we forget when we reside in the safety (and prison) of our mind. It's what we remember and connect with, when we return to the wisdom of our heart.

OVER TO YOU

Identifying your phases of life

Warning: Do not weaponize this tool! It is not a checklist. You do not need to score high on the awakened spectrum in order to feel worthy, be worthy or keep reading. Please don't do that to yourself, not when you've come so far. Please use this list as a prompt to further investigate where you're at, without judgement. Nothing more. Have a think. Note your emotional reactions. See what you can learn.

Clues that suggest you are still in the first phase of your life:

- Life feels very much focused on you and your story.
- You're still blaming your parents for the past.
- You have a strong need to be right.
- You possess an inability to be with your feelings.
- You talk fast and loudly.
- You still believe you are better or less than others.
- Your story feels like the absolute truth.

- You refuse to consider forgiving those who wronged you.
- You are still waiting to be rescued.
- You take life for granted.
- You carry a lot of shame, guilt and secrets.
- You see nature as something separate from you.
- You feel entitled without realizing it.
- You have a strong focus on what you look like and stuff you own.
- You have a strong desire to be liked and approved of.
- You use substances addictively to escape your pain.
- You are easily triggered and reactive.
- You have issues with authority.
- You find it hard to be alone.
- You still believe that love is outside of you and related to another.

Clues that you are entering or are already in the second phase of your life:

- You realize that not much in life is personal.
- You have a strong need to be in nature.
- You have a strong need to serve.
- You view life and your body as a miracle.
- Heartfelt gratitude has become like breathing to you.
- You allow all your feelings the space to be felt.
- You are shame-less.
- You really do love yourself.
- You're not interested in winning; you're not even in the race.
- You talk less and listen more.
- You need less stuff and have a desire to declutter and minimize.

- You have less need to be seen and heard.
- You know there is ultimately nothing to forgive.
- You have less need for people to like or approve of you.
- When you indulge in life's party, you do it consciously and for pleasure (rather than for pain-avoidance or self-destruction).
- You can laugh at yourself and your own stories.
- You remember how precious life really is.
- You laugh and cry a lot.
- You know Love beyond love.

An introduction to spirit-led living

Phase-two living is a spirit-led approach to life rather than the ego-led living of phase one. But what does this actually mean? Now that you're more or less there, or hopefully excited about continuing your journey in that direction, it's time to learn more about the mindset of a grounded spiritual life.

For me, that mindset starts with inquiry. Many people have a sense that there is something more to life, even if they don't know what that 'more' is. Even during the tumultuous first phase of life many of us have a sense that 'there must be better songs to sing than this', as Rita's mum puts it in one of my favourite films, *Educating Rita*. Surveys have shown that 85 per cent of us do believe in some form of higher power. But of course, when we are in a lot of emotional pain (or numbing ourselves from it), it can be very hard to connect to or even consider this bigger dimension to life. Many people are sleepwalking and self-medicating, trying to cope as best they can. I know I was.

When we are in the grip of some form of breakdown, and as we move towards our breakthrough, it's as if we're waking up from a very long slumber. We begin to be able to connect – at first just for a moment, and then increasingly for longer periods of time – to the 'something more' of life. This period is often referred to as a form of awakening, and it naturally (although not inevitably) follows on from deep personal healing.

Awakening is characterized by curiosity and a capacity to see things from a different (deeper) perspective. We notice that the experiences of our life appear to have themes or messages, which can only be discovered by turning towards them. We become aware of and appreciate many instances of guidance and synchronicity that have supported us along the way. These are moments of what some call 'grace', that, when linked together, suggest there is a much deeper story playing out beneath the details of our particular life, even if our intellect and ego cannot fully comprehend it.

As we get more confident that our inner work is taking us somewhere useful and true, we are more able to get in touch with an aspect of our being that seems deeper than our every-day thoughts and feelings. We begin to sense a part of ourselves that is wise and intuitive. This can happen in moments of still-ness and solitude, during a meditation or when we're out for a walk. Or it can arise during times of extreme challenge, such as being diagnosed with a serious illness or the dying and death of a loved one. At such times we can sense ourselves becom-ing more than we believed possible. We might suddenly know exactly what to do in a crisis. We might have complete clarity about the steps we need to take, or understand that we know nothing and feel a rush of excitement and trust about what might happen next.

Can you recall such a time in your own life? Perhaps while

holding the hand of your dying parent or looking into the eyes of your newborn child? Have you ever experienced a moment when you forgot about your past and all of the stories about who you've been and what you've done, and you simply remembered the absolute truth of who you *are* in the bigger scheme of things? I bet you have.

During these moments we are leaning into the deeper dimensions of our being, which many traditions call 'the spiritual self'. The human spirit can be understood as a reflection of the innate goodness in humankind or a representation of the divine in the physical world. The spirit animates our bodies and infuses our thoughts and emotions with awareness and a deeper sense of who we are, way beyond the false-self ego-driven layers of our roles, masks, identity and stories. It's the part that senses, visualizes and understands a world that has more to offer than meets the eye. It is the part that we are drawn to develop if we desire to become a better person. It is the part of ourselves that is revealed to us most clearly as we enter life's second phase. We may have glimpsed it before, but now we begin to embody it and be guided by it. It also seeks to connect to energies beyond itself. People who are on a healing path look to find their way back to this part of themselves, as well as seeking out a resonating space to express it in their life.

Quick question: how are you doing with all this talk of spiritual self and spirit-led living? If you're feeling resistant or you've already rolled your eyes or are nodding off (wake up), I do understand. It definitely can be off-putting for some. Sadly, for many people the spiritual is inextricably linked with religion and if your experiences of religion have been negative ones of an all-seeing, all-punishing 'God', with stories of hell and damnation and feelings of guilt and shame, then no wonder you might reject religion wholeheartedly. Rightly so.

Stick with me a moment though, even if you're eye-rolling because that is SO not what I'm talking about. What I witness in my work is a collective throwing out of the baby of spirituality, along with the bath water of religion. Leaving people shivering and cold in the empty container of their life. Nothing has meaning or depth. Nothing has purpose. A recipe for an empty and fearful existence, if ever I saw one.

I meet a lot of people who come to therapy for what they perceive to be completely material problems. They're prepared to hear about psychology but definitely not spirituality and what they're really looking for is a 'quick fix'. I've come to believe that many of them are suffering from a kind of 'soul sickness' because they do not have a spiritual foundation underpinning their life. I have grown more and more convinced that if we persist in treating all our problems as mechanical issues to be hacked, or diseases to be cured, we limit ourselves terribly. We cut ourselves off from so much power and innate beauty, goodness and joy.

If you're not convinced, no worries. This chapter is an invitation, not a requirement. This book is not about to take an evangelical turn and I myself am not religious. What I am is curious about all things transpersonal. I have experienced too many twists and turns in this illusion called life to close off any avenue of enquiry or communication if it might lead to deeper connection and more positive outcomes.

Inner activism – an invitation

So you are now ready to make a complete change in direction (if you want to). Up until now we have (necessarily) focused the work of this book primarily inwards – on you and your individual wounds and healing. As you know, this is a fundamental and crucial part of your hero's journey and allows the return to the truth of who you are. But it doesn't have to end here. This healing lays strong foundations upon which you can now build your life and uncover its true purpose. Your next step is to realize the power you have and to magnify the positive effect of all this hard work you've been doing.

Does it resonate with you if I suggest that your inner work will benefit your whole family? Imagine this. The changes you have made will (directly or indirectly) impact the lives of all those you love and cherish – your children, siblings, your parents, nieces, nephews and cousins. There will also be a ripple effect further out, in your wider circle, because as you change the world changes in response. So your friends, work colleagues and even strangers, all those whose lives you touch will also be affected. It might be a subtle effect. Perhaps they notice your new boundaries or how much clearer you are in your communication. Perhaps they observe that you are less reactive and more present. That which shifts in you will cause ripples that spread out to those around you, communicating a message of inspiration and the possibility of positive change.

I'd like to invite you to extend the reach of your healing further still. To use what you have gained to make an impact on the wider world. Whether you realize it or not, your work has been your preparation for so much more than just the maintenance of your own increased wellbeing, important though that is. If you accept this invitation, you will officially become what I call an inner activist – that is, somebody who commits to continuing to explore, grieve and integrate any blocks that are holding them back from living through their authentic self, and who also turns their attention to taking action to benefit the wider world.

Step Nine: The Spiritual Dimension – deepening into life

Inner activists view the healing of their individual wounds as being in service to the collective ones, meaning they recognize that as we heal ourselves we are healing the world. One whole heart at a time. Not only do inner activists live an authentic wholehearted and courageous life; they also commit to channel their newly reclaimed positive life force out into the world, for the greater good. They seek ways to live in active service in the world, with love and truth as their compass.

I recently met a woman called Lianne, who had taken precisely this step. When Lianne became a parent she was conscious that she didn't want to perpetuate and pass on family patterns of dysfunction to the next generation. She wanted to ensure that her parenting of her son, who has ADHD, was as healthy as it possibly could be. So she attended therapy, working on healing her own wounds first to ensure she became an emotional grown-up. She then took parenting-skills training and read books and listened to podcasts to learn the necessary skills to be the best possible parent for her son. Inner activism can take many forms, but it always begins with an impulse to be of service to others in the world.

Our wounds make us pay attention, you see, and wake us up from our stupor. We know by now that they are *meant* to be painful and, in daring to face them, we are offered a chance to grow into our greatness. For when we tend to our wounds and allow them to heal, we can learn to carry the scars left behind with pride. Casting aside our victim's crutches and walking strong, shoulders back, head held high, as the heroines that we truly are, we free up our energy to step away from our 'me' focus and move towards our 'we' focus. We naturally start to live more consciously and with greater awareness. We become more tender, compassionate and kind with ourselves and others. That's why I call this work inner activism. It was never meant to be just about you. As we continue to shed the layers of the false self, we can live, love and be guided by our spirit, the true self. We can then head out to love and to serve in the world in whichever way is meaningful to us.

Service – a pillar of spirit-led life

My work is founded on the belief that when we address and resolve our own heartbreaks, losses and hurts, we are lightening the load of what Eckhart Tolle calls the 'pain body' of the whole world. We free ourselves up to focus on living from a place of love and kindness, with service to others at the very core of our being.

I've observed that once people have tended to their own emotional wounds, they often become keen to find a way to 'give something back' to the world. I used to see it as we came to the end of The Bridge Retreat. Participants would be feeling a huge range of emotions, from relief to euphoria and natural nerves about their return to 'normal life'. Many of them were fired up with an exciting new energy. They spoke about a strong motivation to find their purpose and live a more meaningful life. One of the themes we always discussed in the closing sessions was service to others. It is just one of the best ways I know to enhance your joy and connect to your purpose.

Now, when you think of 'service' what images does it conjure up for you? Leaving your job and flying across the world to volunteer in an orphanage or animal sanctuary? Dedicating a large portion of your free time to volunteer in your community?

These are of course important and very precious forms of

service. But the service I'm talking about is essentially a focus on helping, supporting and guiding others. So it doesn't have to be a big event, like flying across the world to volunteer. Your service can be just as impactful and important when it's woven into your daily life. So, for example, committing every day to spread kindness and joy to all those whose lives you touch is an act of true service. Committing to learn about how to become the best mother or father that you can possibly be is a service to the whole world, because what the world needs most of all is more loving, kind, compassionate and secure young people growing up authentically within it.

Whether you have any religious beliefs or not, whether you're agnostic or unsure about spirituality, service is a fundamental aspect of living a truly connected life. When we serve other people by listening to what they need without imposing our own agenda, without expectations, without hopes for advancement, without seeking to rescue or direct those we're working with and for, our service is part of living a wholehearted and loving life. For me it is the absolute definition of a true spiritual life.

So go and give your whole heart away. Offer Love with a capital L to all the people who need it most, with your kindness, attention, care and tenderness. It's the greatest gift you will ever give and receive.

OVER TO YOU

How to serve someone's need, not your ego

The thing about service is that it is at its most powerful when you're doing it for 'altruistic' reasons. That said, the benefits of altruism for the person who's offering the help are also massive, and have been widely studied by psychologists and neuroscientists. People who do regular voluntary service have faster recovery times from illness and report better life satisfaction than those who don't. Being good and useful in the world generates its own buzz of reward. This is why service is such a powerful spiritual win-win.

But for it to endure and become part of your life and mindset rather than a box-ticking exercise, a chore (or worse, a prop to your ego), try to put all the lovely benefits to you on one side and focus on the other person or people.

This is really about trying to flip your own order of priorities. It's fine to start by asking what you could offer in service, because we have to start somewhere and if you can't swim you're not going to be much use as a volunteer lifeguard. But it's good to move closer to uncovering which people and issues need your love and support. Not so much what are you prepared to offer people, but what do they need from you?

Here are a few simple steps you can follow, to support you in finding a way to serve.

- *Identify your skills and interests*
  What can you do? Make an inventory of everything you love to do and all the skills you have to share. Start looking for ways to gift those skills to the wider world. Preferably to lots of people but one will do. Good communicator? Train and volunteer on a helpline. Good cook? Go feed the homeless.

- *Remember that it's not about you*
  Serving others can feel like a challenge. That's a good thing. It's not meant to be comfortable and convenient for you and, if it is, that's a sign you might be putting

your own needs ahead of the other person's. In fact, service is often a more impactful, profound and humbling experience when it includes an element of sacrifice. Hate mornings? Get up early to serve. Bit of an introvert? Get out among people in the community. This will have lots of benefits for you because getting out of our comfort zones is basically the way we build resilience and learn to trust ourselves. But more importantly, it trains your ego to get out of its own way.

- *Service is not for social media*
  Talking of ego, don't go bragging to people on social media and beyond about what you do to serve. Keep it – and your ego – to yourself.

- *Identify the issues that matter to you, then ask yourself what you could do to help*
  Your contribution might be in a high-profile role or it might be more humble. It might be back office rather than front line or the other way around. If you normally lead a team, maybe you could mentor others to lead rather than assume you will take that role yourself. Your service might be highly organized through a big charity or very casual and grassroots. It might be once a month rather than once a week. Whatever your service looks like, so long as it's serving a genuine need, it's all good. Because remember: this is not about you. (Ego weeps . . .)

Prayer – aka active communication with Life

I know the 'P' word makes some people squirm and I know it's a risk even bringing it up here. However, I love a BCC!

(See what I did there?!) I am aware that prayer, like spirituality, can make some people feel defensive, scornful or keen to tell others why the very idea of communicating with a higher power is absurd. (I get all that, I used to be an 'eye-roller' too, you know.) In our culture, prayer is not often viewed as an element of general spiritual practice. It has not floated free of its origins, like meditation or mindfulness. For the vast majority of us, prayer means communicating with God (the one with a capital G). Prayer means religion. If you were made to attend religious services when you were young, or you are a committed atheist, you might understandably baulk at the idea of prayer. But please hear me out because I have a slightly different perspective to offer you.

I believe that prayer, like meditation, is for everyone. You don't need to be religious or to believe in God to pray, and it's so hugely beneficial that I am prepared to risk your scorn by at least presenting it to you as an idea to consider.

As I've said already, I do not define myself as religious and I do not believe in any traditional version of God (although I totally respect it if you do). When I speak of prayer, I mean a practice that connects us to something greater than 'the small story of me'. For some that is God; for others it might be divine energy, love, nature, the universe, your ancestors, or some other form of a higher power. Let's not get hung up on the labels here. I think we all know what we're talking about.

For me, prayer is simply intentional communication with *something* bigger than us. If you can't get past the word itself, feel free to replace it with another word that doesn't jar. Let's face it though, ten or fifteen years ago most people wouldn't have believed that meditation would ever be as normalized as it is today. Back then it was just for hippies or those with a devotional religious practice. Now pretty much everyone knows the benefits of meditation (even if they don't do it). My intention here is to separate prayer from religion (unless religion is meaningful and positive for *you*) and to normalize it enough for you to begin to explore it.

Religion and prayer were absolutely foreign concepts to me before my breakthrough. But in this second phase of life and with the help of some wonderful teachers and guides, I have come to believe that prayer is an essential part of an awakened life. A belief in a traditional version of God isn't essential but prayer practice is. I now pray every morning and evening and this has fundamentally changed how I live and brings with it a sense of peace and harmony. I invite you to consider the possibility that prayer could offer you the same.

Personalize your higher power

For me, the Higher Power to which I pray is Life itself. I'm intentionally communicating with Life through my prayers. This allows me to cultivate a deep and intimate relationship – some might even say a partnership – with Life. I believe Life is talking to us all the time, through the flowers, the trees, the ocean, the birds and the bees, so is it really so strange that we should stop and talk back? My prayers support me to honour Life with every breath, every single thought I have, word I speak and action I take. When we actively communicate with Life in this way, we start to learn to trust in it. Praying becomes a conversation with the best friend we will ever have.

One of the main benefits of my prayer practice has been the way it has allowed me to deeply reconnect with nature and myself as part of an ecosystem. Most of us are profoundly disconnected from our environment; we've forgotten that we are part of the natural world. Prayer has enabled me to remember this fundamental truth. I now trust in Life completely, with all its joys and challenges, just as I trust in the seasons and the phases of the moon. I see the ups and downs of my own life as just another natural cycle.

Prayer offers us a way to rebuild deep faith in Life. It is not about passivity in the face of events. Neither am I suggesting that it's a magic wand that will resolve all our problems. It certainly doesn't mean that we should give up the rest of our personal development work, our activism, service and our resistance to injustice. But when we are in active communication with Life we tend to be able to tell the difference between those challenges we could and should resist and those we should embrace. Prayer supports me to see change as an adventure and an opportunity, rather than a threat. With prayer comes trust and with trust comes faith, which leads to a sense of peace and confidence in the natural order of things.

Prayer acknowledges that there is a power greater than your ego at play, one that doesn't necessarily make sense to the rational mind. If you don't believe in or are blocked by the idea of a higher power, find your 'object of worship' in something you *can* believe in. Pray to the trees if that works for you! Pray to the ocean or to the flowers. Find your own way to communicate with Life, and then once you have prayed, get still enough to listen for the answers, remembering that prayer bypasses the mind and speaks straight to the soul. As Deepak Chopra put it so beautifully, 'Prayer is about looking up and meditation is about looking in. Prayer is talking to "God" and meditation is listening for the answers. Allowing "God" to speak to and through you.'

What are you unintentionally praying for?

I'd like to suggest that even if you believe prayer is not for you, you might be communicating with Life's forces in ways that don't serve your growth or the wider good. The truth is we all pray in one form or another. When we say things like, 'Oh God, this world is such a mess. We're all doomed,' then this, I would suggest, is a form of prayer. Or if you say, 'I really hope so-and-so is recovering and that all will be well,' that too is a form of prayer. Some people pray intentionally, with hope, courage and determination; others pray unknowingly, with fear, blame and doubt. I believe that your thoughts and speech, as well as your actions, are all forms of energy. If you pray with respect and humility to the bigger dimension of Life, you are at the very least sending out a positive energy that just might counterbalance some of the darkness in the world.

The spiritual teacher and mystic Caroline Myss says that all our thoughts and words are 'vessels of [either] darkness or light'. It is up to us to bring awareness to which kind of 'vessels' we are sending out into the world. Do we contribute to Life's vast 'energy pot' by generating light-filled positive energy, or do we unconsciously lower the vibrations, adding to the 'shit pot'?! (Another professional term for you . . . you're welcome.)

The outcomes of our prayers are of course very hard to quantify. Prayer is not easily measurable or evidenced. But I do believe that if we repeat light-filled prayers often enough, we will see them manifesting in the world before our very eyes. The opposite is also true. That's how powerful you and your prayers are.

I guess we all worship a God in some form or another. It might be power, control, money, fame, drugs, perfection, a new idealized partner – or it could be something far more profound.

We all go to 'church' too, whether through music, nature, dancing, silence or visiting a holy temple. For me, my church is nature. This is where I go to celebrate, connect with and praise Life. So your church could be a concert and your prayer might be music or dancing. One way or another, we all find our way to a place of worship. In the words of another great spiritual guru, the singer Sam Smith, 'Everyone prays in the end . . .'

Take a look at the list below. Can you imagine praying in any of these ways, or in these locations? See if you can open up to the idea of trying one or two of these suggestions, in the playful spirit of creative exploration that we've been investigating. To my mind, any activity can be prayerful if it is practised with (good) intention, but sometimes I believe it's important that we have the humility to simply get down on our knees.

- Singing or chanting
- Dance or movement
- Walking or being in nature
- Stillness and silence
- On your knees
- Reading or writing poetry
- Art
- Forgiveness
- Giving heartfelt thanks for things on your gratitude list
- Sending love, both to those you always cherish and to those you suspect are in need of love

How to pray

Are you ready for some practical suggestions? The way I understand it, there are three main elements to prayer: gratitude, celebration (or worship) and requests. I encourage you to include all three and to begin and end every time with one of the most important prayers of all, 'Thank you.'

From there, you can expand on everything for which you feel grateful. After that, you can focus on celebrating or worshipping those things. For me, this is the most joyful and wonder-filled aspect of my prayers. Finally, you might make requests of your God, asking for certain people or groups of people to be looked after, supported or loved. Or you might ask for the strength to face and overcome a difficult challenge.

Above all, I believe that joy is one of the most powerful prayers we can offer to the world. If we can live in joy despite and because of everything, our prayers of joy spread healing far and wide, beyond our wildest dreams. So live your life as if it's one long prayer. Because it is.

OVER TO YOU

A prayer practice to strengthen faith

1. Find a quiet and comfortable space to sit, where you won't be disturbed. Gently hold your hands out in front of you, palms turned up towards the sky. Feel the energy touching your palms. Close your eyes and breathe slowly and consciously. Imagine breathing in and out as if through your heart, feeling it soften and expand with every breath. Give thanks for the gift of this precious moment.

2. Turn your attention to your left hand and, with your eyes still closed, visualize this hand holding your life as

it is today. Imagine that it contains the struggles and challenges as well as the gifts and abundance. Observe which examples of your reality come to your mind's eye and try not to judge. Just notice, and continue to breathe into your heart. Feel the weight of your life held in this left hand.

3. Turn your attention now to your right hand, still with your eyes closed and sending breath to your heart. Imagine that in this hand you are holding life as you pray for it to be. It might contain peace, good health, safety, love, compassion and kindness, perhaps the end to your suffering and that of others. Whatever you wish to pray for today. Once again, feel the weight of your prayers in your right hand. So you have life as it is in the left hand and life as you pray for it to be in your right. Give them both your equal attention. Breathe.

4. Keeping your eyes closed and palms up, notice that in between your two hands, which are holding these two experiences of reality and prayed-for change, there is a space. Imagine that this is a space for your higher power, the universe or your intuitive wisdom to come through. Turn your full attention to this space and be fully present.

5. I invite you to ask for a message from your higher power. A message that will support you in this moment of your life. A message that will allow you to surrender to the reality of your life circumstances, alongside praying for change. (You may receive this message in a word, song, image, colour or energy. It may come immediately or some time later. Trust that whatever comes is exactly what you need.)

6. Now, turn your palms to face each other and very slowly bring them together in front of your heart. Allow your message if it has come, or the energy of your request if it has not yet, to be absorbed into your two hands and mingle with the reality and the change they symbolically contain.
7. Bow your head with humility and gratitude. Take a deep breath and open your eyes.

Make room for silence

If prayer is what happens when we start a conversation with the universe, silence is what we need if we are to pick up on its answers. Silence and solitude are fundamentals of living a connected and awakening life. In our busy, noisy and fast-paced world, acquainting yourself with the power of silence and of periods of solitude may take some practice.

To be in silence requires you to surrender to a wordless place within you. All sorts of things may arise for you when you try to go there. I encourage you to notice and peacefully let go of any judgements, criticism, boredom or incessant planning that surge into your wordless place. If you accept the silence, it will provide you with the essential atmosphere in which to hear the answers to your prayers. This answer might arrive in the form of a message, a bird, an image, intuitive knowing or a person turning up at the perfect moment. With silence, the mind finally gets permission to be still, allowing depth of feeling to emerge. Some call it the doorway to the realm of our essential, true self. It's certainly the best way I know to hear the divine energy of Life speaking to us.

You gotta have faith

Lots of people believe that there's no point in praying if you don't have a religious faith. You need faith in something first, and then it might make sense to pray to it. No faith, no point in prayer. But for me it's the other way round. I have discovered that faith is what inevitably and naturally follows, as a result of consistent prayer practice. As you learn to communicate with, lean into and trust in the perfection of Life itself, your faith in it (and yourself as part of Life) deepens. Your faith in the bigger picture expands and you learn to totally trust in the deeper meaning of existence. Faith brings with it a new perspective on struggle. You develop a kind of certainty that no matter the events occurring outside of you, on the *inside* you will remain full. Your phase two 'container' is overflowing with resilience, worthiness and confidence in your capacity to surf Life's waves. You know for sure that even when you go under, you will not drown. And with that knowledge arrives peace.

For me, faith is like a form of partnership with Life itself. It's as if, after all the years of fighting and resisting and trying to control Life, we finally open and surrender to it. We become partners, loving, living and breathing together as one. When we commit to living in faith we vow to love, honour and cherish ourselves and all beings because there is an unbreakable bond between us. *We* are Life itself. As we come to the end of the book, it is my most profound hope that in surrendering to this simple yet profound truth, you will discover your certainty within all the uncertainty. That, my friends, is worth everything. Because that is true freedom.

May you be safe, May you be well, May you find peace, May you feel loved.

And then one (extra)ordinary day . . .

. . . you will let your faith lead you out into the natural world and
in solitude and silence you will notice with wonder the incredible gifts, not just of *your* life, but of Life itself. You will recognize
that you are a tiny and yet significant part of the whole, and that
how you choose to live affects every single aspect of that whole.
That's how powerful and important you are.

After a while, let yourself be drawn to a specific place,
whether it's beneath the boughs of a tree, in the middle of a
wide open field or on the seashore. Let your intuition guide
you. Then stop, and get really still. Look up at the sky and connect to its expanse and the infinity of the universe beyond.
Take in the incredible vast beauty of it all. Let your heart open
with deep gratitude for everything you have been through,
which has brought you to this moment. Look around and
take in each detail, not just with your eyes but with all of your
senses: the colour of the leaves on the trees, the fresh smell of
early morning, the exquisite perfection of the movement and
sound of the waves of the sea or the leaves of the tree. Bathe
in your awe.

Then, when you're ready, gently close your eyes and feel the
earth beneath your feet (take off your shoes if you can). As
you breathe slowly and deeply, pay attention to how you and
your beautiful body, with all of its scars and hard-won wisdom,
belong here – with and on this earth. Notice how connected
and rooted you feel here. Home within, and home without.
This is what true belonging feels like. Breathe it in. Anchor this
moment.

Now, keep your eyes closed as you connect to your ancestors. Imagine that standing behind you are all the women and

men who came before you. Your mother, father and their parents on both sides . . . then your great-grandparents and back and back, through the generations. Really feel that, see it in your mind's eye: the long line of your tribe, standing behind you like an invisible team of support.

Imagine leaning into this support, knowing that – right from their essence – they've got your back. Because their spirits have prayed for this moment . . . They've prayed that you would be the one who would courageously face the negative legacy passed down through your family, and transform it into riches to offer any future generations and the wider world. They've prayed that *you* would be the one to recognize all they sacrificed, so that you could stand here, free, alive in this moment, belonging to yourself and the Earth.

As you feel their support and your place in the sacred order of things, you know that you are ready. You can open your eyes, breathe deeply and take a conscious step forwards into phase two of your life. And as you do so, if you listen very carefully, you will hear your ancestors cheering you on . . .

In love and service
Donna Lancaster

Finally

To close the book and mark the moment of you stepping into the second phase of your life, here is a prayer. You've seen this before – or rather, you've seen something very similar. At the beginning of your journey I welcomed you – all of you and every part of you – on to the bridge. Now I'd like to offer this version, in which you, dear reader, offer that welcome to yourself and to every part of you. Now that you have done your work you don't need me to tell you that you're worthy. I invite you to use these words in your prayer practice and as a reminder of how far you've come.

The Welcome: A closing prayer for the Worthy

I welcome each and every part of myself.
The part of me that feels anxious and afraid
the part of me that still carries some rage
the part that feels excited and curious
the part of me feeling shut down and disconnected.
You are all welcome here.

I welcome the part of me that feels heartbroken and overwhelmed
the part of me that feels too broken to ever heal
the parts of me that feel fake, and those that I know are real.
You're all welcome.

The parts carrying my trauma; the body carrying my soul.
The abused and violated parts too

the addicted me and my shadowy layers
the secret-carrying, guilt-filled shameful parts.
Guess what? Welcome!

The part of me that has been hurt and that has hurt others
made mistakes, screwed up BIG time.
And the resulting self-loathing and low self-worth.
Oh, you are all so welcome here.

For the parts of me that are confused and lonely
the ones that feel they can't go on another day . . . and yet they do.
And for the courageous me that gets back up again and again.
And those parts of me that yearn to live in love and truth.
The parts that remember everything. Welcome.

And welcome to the Queen in me, as she remembers to collect her crown.
Welcome to the innocence of me and the joyful part, too.
You are all so beyond welcome. Yes! All parts of myself are welcome.
I Belong. I Matter.
I am Worthy. I am Loved.
And I'm so very glad that I came.

Resources

315

Resources

www.grief.com
Website founded by David Kessler, one of the world's foremost experts on loss, with information and resources.

www.griefrecoverymethod.com
The Grief Recovery Method is an action-based, powerful approach to healing from life's heartbreaks.

www.griefworkscourse.com
Useful information and resources from leading grief psychotherapist Julia Samuel.

BODY-BASED SUPPORT AND RELEASE

www.5rhythms.com
A dynamic movement meditation practice offering classes and workshops all over the world.

www.rolfinguk.co.uk
A form of hands-on bodywork and movement training to help the body function more effectively.

www.taichiunion.com
Working to improve and promote Tai Chi in the UK.

www.treuk.com
A programme offering practical tools to support the release of physical, mental and emotional pain.

ADDITIONAL RESOURCES

www.cnvc.org
The Center for Nonviolent Communication is a global organization that supports the learning and sharing of nonviolent communication (NVC).

www.shadowwork.com
Shadowwork® is a personal growth programme which brings your powers out of the shadow and into the light.

www.self-compassion.org
Information and resources from Dr Kristin Neff, one of the world's leading experts on self-compassion.

www.theforgivenessproject.com
Providing resources and experiences to help people examine and overcome their own unresolved grievances.

Recommended further reading

The Apology by V (formerly Eve Ensler)
The Body Keeps the Score by Bessell van der Kolk
The Body Remembers by Babette Rothschild
The Book of Forgiving by Desmond and Mpho Tutu
Daring Greatly by Brené Brown
Falling Upward by Richard Rohr
Finding Meaning: The Sixth Stage of Grief by David Kessler
The Gifts of Imperfection by Brené Brown
The Grief Recovery Handbook by John W. James and Russell Friedman
Healing Through the Dark Emotions by Miriam Greenspan
How to Be an Adult in Relationships by David Richo
Loyalty to Your Soul by Ronald and Mary Hulnick
A Return to Love by Marianne Williamson
Rising Strong by Brené Brown
Triggers: How We Can Stop Reacting and Start Healing by David Richo
Waking the Tiger by Peter Levine

You can continue to follow Donna's work via her Instagram page @donnalancs and her website: www.deepeningintolife.com

Acknowledgements

It felt important to end this book with heartfelt gratitude, given how important we know that this is in living a wholehearted life. As most of us know 'it takes a village', and it is fair to say that each and every person mentioned here has played a meaningful part in the birthing of this book in some form.

I will start at the very beginning with my family. Huge appreciation and gratitude are offered to:

My parents – Julie and Albert. Without those wounds you created, how would I have ever discovered the precious gifts waiting on the other side of the portal? Thank you for everything you could give me and for my very life. I am beyond grateful.

To my daughters – Gemma and Lucy – and my grandsons – Louis, Theo and Jax. You really do complete me.

To my favourite sister Corinne – 'May all your dreams come true . . .'

To my super handsome son-in-law Lucas – eat your heart out Tom Hardy!

And finally deepest heartfelt gratitude to my Ancestors; I bow my head to honour you and hope that I have made you proud. Thank you, thank you, thank you.

To my soulmates Gabi and Vinny – I'm so grateful to share this lifetime with you both and thank you for the lessons, support and giggles.

To my fabulous friends Freddy, Fearne, Lilliana, Gill, Foxy, Michelle, Simon and Jill; you feed my soul.

Acknowledgements

To my agent, Valeria Huerta – thank you for stalking me and refusing to be put off by my numerous (weak) excuses of why I couldn't possibly write a book! Thank you also for your continued trust, championing of me and unshakeable belief in what I have to offer.

To Helen Coyle – we both know that this book was a team effort. Thank you for guiding me, patiently listening to me moan and for helping to shape my many words into something more beautiful.

To everyone at Penguin Life – thank you for your patience, support, enthusiasm and guidance, and for taking a chance on me.

To Sarah Beckwith and Jo Sennett – thank you for your continued loyalty and endless support.

To Hollie Holden – for generously allowing me to include your poem/prayer in this book. Thank you.

To all the many clients, teachers and guides I have worked with along the way. Thank you for showing me the way.

And finally, to you dear readers, especially all the women out there who know what it feels like to 'break'. I am beyond grateful you are here. Shine on.

I love you.

Donna Lancaster